GRANTA

12 Addison Avenue, London W11 4QR | email editorial@granta.com
To subscribe go to www.granta.com, or call 845-267-3031 (toll-free 866-438-6150)
in the United States, 020 8955 7011 in the United Kingdom

ISSUE 122: WINTER 2013

EDITOR	John Freeman
DEPUTY EDITOR	Ellah Allfrey
ARTISTIC DIRECTOR	Michael Salu
ASSOCIATE EDITOR	Patrick Ryan
ONLINE EDITOR	Ted Hodgkinson
EDITORIAL ASSISTANT	Yuka Igarashi
PUBLICITY	Saskia Vogel
ASSISTANT DESIGNER	Daniela Silva
FINANCE	Geoffrey Gordon, Morgan Graver, Craig Nicholson
MARKETING AND SUBSCRIPTIONS	David Robinson
SALES DIRECTOR	Brigid Macleod
SALES MANAGER	Sharon Murphy
TO ADVERTISE CONTACT	Kate Rochester, katerochester@granta.com
IT MANAGER	Mark Williams
PRODUCTION ASSOCIATE	Sarah Wasley
PROOFS	Sarah Barlow, Katherine Fry, Juliette Mitchell, Jessica Rawlinson, Vimbai Shire
PUBLISHER	Sigrid Rausing
CONTRIBUTING EDITORS	Daniel Alarcón, Diana Athill, Peter Carey, Mohsin Hamid, Sophie Harrison, Isabel Hilton, Blake Morrison, John Ryle, Edmund White

Granta, ISSN 173231, is published four times per year by Granta Publications, 12 Addison Avenue, London W11 4QR.

The 2013 US annual subscription price is $48. Airfreight and mailing in the USA by agent named Air Business Ltd, c/o Worldnet Shipping Inc., 156–15, 146th Avenue, 2nd Floor, Jamaica, NY 11434, USA. Periodicals postage paid at Jamaica, NY 11431.

US POSTMASTER: Send address changes to *Granta*, Air Business Ltd. c/o Worldnet Shipping Inc. 156–15, 146th Avenue, 2nd Floor, Jamaica, NY 11434.

Subscription records are maintained at *Granta* Magazine, c/o Abacus e-Media, PO Box 2068, Bushey, Herts WD23 3ZF.

Air Business is acting as our mailing agent.

Granta is printed and bound in Italy by Legoprint. This magazine is printed on paper that fulfils the criteria for 'Paper for permanent document' according to ISO 9706 and the American Library Standard ANSI/NIZO Z39.48-1992 and has been certified by the Forest Stewardship Council (FSC). *Granta* is indexed in the American Humanities Index.

ISBN 978-1-905881-65-9

New Books from Harper Perennial

THE TELL: *A Novel by Hester Kaplan*

"Kaplan is a master of her craft... Every sentence of this book is breathtaking."

—ANN HOOD, author of *The Knitting Circle*

ALL THAT I AM: *A Novel by Anna Funder*

"A sweeping first novel that covers love and war, friendship and betrayal, and the bonds that define a life."

—ANN PATCHETT, author of *State of Wonder*

THE BEAUTIFUL INDIFFERENCE:
Stories by Sarah Hull

"Hall's voice is strong and distinctive—even, in single, elevated passages, exquisite."

—LIONEL SHRIVER, *Financial Times*

AN UNCOMMON EDUCATION:
A Novel by Elizabeth Percer

"Enticing and shyly perceptive."

—*New York Times Book Review*

THE THINGS THEY CANNOT SAY:
Stories Soldiers Won't Tell You About What They've Seen, Done or Failed to Do in War by Kevin Sites

"Riveting and emotionally raw... These gripping stories... are evidence of a profound desire to heal."

—*Publisher's Weekly*

BATH
SPA
UNIVERSITY

WRITE HERE

Join a thriving community of writers in and around the beautiful city of Bath. Work with our award-winning staff including new professors Naomi Alderman, David Almond, Aminatta Forna, Maggie Gee, Tessa Hadley, David Harsent, Philip Hensher, Kate Pullinger and Fay Weldon.

Small groups, specialist workshops, passionate staff and students working in close collaboration: it's no wonder so many of our graduates see their work published by companies such as Random House, Oxford University Press, Hodder & Stoughton, Bloomsbury and HarperCollins.

MA CREATIVE WRITING
MA WRITING FOR YOUNG PEOPLE
MA TRAVEL AND NATURE WRITING
PHD CREATIVE WRITING

admissions@bathspa.ac.uk
www.bathspa.ac.uk

CONTENTS

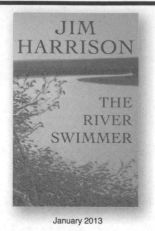

SEVEN DAYS IN SYRIA

Janine di Giovanni

1. Hossam

When my son was born, I was unable to cut his nails. It was a visceral rather than rational reaction. I would pick up the tiny baby scissors, look at his translucent fingers, clean and pink as seashells, and feel as though I would retch.

One night, in the hours between darkness and light, the time when the subconscious allows the source of such neuroses to become clear, I understood my inability to perform such a straightforward task. I had a vision of the Iraqi man I once knew who had no fingernails.

In the dying days of the Saddam regime, I had an office inside the Ministry of Information. It was a sinister, paranoid place. Journalists begged, bribed and pleaded to stay inside the country to report. We were followed, videotaped; our phones were tapped. We all knew that our hotel rooms were equipped with hidden cameras. I dressed and undressed in the darkened bathroom.

Every Monday morning, the man with no fingernails arrived in my office and stretched out his hands, utterly unselfconscious that in place of nails were raw beds of flesh. He had come for his weekly baksheesh. His job was to get the money to seal my satellite phone so I could not use it unless the ministry listened in. Most of us had to pay our way to get anything done, and aside from the fee the ministry charged, we gave a baksheesh to get it done faster.

Every time the man arrived and I looked at his hands spread out, I immediately felt a wave of panic, which turned to nausea, and yet I could not take my eyes off the place where his fingernails had been ripped off. Questions that I could not ask him raced through my mind. What had he done to deserve such agony? Was he an informer? Had he tried to escape Iraq and been caught? Was he part of the secret network attempting to overthrow the dictator? I never asked. Nor would he have answered. We were living in a republic of fear. He became one of those shadowy figures one holds in one's mind forever, hovering on the fringes.

The man, whose name I never knew, seemed to bear no resentment that he had been disfigured in such a public way. Because hands are one of the first things we usually notice about someone, every time he stretched out his, one knew immediately he had done something.

Or perhaps he had done nothing at all. Perhaps it was a horrible mistake. Such things happen all the time under dictatorships. People get locked up for years, forgotten, then the key turns and a jailer says, 'You can go now.' They never know why.

The day Saddam's regime fell, in the feverish chaos, I went to search for the man with no fingernails to open the seal so I could use my sat phone. But he, like most of the regime staff, had fled.

I went back to Iraq many times after that, but I never saw the man with no fingernails again – except in my dreams.

In northern Lebanon, in a town now inhabited by the Free Syrian Army (FSA) and many fighters who are recovering from severe injuries, I do what I do in most war zones: I go to the nearest hospital. In the hallway of a small rehabilitation clinic, I pass a man who recently had twenty-nine bullets removed from his body. Then I meet a paralysed man strapped to a board who is playing with a child – an orphaned child. The man had been badly beaten and left with a fractured spinal cord.

'Every time they hit me,' he said, 'they screamed, "You want freedom? OK, take this! Here is your great freedom!"'

Then I meet a man I am going to call Hossam, a student of human rights law, who sits on a bed trying to re-enter the human race.

He is twenty-four years old and dressed in baggy dark trousers, a T-shirt, and has a full beard and a shy but gentle demeanour. He keeps trying to buy me packs of Winston cigarettes, but I keep refusing, and he keeps insisting, gently, that he must give me a gift. On his hands and arms I see cigarette burns that I suspect are not self-inflicted.

On another bed, pushed against a wall, a fourteen-year-old boy sits and listens. When I suggest he leave the room for the interview, which I know is going to be painful, the boy explains that his father was killed in front of him, so he can take whatever else is about to come.

Hossam is Sunni and religious, but he still shakes my hand and gets off his bed, limping, to get me a chair. He tells me that he comes from an educated family – his father a civil servant, his brothers all university-educated.

Then he begins to tell his story without words. Slowly he removes his T-shirt. A thick, angry scar that begins under his mid-breastbone swims down to the proximity of his groin. He sighs, lights a cigarette and starts to talk in a low voice.

Hossam comes from Baba Amr, the district of Homs, Syria's third-largest city, which became an icon for the suffering of civilians when it got pummelled and overrun by Syrian government troops and paramilitary units beginning in December 2011. He admits that he was one of the organizers of the at first peaceful demonstrations against the government, but denies that he is a member of the FSA.

'It was about freedom and rights at first,' he says. 'Then came bullets.'

On 8 March 2012 at about 7.30 p.m., there were shouts outside the door of his family home. He heard men speaking a foreign language that he believes may have been Farsi. At first he refused to open the door. 'I said, "We are civilians! We have rights!"'

But the soldiers – who he said were not wearing uniforms, meaning they could have been paramilitary – fired intimidating shots, and his brother opened the door. The men shot the young man through the chest at close range, and the force of the bullet pushed him against a far wall where he fell, dying.

They swarmed into the house like bees. Hossam thinks there were about thirty of them. They shot Hossam in the shoulder and in the hand as he tried to cover his face for protection from the blow he thought was coming. He holds up his deformed fingers, and touches the angry red circle on his shoulder blade. The impact of the bullet made Hossam reel backwards, and he ended up lying next to his dying brother, looking him straight in the eye.

'I was watching the life go out of him,' he says quietly.

The men then picked him and his brother up by their feet and hands and hauled them, along with several dozen men from the neighbourhood, into a truck and threw them in, one on top of the other. They said they were going to use them as human shields. Some of the men in the truck were already dead, many were badly beaten and lay groaning in agony. Others had been shot.

'One guard pulled a man up by his ear and said, "Say Bashar al-Assad is your God." The man replied, "I have no God but God," and the guard shot him and tossed him onto the pile of bodies.'

Hossam was bleeding but his brother was closer to death. They took all of them off the truck when they reached the military hospital, and the minute they closed the doors, they began to beat Hossam brutally with sticks of plastic and wood.

Hossam's brother and the other men were flung into an underground room that served as a morgue. This was the same room where, from then on, Hossam was thrown every night to sleep after he was tortured, on top of the dead bodies. He described how he would lie awake listening to people breathing their last breath.

On the first day, Hossam's torturers, who were Syrian and told him they were doctors, brought him to something like an operating room. There were about four of them. They strapped him down.

'Are you a fighter?'

'No, I'm a student.'

'Are you a fighter?'

They held his penis and took a blade and said, 'OK, cut it off.'

They pressed the blade into his flesh, enough to draw blood, then began leaning painfully on his bladder, forcing him to urinate.

'Why do you want to kill me?' Hossam asked.

'Because your people are killing us,' he was told.

Then they electrocuted him. This went on for three days. Beatings, burnings, cuttings. The worst, he says, was 'the cutting'.

'They came for me. I lay down on a table and closed my eyes. I saw them cut my gut with a scalpel.' He tells me that he must have been in shock because the pain did not seem to reach his brain. 'Then they lifted something out of my body – I felt pulling. It was my intestine. They stretched it. They held it in their hands and laid it on the outside of my body. They made jokes about how much the rebels ate, how much food was inside my intestines. Then they sewed me back up, but in a rough way so that there was skin and blood everywhere.'

He tells me his stomach was 'open' for two days before they properly stitched the wound closed.

The next day the torturers – who clearly must have had medical knowledge – punctured Hossam's lung. They cut an incision that runs from under his nipple to the middle of his back. They inserted what he described as a small plastic suction tube.

'I felt the air go out of my lung,' he says quietly. 'My right lung had collapsed. I could not breathe.'

Hossam is alive only because on the third day of his torture he was left hanging upside down for nearly five hours. He tells me how he was 'used as a punchbag by nearly everyone that went by as a way of having fun', until, later that day, when it was quiet, a doctor suddenly knelt before him.

He whispered, 'My job is to make sure that you are still alive and can sustain more torture. But I can't watch this anymore.' The doctor shook his head.

'Your heart has technically stopped twice, once for ten seconds and once for fifteen.' He leaned forward and opened a notebook.

'I am going to close your file and write that on the second attempt to revive you, I failed. Do you understand what I am saying? You are dead.'

As the doctor walked away, he said, 'If Allah intends you to live, you will find a way to get out of here.'

It took several minutes for Hossam to understand what the doctor meant. He was giving him a chance to escape, to live. The doctor ordered that Hossam be taken down from his ropes, and he was tossed back into the morgue. As he lay there, he thought of his dead brother, somewhere under the pile of bodies.

Hossam's story is so grisly that, in spite of his obvious wounds, part of me, a small part of me, wonders if it can be true. How can someone actually survive such treatment? This is what torture also does. In its worst form, it makes us doubt the victims.

After an hour among the dead, in pain so brutal that he could think of nothing but the blood coursing through his ears, a nurse came into the room. She whispered that she had been paid by the FSA to bring out any men who were still alive. She told Hossam to follow her instructions carefully: she would give him a Syrian government uniform, and a number, which he must memorize. She made him say it twice. He mumbled that he could stand no more, and she gave him an injection of painkiller. Then, she gently lifted him up and helped him put on the uniform.

With his arm around the nurse for support, they walked out of the courtyard of the military hospital. It took twenty minutes to walk a few feet; but he tells me that it felt like days. A guard asked him for his serial number. He gave the number the nurse had rehearsed with him while she looked on nervously.

At the gate, a car was waiting. It was someone sent by the FSA. They opened the door and the nurse helped him in and turned away without looking back.

He was free.

2. Daraya

Daraya, a suburb seven kilometres south-west of Damascus, was once known for its handmade wooden furniture. It is also allegedly the place where Saul had a vision of God, became a believer and apostle and headed for Damascus.

In August 2012, more than 300 people, including women and children, were killed – the town was 'cleansed'. It marked a turning point in the war. I was driven by a Sunni resident, Maryam (not her real name), and we passed easily through the government military checkpoints manned by young boys with stubble and Kalashnikovs who looked as though they would be more comfortable in discos than in this war zone.

Maryam's family came from Daraya, but they had been at their holiday home near the coast when the massacre took place between 23 and 25 August. As we drove, she took in the destruction with a certain sangfroid, but it was clear that she was shocked. She had not yet decided if she supported the government or the rebels. But as an open-minded, educated woman, she wanted to see for herself what was happening in her country.

The government line was that the massacre was a prisoner exchange gone wrong; the FSA said it was an attack and cleansing operation.

'Syrians could not do this to other Syrians,' she said, her voice shaking. It appeared as though the government tanks had rolled right through the centre of town, destroying everything in sight, crushing the street lights, the houses, even the graveyard walls.

There were shattered windows and glass everywhere and I saw a lone cyclist with a cardboard box of tinned groceries strapped to a rack over his back wheel. But there were no other civilians on the streets. The buildings appeared crushed like accordions; it looked as though people had either hidden or run away as fast as they could.

The Syrian opposition was giving figures as high as 2,500 massacred, but the local people I managed to find told me the number was closer to 1,000 people killed, mainly men and boys.

One month on, there are still no clear figures, but the number 330 is usually quoted. But everywhere I went that day in Daraya, I encountered the distinctive smell of the dead decaying.

I met one of the witnesses, a man who had just been released after six months in prison. His crime? There were often demonstrations in the streets. But this man said he wasn't even at a demonstration when he was arrested.

'They picked up the wrong guy and forgot about me.' He had been led outside in the prison yard, naked but for his underwear in the freezing winter cold, doused with icy water, then left hanging from ropes for hours and beaten. But somehow, he survived.

After a while, Maryam and I went to look for the gravedigger to see if he could give us a count of the dead. There was a crowd of people gathered who were reading a sign put up by desperate families – a list of the missing. They told us that they came every day to see if they could find their loved ones. One man told me he had been looking for his elderly father for three days before finally finding his body decaying in the heat on a farm outside Daraya, along with the bodies of several young men.

'But why kill an old man? Why?' Then he said what I kept hearing, over and over on this trip: 'Syrians cannot do this to other Syrians.'

3. The Balloon Has Not Yet Burst

My first trip to Syria was in the stifling heat of summer. I arrived in a local taxi from Beirut. The first thing I saw once I crossed the border was the enormous colour portrait of the leader, common to all autocratic regimes. This was of the youthful, triangular face of Bashar al-Assad.

The second thing that attracted my attention was a Dunkin' Donuts, which seemed odd, even in a sophisticated country like Syria. I was aware I was entering what has been called the second most dangerous regime next to North Korea, so I was shocked to see such an American symbol. It's the kind of thing one would expect to find on a US airbase in Kandahar, for example, with well-fed American soldiers, rather than skinny, suspicious-looking Syrians, lined up to buy pink-sprinkled donuts.

As it turned out, the Dunkin' Donuts was a fake. It only sold toasted cheese sandwiches. I bought one, watched all the while by three men with moustaches, smoking cigarettes – clearly Mukhābarāt, the infamous Secret Police.

In Damascus, people whisper when out in public. When a waiter arrives at a table, people stop talking. The Mukhābarāt are often so obvious that they could have come straight from central casting. They could easily have been the same men who followed me in Iraq a decade before – the same cheap leather jackets, the same badly trimmed, downward-turned moustaches.

I had come to Syria because I wanted to see the country before it tumbled down the rabbit hole of war. That first trip in June 2012, Syria was on the brink. I checked into a hotel where the United Nations military observers who were there to monitor Kofi Annan's six-point plan in an attempt to bring peace – glum-faced men who were no longer allowed to operate because they had been shot at too often – sat drinking coffee after coffee and making jokes about the Russian hooker bar downstairs.

One Thursday – the start of the Muslim weekend – I came in after an exhausting day of talking to people who were uncertain whether or not their country would exist in a year or two. They were Christians, but liberal. They did not support the government's crushing of peaceful protests at the beginning of the uprising; on the other hand, they were terrified of what was coming next.

'Jihadists?' they asked. 'Salifists?' This is what everyone was worried about, what everyone claimed to distrust: 'Who's next?' Syria, like Bosnia, is multi-ethnic: home to generations of Greek Orthodox, Christians, Sunni Kurds, Shias, Alawites and even a residual population of Jews – 'a melting pot', as the foreign minister's spokesperson, Jihad Makdissi, a Christian with an Islamic name, has called it. But for how much longer was that melting pot going to hold?

To get the weekend going, the hotel sponsored a pool party that looked to me, with the smoke rising in the background from shelling in the southern suburbs, like a re-enactment of Sodom and Gomorrah.

A half-dressed Russian woman danced onstage by the pool, gyrating her skinny hips. Voluptuous wealthy Syrian ladies – all teased hair, glossy lips and silicone-enhanced bosoms – strutted in bikinis and high heels. Men also wore the briefest of swimming trunks and drank what the Levants call 'Mexican beer' – Lebanese beer served with a slice of lime in a salt-rimmed glass.

The party was obscene in a city that was verging on civil war. I stood on my balcony and watched this denial of the drum roll of impending carnage. These people's lives were falling apart. But the balloon had not yet burst.

4. The Believers

For two weeks running, I witnessed the fevered hedonism of the Thursday-afternoon pool parties at the Dama Rose Hotel. The first week was like every other. The hairdresser's were full of ladies of leisure getting hair extensions, mani/pedis and false eyelashes. The roads were clogged with luxury cars heading outside the city to amusement parks – the ones that were still open – en route to country villas for parties, weekend picnics or dinners. Restaurants such as Naranj, which takes up nearly half a block in the Old City and serves traditional Arabic food to the elite, were packed.

But what was unusual about the Dama Rose pool parties was that they were taking place in a hotel that was, ironically, also home to those 300 frustrated United Nations soldiers from fifty different countries who had been brought in to monitor the situation.

From 14 June onwards, when their operations were suspended because it became too dangerous for them to work – their convoys had been attacked, shot at and harassed – the men sat around in the hotel lobby, looking bored, just like the Mukhābarāt.

The blasting house music wafted up to the third floor where Major General Robert Mood, who was then head of the UN Supervision Mission in Syria, tried to negotiate ceasefires, and where his civilian staff shut the windows, put their heads in their hands and wondered what the hell was going to happen to their mission. It would be suspended a few weeks later and Syria would be added to the long list of United Nations failures.

That first week, people danced around to a pumped-up version of Adele's 'Someone Like You', but by the second week, there was an air of sombre reflection to the party. People drank, the house music blared, the UN staff complained about the noise, but the Russian dancer was gone. And this week, people left early, rushing to their 4x4s with distinctly worried looks on their faces.

In the distance, beyond the pool, towards the al-Marjeh neighbourhood, just across from the Justice Courts, there was a larger curl of smoke: two car bombs had exploded earlier that day in the centre of Damascus.

I had left town that morning to visit a remote convent where pro-government – meaning those who support the regime of President Bashar al-Assad – nuns made apricot jam and spent their days praying to the relics of Takla, an ancient Christian saint.

Takla had been an early convert of St Paul, who was running from the Romans when she found herself facing an enormous mountain. Miraculously, the mountain opened to let her pass and make her escape. Syrians and others from all over the Middle East came to be healed at the place of that miracle.

Like many people who support Assad, the Greek Orthodox nuns feared a fundamentalist Islamic regime in their country. I sat with one sister who wore an old-fashioned wimple and served me sugared coffee and biscuits. She spoke Aramaic, the ancient language of Christ, and vehemently defended the regime.

The nuns would not believe that Syrians could massacre each other, she said. When I pointed out that earlier in the summer the United Nations had released a report pointing a finger at the Assad regime for the massacre of civilians at al-Houla, she ignored me, asking a younger nun to bring in a plate of sugared apricots.

This was the same week that the offices of a pro-government television station had been bombed and a firefight had broken out between opposition and pro-government forces. And yet, in Maaloula where the convent was situated, in this village that lay on the road between Damascus and Homs, I felt an unexpected sense of peace.

I remember thinking this would be a good place to hide if full-scale war broke out, and I slipped away from the nuns to explore the convent. Downstairs, the nuns slept in monastic cells, which looked out over the mountains where St Takla had fled. In the courtyard, I saw Syrian couples who had come here to pray for fertility or for the healing of various ailments: you went into a candlelit cave and held a wooden foot, or stomach, or arm, or whatever part of the body ailed you, and prayed to St Takla.

The sun bore down on the car on the road back, and in contrast to the cool convent with its sense of hushed protection, the Damascus bomb site stank of burned rubber. Skeletons of charred cars remained. It was a miracle that no one had been hurt by these explosions caused by 'sticky bombs' – handmade bombs taped to the bottom of a car at the height of rush hour, just across from the Justice Courts.

'Real amateur hour,' one UN official said to me later. 'The bombers didn't know what they were doing – it's just a scare tactic to make the people hate the opposition.'

And it worked. People blamed the opposition and 'foreign interventionists' for the explosions. Crowds of people gathered, angry that their city was quickly falling victim to the devastation that was spreading across the country.

'Our only friend is Russia!' one well-dressed man shouted, his face contorted with rage. 'These are foreigners that are exploding our country! Syria is for Syrians!'

It is a common belief that the bombs and the chaos spreading throughout the country are being caused by a 'third element'. Especially in Damascus, which has long been an Assad stronghold, people refuse to believe that the opposition will rule their country without turning it into a fundamentalist Muslim state.

Damascus has many faces. There are the opposition activists who are working night and day to bring down Assad, the ones who meet me in secret. Sometimes, when I return to my home in Paris, I hear news through the grapevine that they have disappeared. These are the ones who risk going to jail for up to forty-five days without charge. Even peaceful protesters have been thrown in jail simply for demonstrating. Their families are not told of their whereabouts.

Twice I visited the Damascus Opera House – the second-grandest in the Middle East, in this city named by UNESCO in 2008 as the Arab Capital of Culture.

'I do not want to give the impression that we are like the *Titanic* – the orchestra plays on while the ship sinks,' explained one classical musician. We were sitting in her office and she motioned overhead, meaning the room was probably bugged.

On another visit, I went to see the Children's Orchestra practising, led by a visiting British conductor. When I mentioned that he was brave to be there, he said, with a worried look, 'Should I get out soon? How long do you give it before all-out war?'

I reassured him, but in fact, I thought, the country was already in a full-scale, if guerrilla, war.

Some of the musicians were very young – around eight – with tiny hands holding their instruments, but others looked like teenage kids anywhere – Brazilian surfing bracelets, baggy jeans, long flowing hair. They practised the incredibly touching song of innocence, 'Evening Prayer', from Humperdinck's *Hansel and Gretel*.

I sat for a good while watching the fresh young faces of the children intently reading the musical scores and holding their instruments with care, and wondered what this room would look like if I returned at exactly this time next year. How many of these boys would be sent to mandatory military service? How many would flee the country? I tried not to think about whether any would no longer be living.

Maria Saadeh (Arabic for 'happiness') lives in Star Square in the old French mandate section of Damascus, in a 1920s building that she helped renovate. A restoration architect by training (educated in Syria and France), she was recently elected, without any experience, as the only Christian independent female parliamentarian.

The Christians are frightened. On Sundays during my stay, I go to their churches – Eastern Christian or Orthodox – and watch them kneel and pray, smell the intense wax of the candles and see the fear on their faces. Will we be wiped out?

The Christian minority fears that if a new government – and perhaps a Muslim fundamentalist one – takes over, they will be cleared off the face of Syria, off the face of the Middle East, the way the Armenians were driven out of Turkey and massacred in 1914.

'Christians to Beirut, Alawites to the coffin,' is one of the chants of the more radical opposition members.

Maria seems confident for the moment. She sits on her roof terrace in a chic apartment building, her two adorable children, Perla and Roland, peeking their heads through the windows and a Filipina maid serving tea. It could be an ordinary day in peacetime – except that, earlier that day, in another Damascus neighbourhood, there was a car bomb and no one yet knows the number of people killed.

Earlier in the week, I had gone to a private Saturday-night piano and violin concert where the director-general of the Opera House, an elegant woman of mixed European and Syrian background, performed Bach, Gluck and Beethoven.

The concert was held at the Art House, an elegant boutique hotel built on the site of an old mill that has water streaming over glass panels on parts of the floor. The audience was sophisticated. There were women in spiky heels and strapless black evening gowns mingling with artistic-looking bohemian men in sandals and casual chinos, and their children.

Everyone rose at the beginning of the concert to pay homage to the 'war dead' with a minute of silence. The violinist wore a strapless red silk dress and high heels, and received a standing ovation. Afterwards, the audience filed out to an open-air restaurant where champagne was served. I overheard several people talking in hushed voices about what had happened around the city that day: explosions, fighting near the suburbs.

'A symphony,' one man said, toasting hopefully with his glass of champagne, 'that we will live through for the next few years.'

5. Firis

One steaming Saturday morning, I drove to the neighbourhood of Berzah, which is a toehold of the opposition inside Damascus. There are frequent protests here, and the government soldiers crack down with arrests, shootings, injuries and deaths. Berzah is known as one of the 'hot spots': areas around Damascus where it is evident that the war is now creeping closer. Douma, where dozens of people were killed in one day in July, is another hot spot. These days the hot spots are engulfing Damascus.

Berzah is also the site of the government-run Tishreen military hospital. One morning, I go to a funeral for fifty soldiers, all killed fighting for Assad. I watch silently as men load the mangled bodies – disfigured and broken by car bombs, IEDs, bullets and shrapnel – into simple wooden coffins, which are then secured with nails before being draped with Syrian flags. The men then march with the coffins, in full military style, to the sound of a marching band, into a courtyard, where families and members of their regiment wait, many of them weeping. It is an acute reminder of how hard Assad's forces are getting hit by the opposition, who are resorting more and more to guerrilla tactics. A senior official at the hospital, who refuses to give his name, says that 105 soldiers are dying every week.

Upstairs, on the seventh floor of the hospital, a thirty-year-old major lies under a sheet, his right leg and arm missing. At the end of May, Firis Jabr was in a battle in Homs where he says he was ambushed and gravely injured by 'foreign fighters: Libyans, Lebanese, Yemeni'.

Despite the fact that he is now missing nearly half his body, and his anxious fiancée is standing attentively near his bed, Firis, who is

Alawite – an offshoot of the Shia religion to which the Assad clan and many of his followers belong – has a huge smile on his face. He introduces me to his mother, whom he calls 'Mama' when I ask her name, and she makes us coffee from a small hotplate in the corner of the room. She serves Arabic pastries with pistachios. She tells me that she is a widow and Firis is her eldest son.

Like nearly all the government supporters I meet, Firis says that he believes in Assad and will continue to fight, as soon as he is fitted with his prosthetics.

'I have two loves,' he tells me, trying to lift himself up with his useless side, 'my fiancée and Syria.'

Later I meet a Syrian friend for tea. She shakes her head sadly when I tell her about Firis.

'It has started,' she whispers sadly. 'The beginning of the end of what was Syria.'

6. Among the Alawites

On my second trip to Syria, a little more than a month later, I felt I was in a different country. The evolving war had become a real war. The faux light-heartedness that had existed – like a balloon – had been popped. Four men in Assad's closest circle had been assassinated, probably with the help of FSA members who had infiltrated the government. People were expecting the fall of Damascus, or worse. There was heavy fighting in other parts of Syria – in Idlib, Aleppo and in the suburbs of Damascus.

I was told by a local reporter that two thousand people had fled the capital alone. Refugees were flooding the Turkish, Jordanian and Lebanese borders. There were fears for the winter.

The Dama Rose Hotel pool parties had halted. The UN had been pulled out except for a skeleton staff; one night I watched a strange karaoke evening – an attempt to be jolly in a miserable place – in the bar. I sat smoking a narghile – a water pipe – and listened to shelling coming from inside Damascus.

I went back to Homs to see some of my Syrian friend Maryam's relatives, and had lunch with her family. Everyone ate quietly while we heard the shelling emanating from a nearby government base. Then, while the older ladies rested on sofas for their after-meal repose, I spoke quietly to the men, asking if they were frightened.

Many people had left, they told me, or were leaving, and they pointed in the direction of the sound of the shelling: 'This is the background music of our lives.'

The next day, we drove towards Latakia, in the Alawite heartland, to see the mausoleum of Hafez al-Assad, the father of Bashar, who had been president from 1971 until his death in 2000. I drove down with Maryam and her husband, passing through checkpoint after checkpoint, and as we got closer to Qardaha, where Assad is buried, there were stone lions everywhere – *assad* means 'lion' in Arabic and it's the name Bashar's grandfather had adopted.

Maryam, who wears a hijab, said, 'We are in the land of Alawites now.' She paused. 'I feel uncomfortable.'

But at the Assad family mausoleum, the guards – young men in sombre blue suits – were friendly; shocked, even, to see a foreigner. They gave me tea and escorted me inside to the green-covered graves where Hafez and two of his sons are buried. They said Hafez had been the first Alawite to go to high school. The air was heavy with the scent of roses and incense. I looked at an empty corner and wondered if the current president, Bashar, was going to find his place there, sooner rather than later.

'We may never see this again,' Maryam's husband said as we left, passing another lion. 'If the regime crumbles, the opposition will tear this place down to the ground.'

When we left, we climbed higher into the green Jibal al-Alawiyin mountains and stopped to eat at a roadside restaurant. A river rushed below us. The waiter was blue-eyed – many Arabs in the Levant are, but in particular Alawites – and said he had moved to Latakia when he was a child. As an Alawite he constantly felt marginalized: even as part of the minority that controlled the country. Seventy-four per cent of the country are Sunni Muslims, yet the Alawites control most of the government jobs and postings.

'The Europeans don't understand us,' the waiter said as he brought platters of barbecued chicken and bottles of beer. 'As Syrians, we are all losing so much.'

At another table, two Alawite businessmen offered us *rakija*, a form of brandy made with anise, and came to join our table. We spoke openly of politics, but when I mentioned the regime's reputation for torture and detention, there was visible stiffening.

'That does not happen,' one of the businessmen said. 'It's propaganda.'

Then the men excused themselves politely and left; Maryam was embarrassed.

'You should not have asked that,' she remonstrated quietly.

'But it's true,' I said.

She turned her face away, and in a cloud of narghile smoke replied, 'Syrians cannot bear that we are doing this to each other. Once we had a common enemy – Israel. Now we are each other's enemy.'

7. The Shabaab

The war had come to Damascus – hit-and-run operations by the opposition; bombings in defence of their minute strongholds. The government, which has tanks and aircraft, kept to the high ground and pummelled opposition fighters from above. The FSA are said to be armed by Qatar, Saudi Arabia and to some extent by the United States, but when you see the fighters – the *shabaab*, the guys – you see what they need is anti-tank weapons and anti-aircraft guns. They have none. Their weapons are old. Their uniforms are shabby. They fight wearing trainers.

Zabadani, a town close to the Lebanese border on the old smugglers' route, had once been a tourist attraction but is now empty except for government gunners on the hills and FSA fighters in the centre of town. Before the war, the town was more or less a model community: mainly populated by Sunnis but a friendly place where people were welcomed, and where ethnicity and religion did not matter.

'There is a feeling of belonging in Zabadani that the regime deprived us of,' said Mohammed, a young journalist I had met in Beirut who was born and raised in Zabadani, but who had been forced to flee. 'We felt *Syrian*. Not any ethnic or religious denomination.'

I crowded into a courtyard of an old building in town, which was protected from shelling on all sides, with a group of fighters on what they counted as the fifty-second day of straight shelling in Zabadani. They did the universal thing soldiers do when they wait for the next attack: drink tea, smoke cigarettes and complain.

'What did you do in your former life?' I asked this ragtag bunch.

One was a mason; another a truck driver; another a teacher; another a smuggler. Thirty years ago, the roads from Damascus to Zabadani were infamous for smuggling.

'You could buy real Lacoste T-shirts, anything, for the cheapest price.' Everyone laughed. Then there was the sound of machine-gun fire and the smiles disappeared.

At the Zabadani triage hospital, which keeps getting moved because it keeps getting targeted and blown up, the sole doctor was stitching up a soldier who had been hit in a mortar attack. The current hospital location had been a furniture shop and was well hidden in the winding streets of the Old City, which had been taken over by the FSA. As the doctor stitched in the dark, he talked: 'Both sides feel demoralized now,' he said. 'But both sides said after Daraya' – referring to the massacre – 'there is no going back.'

The doctor insisted on taking me back to his house and giving me a medical kit for my safe keeping. 'You need it,' he said. As I left, his wife gave me three freshly washed pears.

'The symbol of Zabadani,' said the doctor. 'They used to be the sweetest thing.'

There are no templates for war – the only thing that is the same from Vietnam to East Timor to Sierra Leone is the agony it creates. Syria reminds me of Bosnia: the abuse, the torture, the ethnic cleansing and the fighting among former neighbours. And the sorrow of war too is universal – the inevitable end of a life that one knows and holds dear, and the beginning of pain and loss.

War is this: the end of the daily routine – walking children to schools that are now closed; the morning coffee in the same cafe, now empty with shattered glass; the friends and family who have fled to uncertain futures. The constant, gnawing fear in the pit of one's stomach that the door is going to be kicked in and you will be dragged away.

I returned to Paris after that second trip, and thought often of a small child I met in Homs, with whom I had passed a gentle afternoon. At night, the sniping started and his grandmother began to cry with fear that a foreigner was in the house, and she made me leave in the dark.

I did not blame her. She did not want to die. She did not want to get raided by the Mukhābarāt for harbouring a foreign reporter.

The boy had been inside for some months and he was bored: he missed his friends; he missed the life that had ended for him when the protests began.

For entertainment, he watched, over and over, the single video in the house, *Home Alone* – like Groundhog Day, waiting for normality to return so he could go out and play, find the school friends who months ago had been sent to Beirut or London or Paris to escape the war, and resume his lessons.

'When will it end?' he asked earnestly. For children, there must always be a time sequence, an order, for their stability. I know this as a mother. My son is confused by whether he sleeps at his father's apartment or his mother's and who is picking him up from school.

'And Wednesday is how many days away?' he always asks me. 'And Christmas is how many months? And when is summer?'

'So when is the war over?' this little boy asked me.

'Soon,' I said, knowing that I was lying.

I knelt down and took his tiny face in my hands. 'I don't know when, but it will end,' I said. I kissed his cheek goodbye. 'Everything is going to be fine.' ■

DON'T FALL
IN LOVE

Mohsin Hamid

So it is worrisome that you, in the late middle of your teenage years, are infatuated with a pretty girl. Her looks would not traditionally have been considered beautiful. No milky complexion, raven tresses, bountiful bosom or soft, moonlike face for her. Her skin is darker than average, her hair and eyes lighter, making all three features a strikingly similar shade of brown. This bestows upon her a smoky quality, as though she has been drawn with charcoal. She is also lean, tall and flat-chested, her breasts the size, as your mother notes dismissively, of two cheap little squashed mangoes.

'A boy who wants to fuck a thing like that,' your mother says, 'just wants to fuck another boy.'

Perhaps. But you are not the pretty girl's only admirer. In fact, legions of boys your age turn to watch her as she walks by, her jaunty strut sticking out in your neighbourhood like a bikini in a seminary. Maybe it's a generational thing. You boys, unlike your fathers, have grown up in the city, bombarded by imagery from television and billboards. Excessive fertility is here a liability, not an asset as historically it has been in the countryside, where food was for the most part grown rather than bought, and work could be found even for unskilled pairs of hands, though now there too that time is coming to an end.

Whatever the reason, the pretty girl is the object of much desire, anguish and masturbatory activity. And she seems for her part to have some mild degree of interest in you. You have always been a sturdy fellow, but you are currently impressively fit. This is partly the consequence of a daily regimen of decline feet-on-cot push-ups, hang-from-stair pull-ups, and weighted brick-in-hand crunches and back extensions taught to you by the former competitive bodybuilder, now middle-aged gunman, who lives next door. And it is partly the consequence of your night job as a DVD delivery boy.

Beyond your neighbourhood is a strip of factories, and beyond that is a market at the edge of a more prosperous bit of town. The market is built on a roundabout, and among its shops is a video retailer, dark and dimly lit, barely large enough to accommodate three customers at the same time, with two walls entirely covered in movie posters and a third obscured by a single, moderately packed shelf of DVDs. All sell for the same low price, a mere twofold markup on the retail price of a blank DVD. It goes without saying that they are pirated.

Because of splintering consumer tastes, the proprietor keeps only a hundred or so best-selling titles in stock at any given time. But, recognizing the substantial combined demand for films that each sell just one or two copies a year, he has established in his back room a dedicated high-speed broadband connection, disc-burning equipment and a photo-quality colour printer. Customers can ask for virtually any film and he will have it dropped off to them the same day.

Which is where you come in. The proprietor has divided his delivery area into two zones. For the first zone, reachable on bicycle within a maximum of fifteen minutes, he has his junior delivery boy, you. For the second zone, parts of the city beyond that, he has his senior delivery boy, a man who zooms through town on his motorcycle. This man's salary is twice yours, and his tips several times greater, for although your work is more strenuous, a man on a motorcycle is immediately perceived as a higher-end proposition than a boy on a bicycle. Unfair, possibly, but you at least do not have to pay monthly instalments to a viciously scarred and dangerously unforgiving moneylender for your conveyance.

Your shift is six hours long, in the evening from seven to one, its brief periods of intense activity interspersed with lengthy lulls, and because of this you have developed speed as well as stamina.

You have also been exposed to a wide range of people, including women, who in the homes of the rich think nothing of meeting you alone at the door, alone, that is, if you do not count their watchful guards and drivers and other outdoor servants, and then asking you questions, often about image and sound quality but also sometimes about whether a movie is good or not. As a result you know the names of actors and directors from all over the world, and what film should be compared with what, even in the cases of actors and directors and films you have not yourself seen, there being only so much off time during your shifts to watch what happens to be playing at the shop.

In the same market works the pretty girl. Her father, a notorious drunk and gambler rarely sighted during the day, sends his wife and daughter out to earn back what he has lost the night before or will lose the night to come. The pretty girl is an assistant in a beauty salon where she carries towels, handles chemicals, brings tea, sweeps hair off the floor and massages the heads, backs, buttocks, thighs and feet of women of all ages who are either wealthy or wish to appear wealthy. She also provides soft drinks to men waiting in cars for their wives and mistresses.

Her shift ends around the time yours begins, and since you live on adjacent streets, you frequently pass each other on your ways to and from work. Sometimes you don't, and then you walk your bicycle by the salon to catch a glimpse of her inside. For her part, she seems fascinated by the video shop, and stares with particular interest at the ever-changing posters and DVD covers. She does not stare at you, but when your eyes meet, she does not look away.

Every so often it happens that you don't pass her on your way to work and also don't see her when you walk by the windows of the salon. On these occasions you wonder where she might have gone. Perhaps she has a rotating day off in addition to the day the salon shuts. Such arrangements are, after all, not unheard of.

One winter evening, when it is already dark, and the two of you approach each other in the unlit alley that cuts through the factories, she speaks to you.

'You know a lot about movies?' she asks.

You get off your bicycle. 'I know everything about movies.'

She doesn't slow down. 'Can you get me the best one? The one that's most popular?'

'Sure.' You turn to keep pace with her. 'You have a player to watch it on?'

'I will. Stop following me.'

You halt as though at the lip of a precipice.

That night a video is quietly stolen from your shop. You carry it under your tunic the following day, but there is no sign of the pretty girl, neither on the way to work nor at her salon. You next see her the day after, her shawl half-heartedly draped over her head in a disdainful nod to the accepted norms of your neighbourhood, as it always is when she is out on the street. She walks awkwardly, burdened with a large plastic bag containing a carton for a combination television and DVD player.

'Where did you get that?' you ask.

'A gift. My movie?'

'Here.'

'Drop it in the bag.'

You do. 'That looks heavy. Can I help?'

'No. Anyway you're like me. Skinny.'

'I'm strong.'

'I didn't say we weren't strong.'

She continues on her way, adding nothing further, not even a thank you. You spend the rest of the evening in turmoil. Yes, you have spoken to the pretty girl twice. But she has given you no sign that she intends to speak to you again. Moreover, the strong-versus-skinny debate has been raging in your head for some time, so her comments cut close to the bone.

When asked why, despite your regular workouts, your physique looks nothing like his in photos of him at his competitive prime, your neighbour, the bodybuilder turned gunman, blames your diet. You are not getting enough protein.

'You're also young,' he says, leaning against his doorway and taking a hit on his joint while a little girl clings to his leg. 'You won't be at your max for another few years. But don't worry about it. You're tough. Not just here.' He taps your bicep, which you flex surreptitiously beneath your tunic. 'But here.' He taps you between the eyes. 'That's why the other kids usually don't mess with you.'

'Not because they know I know you?'

He winks. 'That too.'

It's true that you have earned a savage reputation in the street brawls that break out among the boys of your neighbourhood. But the issue of protein is one that rankles. These are relatively good times for your family. With one less mouth to feed since your sister returned to the village, and three earners since you joined your father and brother in employment, your household's per-capita income is at an all-time high.

Still, protein is prohibitively expensive. Chicken is served in your home on the rarest of occasions, and red meat is a luxury to be enjoyed solely at grand celebrations, such as weddings, for which hosts save for many years. Lentils and spinach are of course staples of your diet, but vegetable protein is not the same thing as the animal stuff. After debt payments and donations to needy extended relatives, your immediate family is only able to afford a dozen eggs per week, or four each for your mother, brother and you, and a half-litre of milk per day, of which your share works out to half a glass.

For the past several months, your one secret indulgence, which you are both deeply guilty about and fiercely committed to, has been the daily purchase of a quarter-litre packet of milk. This consumes 10 per cent of your salary, the precise amount of a raise you neglected to inform your father you had received. Per week, your milk habit is also roughly equivalent to the price your employer's customers are willing to pay for the delivery of one pirated DVD, a fact that alternately angers you in its preposterousness and soothes you by putting your theft from your family into diminished perspective. The daily sum of money involved is, after all, worth a mere thumb's-width slice of a disc of plastic.

You are thinking of your complicated protein situation when you spy the pretty girl the next evening. This time she stops in the alley, produces the DVD you gave her and thumps it without a word against your chest.

'You didn't like it?'

'I liked it.'

'You can keep it. It's a gift.'

Her face hardens. 'I don't want gifts from you.'

'I'm sorry.'

'Do you have a phone?'

'Yes.'

'Give it to me.'

'Well, the problem is it's from work . . .'

She laughs. It is the first time you have seen her do so. It makes her look young. Or rather, since she is in fact young and normally appears more mature than her years, it makes her look her age.

She says, 'Don't worry. I'm not going to take it with me.'

You hand over your phone. She presses the keys and a single note emerges from her bag before she hangs up.

She says, 'Now I have your number.'

'And I have yours.' You try to match her cool tone. It is unclear to you if you succeed, but in any case she is already walking away.

Because of the nature of your work and the need to be able to reach you on your delivery rounds at any moment, your employer has provided you with a mobile. It is a flimsy, third-hand device, but a source of considerable pride nonetheless. Paying for outbound calls is your own responsibility, so you maintain a bare minimum of credit in your account. Tonight, though, you rush to buy a sizeable refill card in anticipation.

But the call you are waiting for does not come. And when you try calling the pretty girl, she does not answer.

Deflated, you go about the rest of your deliveries without enthusiasm. Only at the end of your shift, after midnight, does she ring.

'Hi,' she says.

'Hi.'

'I want another movie.'

'Which one?'

'I don't know. Tell me about the one I just saw.'

'You want to see it again?'

She laughs. Twice in one night. You are pleased.

'No, you idiot. I want to know more about it.'

'Like what?'

'Like everything. Who's in it? What else have they done? What do people talk about when they talk about it? Why is it popular?'

So you tell her. At first you stick to what you know, and when that runs out, and she asks for more, you say what you imagine could be plausible, and when she asks for even more, you venture into outright invention until she tells you she has heard enough.

'So how much of that was true?' she asks.

'Less than half. But definitely some.'

She laughs again. 'An honest boy.'

'Where are your parents?'

'Why?'

'Just that they let you speak on the phone at this time.'

'My father's out. And my mother's asleep.'

'She doesn't wake up when you talk?'

'I'm on the roof.'

You consider this. The image of her alone on a rooftop makes you somewhat breathless. But before you can think of anything appropriate to say, she speaks again.

'I'll take another tomorrow. You pick. But a popular one.'

Thus begins a ritual that will last for several months. You meet on the way to work. Without stopping or exchanging a word, you either hand her a DVD or receive one she has just seen. At night you speak. Initially you feel like a professor of a subject in which you are barely literate, but because you give her only movies you have already partly seen, you are at least able to offer opinions of your own. Soon you find that she is helpfully filling in gaps in plot for you, telling you entire storylines, in fact. And your debates grow richer, and sometimes more heated. Your phone charges ought to be considerable, eating up most if not all of your tips, but she insists on being the one to call you, and so you spend nothing. She also insists that the two of you do not discuss yourselves or your families.

The pretty girl's father is a trained stenographer who has not taken dictation, or held any other kind of employment, for some time. He always had weaknesses for cards and moonshine, but a lack of funds ensured in his case that these remained minor vices. His undoing came when his employer, the owner of a small plastic-bottle-manufacturing business, sold the company and rewarded the workers with bonuses. The pretty girl's father, having been in close daily contact with his departing boss, was treated with particular generosity, receiving over a year of his modest salary in a single lump sum. He never worked again.

A day in the life of the pretty girl's father now begins with him going to sleep, which he does at dawn, rising at dusk or even later. He seizes what money he can from his wife and daughter and heads out to the bar, an underground establishment run by illegal African immigrants in a room that moves around the neighbourhood, relocating each time the police, despite the bribes they receive, feel enough pressure from religious activists to make a show of shutting it down. He drinks alone until about midnight, when the game begins. Then he makes his way to the shuttered stall where his friends deal him in. Some of them have beaten him brutally in the past, one of the consequences of this being that he cannot bend three fingers on his left hand. He currently owes a substantial sum to a local gangster, an unsmiling man who is decidedly not his friend, and he plays in the hope of winning back this amount, and in the fear of what will happen if he does not.

His wife, the pretty girl's mother, suffers from severe and premature arthritis, a condition that makes her work as a sweepress, the only work she could find when circumstance thrust her relatively late in life into the paid labour force, an exercise in unmitigated agony. She no longer speaks to her husband, rarely speaks to the pretty girl except in occasional shrieks that can be heard up and down their street and, at her job, pretends to be mute. She does speak to the divine, requesting to be released from her pain, and since she does so in public, mumbling seemingly to herself as she shuffles along, she is thought to be insane.

The pretty girl, not surprisingly, is planning her escape from her family. Her salary at the beauty salon is far more than what her mother makes, and she surrenders all of it to her parents without resistance. But the salon also caters to the needs of a number of lesser-known fashion photographers, so she has been exposed to their world, and has even been taken along to assist with hair and make-up on a few low-budget shoots. Through this she has become the mistress of a marketing manager responsible for a line of shampoo. He says he recognizes her potential to be a model, promises to make this happen and in the meantime gives her gifts and cash. This cash the pretty girl has been saving, without telling either her parents or the marketing manager, believing that it represents her independence.

In exchange, the marketing manager demands physical favours. Initially these were kisses and permission to fondle her body. Then oral sex was required. This was followed by anal sex, which she believed, much to his surprise and delight, would allow her to preserve her virginity. But as the months passed, she came to doubt this logic, and eventually she permitted vaginal sex as well.

Whatever excitement and warmth the marketing manager once evoked in the pretty girl are now long gone. Her goal is sufficient funds to afford the rent of a place of her own, a goal she is now close to achieving. She also holds out some hope that the marketing manager will come through on his commitments to put her face in an ad and to introduce her to others who could further her career. But she is no fool, and she has been getting to know some of the photographers who use the services of her salon, more than one of whom has told her in no uncertain terms that she has potential.

What is clear to the pretty girl is that she must bridge a significant cultural and class divide to enter even the lower realms of the world of fashion. Hence her initial interest in movies, and in you. But she has discovered, beyond their educational value, that she actually enjoys films, and even more surprisingly that she actually enjoys talking to you. In you she has made a friend, a person who renders her life in the neighbourhood she hates more bearable.

She recognizes your feelings for her, however. She sees the way you look at her as you pass each other in the alley. Her own feelings for you, she tells herself, are rather different. She thinks of you with warmth and fondness, like a little brother, except of course that you are the same age, and not her brother at all. And you do have beautiful eyes.

Yes, she knows there is something. She is happy during her conversations with you, happier than at other times. She appreciates the lines of your body and how you carry yourself. She is amused by your manner. She is touched by your evident commitment. You are a door to an existence she does not desire, but even if the room beyond is repugnant, that door has won a portion of her affection.

So before she leaves the neighbourhood for good, she gives you a call. This is itself not at all unusual. What she says, though, is.

'Come over.'

'Where?'

'Meet me on my roof.'

'Now?'

'Now.'

'Where is it?'

'You know where it is.'

You do not bother denying it. You have walked by her house many, many times. Every boy in your neighbourhood knows where she lives. Though you have an hour left in your shift, you jump on your bicycle and pedal hard.

You climb the outside of her building carefully, moving from wall to windowsill to ledge, trying not to be seen. When you get to the top she does not speak, and you, out of habit from your many unspeaking encounters, remain silent as well. She undresses you and lays you flat on the roof, and then she undresses herself. You see her navel, her ribs, her breasts, her clavicles. You watch her expose her body, taking in the shock of her nudity. A thigh flexes as she kneels. A brush strokes your belly. She mounts you, and you lie still, your arms stiff at your sides. She rides you slowly. Above her you see the lights of circling aircraft, a pair of stars able to burn through the city's pollution, lines of electrical wires dark against the glow of the night sky. She stares into your face and you look back until the pressure builds so strong that you have to look away. She pulls off before you ejaculate and finishes you with her hand.

After she has dressed, she says with a small smile, 'I'm leaving.'

She disappears downstairs. You have not kissed her. You have not even spoken.

The next day she is gone. You know it well before you fail to cross her on your way to work, word spreading quickly in your neighbourhood that she has surrendered her honour and run away with her deflowerer. You are distraught. You are the sort of man who discovers love through his penis. You think the first woman you make love to should also be the last. Fortunately for you, for your financial prospects, she thinks of her second man as the one between her first and her third.

There are times when the currents leading to wealth can manage to pull you along regardless of whether you kick and paddle in the opposite direction.

Over dinner one night your mother calls the pretty girl a slut. You are so angry that you leave the room without finishing your egg, not hearing that in your mother's otherwise excoriating tone is a hint of wistfulness, and perhaps even of admiration. ∎

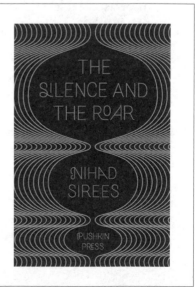

ONE MORE LAST STAND

Callan Wink

Pencil drawing on the wall of the home of Rudy Vargas in Pine Ridge village, Pine Ridge Indian Reservation.
© Aaron Huey

At the last rest stop before Crow Agency, Perry pulled off and donned the uniform in a stall in the men's restroom. Navy-blue wool pants and high-topped leather riding boots. A navy-blue wool tunic with gaudy chevrons and large gilt buttons. Elbow-length calfskin gloves. A broad-brimmed hat with one side pinned up rakishly. He smoothed his drooping moustache and ran his fingers through his long blonde hair. When he got back into his car he had to take off the hat. He was tall and the crown crushed against his Camry's low ceiling.

Out over the Bighorn range the sky was going red, a red shot through with soot-black tendrils of cirrus horsetail. He came in fast, pushing the Camry up to ninety just past the last hill into the Little Bighorn valley. It felt like a charge, headlong and headstrong, brash, driving hard into the final waning moments of a Martian sunset. He rolled the windows down to feel the rush of air. Only in this place, Perry thought, could the sky look like an expanse of infected flesh. What was the saying?

Red sky at night – sailors take fright?

Red sky at night – keep your woman in sight?

How about: red sky at night – bad men delight?

He'd reserved his usual room at the War Bonnet Motel and Casino. There was a king-sized bed and an ironing board that folded down from the wall, and an unplugged mini-fridge. The first thing he did was plug in the mini-fridge. The second thing he did was take off and hang up the uniform. Then Perry stretched out on the bed in his boxer shorts and undershirt and fell asleep.

When he woke an hour later it was full dark. He drank a beer and flipped through the channels until he found the weather and was pleased to see the weekend forecast called for high eighties and almost no chance of rain. It was going to be hot and dusty out there but better that than rain. Nothing like rain to ruin a re-enactment.

Perry called home. It was only nine but Andy sounded sleepy when she answered.

'Did I wake you?'

'No, it's OK.'

'It's only nine; I didn't think you'd be asleep.'

'It's OK, it's just I had a feeling like I wasn't going to be able to sleep tonight so I took something and then there was this documentary about meerkats on PBS and I started watching that and fell asleep and was having these absolutely insane rodent dreams. You know, that's the problem with when you take something, you fall asleep and then you dream so hard it's like you have a full day or sometimes it seems like a year and then, just as you're ready to lie down for sleep, you wake up. You know what I mean? You take something and you sleep but you're not rested. Anyway, how was the drive?'

'Fine. Long. I got an audiobook at a truck stop in Sioux Falls. It was about this guy in New York who tried for a year to follow the Bible exact. Did you know that the Bible says you shouldn't wear clothing that is made of fabric that mixes wool and linen?'

'I had no idea.'

'Seriously. Also you shouldn't trim your sideburns and the corners of your garments should have tassels.'

'Tassels?'

'Yes.'

'Why?'

'I'm not sure. But, according to the book, there's a store in New York City that sells nothing but tassels. Tassels without Hassles.'

'What?'

'That's what it's called. The store. Tassels without Hassles.'

'Huh. Why was this guy doing this? Trying to follow the Bible exact, I mean. What was his reason outside of trying to come up with an idea for a book?'

'To awaken his spiritual side I guess. Connect to his Old Testament ancestors.'

'Is he Jewish, the author?'

'Yeah. In the book he went to a Hasidic dance in Crown Heights in New York, which, from what I gather, is like an Indian reservation but for Orthodox Jews. There weren't any women there – they didn't allow them to come to the dance. It was a life-changing experience, he said.'

'Sweet, sounds fun.'

'Yeah.'

'I think if I were a Hasidic woman I'd have a big problem with not being allowed at the dance. Perry, I think I'm going to go to bed now.'

'Sounds like it might be a good idea. I'm tired myself from all the driving.'

'Love . . .'

'Love.'

Perry drank another beer then put on the uniform and headed down to the War Bonnet Lounge. He was surprised to see a new bartender this year, a young guy with a black goatee and a spiderweb tattooed over his elbow. 'Well,' the bartender said when Perry bellied up, 'looks like the re-enactment is in town. Either that or you're lost. In the wrong century.' He laughed.

'Maybe both,' said Perry. 'Where's Nolan?'

'He died.'

'No shit. When?'

'April.'

'How?'

'He was old. And diabetic. And Indian. How do you think he died?'

'I was accustomed to seeing him here. We were kind of friends. I didn't know. How old was he anyway?'

'I have no idea, old enough to die and not have it be much of a surprise to anyone that actually knew him.'

'OK, fair enough.'

'Beer?'

'PBR with a shot of Evan.'

Perry shot the Evan and chased it with a small sip of Pabst. He scanned the slot machines. When the bartender came around Perry asked about Kat.

'Kat who?' the bartender said, narrowing his eyes. 'Kat Realbird?'

'Yes, Kat Realbird. She been around tonight?'

The bartender leaned his elbows on the bar and spun an empty shot glass around on the bar top.

'Not tonight. Last night though.'

'How was she? I mean how did she look? How did she seem?'

'What do you mean how did she seem? She came in and played nickel slots with her old grandmother. She had two Coronas with lime. She looked fine. She wore pants. And a shirt. And she had black hair. She looked Indian. I mean what the fuck do you want from me here?'

'Nothing. That's it. That's all I wanted. Thank you.'

Perry finished his beer, and when he did, he flagged the bartender down.

'Another?'

'No, I'm done. But a quick favour for me if you would. When you see Kat Realbird give her a message for me. Tell her the General is back in town.'

That night Perry fell asleep waiting, nursing a beer, still in full uniform on the king-sized bed. When the knock on the door came he thrashed awake and spilled the beer down the side of his tunic.

She stood in the shadows thrown by the motel vapour lights. She was in full regalia – a turkey-bone breastplate, a fawn leather breechclout – her hair braided and adorned with a single raven's feather. Her paint was different this year, the left side of her face starting below the eye was chalk white, the right side was unpainted except for a red, quarter-sized circle on her high cheekbone.

She crossed the threshold and was on him hard, her fingers twisting in his tunic, her lips dampening his full moustache. She drove him back onto the bed and her smell – a mixture of leather, bear-grease face paint and knock-off Chanel No. 5 – came over him. He breathed in where her neck met her shoulder and it was like a return home after a long journey fraught with uncertainty and peril.

'I think about you,' he said. 'Back home at work I sometimes put on my uniform and imagine this. I'll spend whole days downstairs in my office, in full dress. I do conference calls in my hat and gloves and cavalry pants. It makes me feel closer to you – to this.'

He was still on the bed. She was in the room's small bathroom washing off the face paint and rinsing the grease from her hair. She came out towelling her hair, her face clean and bare. He could see the faint pockmarks on her cheeks.

'I have to wash that stuff off, or I break out terribly.'

'Kat, did you hear me?'

'Yes.'

'And? Do you think of me? During the year, in your real life?'

'I do. But it doesn't change anything, so I try not to.'

She got in bed and put her body tight next to his, her face on his bare chest. She twisted a lock of his long blonde hair between her fingers and then put the ends in her mouth, wetting it to a tip like a paintbrush. She traced invisible designs on his chest.

'You painted your face different this year,' he said. 'I almost didn't recognize you.'

'Oh? You have a lot of half-naked Indian women in traditional dress coming to your hotel rooms these days?'

'Of course. But I send them all away.'

'*Sha*, you know no one but me is crazy enough to do this with you. Just so you know, I wasn't going to do it this year, the re-enactment. But when I came to the War Bonnet and heard you were back, I just couldn't not come. I gave John some half-assed excuse and came up to my cousin's. You realize that I just snuck out and walked a mile across Crow Agency in the dark in a breechclout with no panties or bra?'

'Thank you. You were beautiful. You *are* beautiful.'

'*Sha*, you say. General?'

'Hmm?'

'I've had a bad year.'

The first day of the re-enactment went as well as could be expected. They did three shows each day of the weekend and the first was always the roughest. There were always logistics to be straightened out. Horses that acted up. That was Perry's least favourite part about the whole thing. The horses. Inevitably he got stuck on some spavined nag that wanted to stop in mid-battle to take a mouthful of grass or take a shit right where Perry was supposed to lie after being killed.

As had become their custom, on the first day Perry waited on Last Stand Ridge until Kat had time to get there and kill him. He knew it pissed some of the guys off, the way he refused to go down until Kat came flying up the ridge and vaulted from her horse with a piercing war cry – but so what, tough shit for them. She would run at him and he would fall under her weight. As she pretended to slit his throat she always gave him a full kiss on the lips, her body shielding this from the people watching in the grandstands. He never wanted her more than right then. Pretend dead on his back in the dust and horseshit, an erection straining the front of his blue cavalry trousers.

This year was different, but only a little. Perry staggered and gestured as if he were in agony. The field was littered with the bodies of the fallen and he could sense their annoyance. Fucking go down already, man, one of the dead bluecoats lying in the dust near him muttered. It's hotter than hell out here. Show's over. Warriors on horseback were circling and Perry stumbled and then rose slowly to his feet. The crowd was clapping and cheering and he was scanning the ridge-line for Kat. And then she came and it was a sight to see. She and her horse were cast from the same mould. Her brown thighs rippled and tensed, echoing the muscled brown haunches of her mount. Everything was black streaming hair, black flowing mane. He turned to face her, and when she swung one leg and sprung from the horse, he caught a fast glimpse of taut inner thigh. His heart hiccuped. She rushed him and tackled him full force. He tried to get a quick feel of breast as he went down but she made a show of pinning his arms as she straddled him with her knife between her teeth. She brought the dulled blade across his throat theatrically and when she leaned in close for the kiss he thought he saw tears smearing the paint on her cheeks. It could have been sweat. But then he saw her sad smile.

There were no good restaurants in Crow Agency – actually no restaurants at all if you didn't consider fast food a viable option – so he bought steaks and they grilled them on the small fenced patio off the back of his hotel room. It didn't matter, about the lack of restaurants, because they couldn't have been seen like that anyway, out together. The reservation was small. Word would have travelled.

Perry got the beer she liked, Corona, and they drank them while he messed with the steaks. Kat painted her toenails, her knees drawn up to her chest. Over the top of the warped vinyl patio fence Perry could just make out a ragged flock of turkey vultures circling over the battlefield, searching for stray hot dogs and partially eaten Indian tacos left by the tourists.

'Do you mind if I call my wife quickly?'

'You know I don't.'

'OK, we'll eat soon.'

He went into the room and left the door open behind him. He sat on the edge of the bed and called.

'Andy. Hi, it's me.'

'Oh, hi. I was just loading the dishwasher, just a minute.' Perry heard the phone being fumbled. He could see her fumbling it, her hands wet with soap.

'OK, I'm back. How did it go today?'

'Pretty good. Hot and dusty. But we put on a good show. I think people were happy. During the second act the guy that finally killed me was a little rough with the takedown. I've got some bruises.'

'Geez, my poor banged-up man. What do these guys think? It's not your fault how everything worked out, you know, the scope of history and all that. They won the battle, we won the war. No need to take it out on you. Actually, I don't know how you do it, I think it would start to get to me, you know, dying every day. It's like you're a sacrifice.'

'Or a martyr for the greater American conscience.'

'Yeah, that's it. Jesus H. Custer dying for our sins. Three times a day.'

'Whose sins exactly, do you suppose?'

'I'm not sure, everyone's I guess. What are we even talking about?'

'I don't know either, never mind. How are you feeling today? Yesterday you seemed tired.'

'Yeah, to tell you the truth I hardly remember our conversation. I was a little whacked out. This new stuff they've got me on is potent.' There was a pause, her sharp intake of breath and a soft laugh that couldn't mask what lay underneath.

'Jesus, I feel like shit.'

'I'm sorry. Maybe I shouldn't have left.'

'No, it's not your fault, it's just the thought of another round of this next month makes me want to die. I mean seriously. I'm actually surprised that I'm saying this but maybe they should just cut the fucking thing off and be done with it. I could get a prosthetic. I could still wear bikinis.'

'They make those? Prosthetic breasts?'

'Yeah. You can pretty much get a prosthetic anything these days.'

Perry could tell she was crying and trying to hide it. He could smell the steaks cooking on the grill, could hear Kat humming tunelessly to herself out on the patio.

'I know it sucks now but it will all work out. You won't need a prosthetic anything.'

'Promise?'

'Yes.'

'OK, I'm being depressing. Let's say goodnight.'

'Love.'

'Love.'

They ate their steaks out on the patio. There was no furniture so they sat on the bare concrete with their plates balanced on their laps, cutting their meat while a dusky swarm of moths batted around the single halogen bulb.

'We've been doing this for a long time now,' he said finally.

'Yes. Seven years. And?'

'And, it's funny to think that we existed, us together, before either of our marriages.'

'So?'

'Doesn't that beg the question: which is the marriage, which is the affair?'

'I married John at the First Church of Christ in Hardin. We live together. Every day. That's the marriage. Don't be dumb, General.'

Kat was right of course. She had a smear of steak juice on her upper lip. Perry thought that was unbearable.

Later, she emerged from the bathroom in a one-piece dress of white beaded deerskin, cinched at the waist with a wide, quill-stitched belt. Her face was scrubbed clean and she had used a thin plait of her own hair to tie the rest back into a ponytail. The dress was short and ended in fringe at her upper thighs. Strong thighs, horse-squeezing thighs. The dress was new. A new thing for them.

'Christ, you are beautiful.'

'*Sha*, you say.'

And then she straddled him on the bed. Rode him like she had stolen him and God himself was in pursuit.

After another hot day on Last Stand Ridge, Perry spent an hour posing for photographs with tourists. He put his arms around two rotund sixty-something women and they all smiled for the photographer.

'We're twins,' one of them said. 'And we're from Michigan. Did you know Custer was from Michigan?'

Perry smiled behind his moustache and made a show of examining the women. He thought they only looked like twins the way all fat older women looked like twins. He wanted a beer, he wanted a steak and he wanted Kat's head in his lap.

'We love Custer trivia,' one of the twins said. 'Did you know he graduated from West Point at the top of his class and would probably have been made president one day if his career had continued on its natural path?'

'I did know that. In fact I have a PhD in Custer Studies and my dissertation was a theoretical projection of the scope of American politics had Custer survived the battle and gone on to be elected president.' Perry thought this to be sufficiently lofty to discourage further conversation.

'Oh, how interesting! Did you know that Custer had size twelve feet and was married to Elizabeth Bacon?'

Perry was developing a headache. He could feel hot rivulets of sweat roll from his underarms.

'I did know that,' he said. 'Now I have one for you ladies. Did you know that when a reinforcement cavalry regiment finally arrived on the scene of the battle, they found Custer had received over thirty-two assorted stab wounds, arrow punctures and rifle shots, was scalped, and had his penis and scrotum cut off and stuffed in his mouth?'

That night, after dinner, they walked together on a path along the bank of the Little Bighorn River. They slapped mosquitoes off each other's necks and Perry threw pebbles into the air to make the bats dive to the ground in pursuit. 'It's because they can't see,' he said. 'That's why they chase a pebble. They emit noises too high for the human ear to hear and it's like sonar. The sound bounces back to the bat and that's why they think any small thing flying in the air is probably a bug.'

'Bats have eyes, don't they?'

'I think so.'

'Well, they must be able to see a little then. I'm nearsighted too; I know what that's like. It's not the same as blind. General?'

'Yeah?'

'Do you think you could catch a bat that way, if you wanted to? Like have a net ready and when one swooped down for the pebble you could snag it?'

'Maybe. But what would you do with a bat after you caught it?'

'I don't know, keep it for a pet. Let it hang upside down from a hanger in my closet. Nice and dark in there. They're kind of cute, especially when they're babies.'

'Bats? Cute? I don't see it.'

'Pretty much anything that's a baby is cute. I read somewhere that's Mother Nature's way of helping something defenceless survive. Like, when I was a kid and we had cats that lived out in the barn. My dad always hated those cats and bitched at the way they kept producing litters left and right up in the haymow. But I remember one time I came out to the barn to get him for supper. He was sitting on a hay bale playing with a little calico kitten that was barely half the size of one of his boots. The rest of the litter mewled and rolled over each other in a pile of hay and my dad had a gunny sack and a piece of twine in one hand and that little calico licking the other. I was young, maybe seven or eight, but even then I knew what he was going to do. He looked at me standing there in my barn boots, I was probably crying, I don't remember. Anyway, he didn't say anything, just pitched the calico back in the pile with its brothers and sisters. He threw the gunny sack and twine in the trash on the way out of the barn and he carried me on his shoulders all the way up to the house. I don't remember him doing that very much.'

They had been holding hands but Kat pulled away and walked on a few steps.

'Let's head back. These bats suck at what they do. The damn mosquitoes are eating me alive.'

In Perry's room at the War Bonnet she stopped him when he went to put on the uniform.

'Let's just do it like normal people tonight. If you don't mind.'

'Normal people? I thought you liked what we do.'

'General, you know I do. It's just tonight, I don't want to be your Indian tonight. How about we do something different? How about you pretend I'm your wife? How about we do it like that?'

'I don't know.'

'Please? What does she wear to bed? How does she like it?'

'I don't know, Kat. It feels like a wrong thing. Dishonest.'

'Just once, General. Then we can go back to the old way until you leave. You said yourself that you were unsure what was the affair, what was the marriage.'

She had her arms around him and was rubbing her fingers in tight circles down his back. Looking down on her he could see where she had missed some white face paint behind her ear.

'OK. Fine. She wears one of my T-shirts and a pair of my boxer shorts. I usually work late and she likes to read. Most of the time she's asleep with her book by the time I get to bed.'

'Sometimes do you wake her up?'

'Sometimes.'

'*Sha*, I bet you do. OK. Go into the bathroom and come out in five minutes.'

Perry went into the bathroom and sat on the toilet seat. It was a small bathroom and his bent knees hit the shower door. He realized he had forgotten to call Andy. He waited as long as he could and when he emerged, the lights were off in the room except for the small bedside lamp. Kat had let her hair down. She was on her back on top of the comforter and her black hair spilled across the pillow. She had the hotel Bible split open, face down on her stomach. She was wearing one of his white T-shirts, a pair of his white-and-red-striped boxer shorts. Her skin was very dark against the white cotton, her nipples erect and visible through the thin material. She had her eyes closed and her arms laid out by her sides.

'Oh, hi,' she said drowsily. 'I was asleep. I must have just nodded off while reading.'

On the final day of the re-enactment, clouds came down across the Bighorn Mountains and the sky opened up. It was a mud bath. Between acts everyone stood under the pavilion at the visitors' centre. The warriors' painted faces streaked. Their feathers sodden. Soldiers drank coffee, miserable in wet wool tunics and pants. During a short break in the rain, Perry found Kat retouching her paint, using the side mirror of a Winnebago in the overflow parking lot.

'Can you believe this?' he said. 'I checked the weather and there was no mention of rain.'

'Imagine that, the weatherman being wrong.' She was using two fingers to rub the white paint over her cheek and the side of her jaw.

'In the last show I got killed in a puddle and had to lie there for fifteen minutes while the crowd cleared the grandstands.'

'Poor General.' She flashed him a quick smile.

'Kat?'

'Yeah?'

'My wife has breast cancer.'

She turned to him slowly. She put her arms around him and her painted face left a dull smear on the rough wool of his tunic.

'But it's going to be OK. I think we're going to be all right.'

After the last show everyone went down to the War Bonnet Lounge and got drunk. It was an annual tradition on the final day of the re-enactment. All the re-enactors piled into the dim bar, most still in full dress. The place was hazy with cigarette smoke and the stink of slow-drying wool. A grey-haired man in a full eagle-feathered headdress played the jukebox. Grimy cavalry soldiers played pool with shirtless warriors. Perry ordered a beer and when the bartender – the same goateed guy from the other night – extended the bottle, he didn't release his grip when Perry tried to take it from his hand.

'Don't think people don't know about you, man.'

'What?' Perry said, unsure he'd heard correctly in the noisy bar.

'Don't *what* me, man. You come to get you some red pussy? Is that your deal? John Realbird is my cousin, man. You think you can come here and do whatever the fuck you want?'

Perry felt the blood rising to his face. He looked to see if anyone else was hearing the conversation. 'I don't know what you're talking about, pal. I'm just here for the re-enactment like everyone else. They pay me to come. I've been coming here for years.' Perry backed away from the bar and the bartender said something but Perry couldn't hear over the jukebox and raised voices. Someone clapped Perry on the shoulder and pressed a drink in his hand. When Kat came in he nodded at her and left out the back door. After a while she followed.

They were both a little drunk and in the room they got drunker. Kat perched precariously on the shaky fold-out ironing board and Perry sat on the end of the bed. They passed a pint of J&B.

'My paint is different this year,' she said.

'I know, I asked before. What does it mean?'

'I've been wanting to tell you, I just didn't know how.'

She touched her cheek, the red circle. 'This is a part of me, a piece of my heart that is gone forever.' She touched the other cheek, the chalky white paint. 'This is my soul, blank as a field of snow, white like a ghost wandering the world.' Perry nodded solemnly. Kat gave a snort and shook her head. 'You white people are suckers for that Indian shit. Hand me the bottle.' She drank deeply and laughed like none of it was true.

He nearly forgot to call Andy again, and when he remembered it was late. Kat was slid up against him on the bed, maybe asleep, maybe just being quiet. He dialled with one hand not to disturb her.

'Hello?' Andy's voice was groggy with sleep.

'Hi, it's me. Sorry it's late.'

'Jesus, it's late.'

'I know, I just got caught up with everything here and forgot to call you yesterday and I just wanted to see how you were doing and so I'm sorry but I called you anyway.'

'You sound kind of drunk.'

'I am kind of drunk. End of re-enactment party. Drinking firewater with the locals. That kind of thing.'

'Sounds fun, I'm kind of jealous. Tonight I tried to make a tofu stir-fry. I'm not sure what happened but the tofu ended up scorched and the vegetables were still raw.'

'Tofu can be tricky.'

'Apparently. You know what else I did?'

'Hmm?'

'I bought a pack of cigarettes and smoked almost half of them.'

'Really?'

'Yes.'

'What kind?'

'Don't laugh.'

'What kind?'

'Virginia Slims. Long skinny girly ones.'

'I've never seen you smoke before. I'm having a hard time picturing it.'

'I'm new to it, so I'm not very good at it yet, but maybe I'll do it for you when you get back.'

'Wearing something sexy, holding a glass of wine?'

'If you'd like.'

Kat had reached one arm across Perry's chest and pushed her face down against his neck. The raven feather in her hair brushed his cheek. Her hand found his, the one that wasn't holding the phone.

'OK. I look forward to it. Have you tried blowing smoke rings yet?'

'No.'

'Well, practise.'

'I will. I was going to make it a surprise. You know, you come home from your re-enactment and all of a sudden you have a smoking wife. A wife that smokes. That is something you'd probably never expect.'

'Well, it's still a surprise this way, I almost don't believe it.'

'Yeah, you know why I started?'

'It is a question I had considered asking. Why?'

'Because what's the point of not smoking? I've been not smoking for thirty-three years. Look at where it has gotten me. Now I'm going to be smoking. Make sense?'

'Perfectly.'

'OK, I'm going to let you go, very tired.'

'OK.'

'Love.'

'Love.'

'Love.'

Kat's lips brushed his ear in her whisper. He hung up the phone. He was a scalped and bloody mess.

Before dawn Perry woke to find Kat's side of the bed empty. He turned and saw her standing over him in the dark, fully clothed in jeans and T-shirt. She brought her fingers to his face and smoothed his moustache. When she moved her head down to him, her hair folded like black wings around them.

In the morning Perry crammed the uniform, now smelly and stained, into his suitcase and gave a final look around the room to make sure he wasn't forgetting anything. He put the empty bottle of J&B in the trash can. When he went out to the parking lot he found a fluorescent-orange aluminium arrow shaft protruding from the rear passenger tyre of his Camry. Perry considered the arrow for a moment and then pulled it, with some difficulty, from the tyre. The fletches were glued-on pieces of hot-pink vinyl. The shaft had the word WHACKMASTER printed down the side, and black squiggly lines, which, coupled with the orange, were supposed to give the appearance of tiger stripes. The edges of the broad-head were chipped and rusty. Perry got the spare tyre from the trunk and switched out the flat. He put the arrow in the back seat and left the War Bonnet, driving slowly on the small spare.

The only repair shop in Crow Agency was Robidoux's Fix-It, a lean-to built off the back of a double-wide trailer. Perry pulled in and Ted Robidoux came down the trailer steps in his bathrobe. Ted occasionally rode in the re-enactment. Three years ago he had taken care of a clogged fuel line in Perry's car.

'Morning, Ted. It's Perry. Remember me, the General?'

'Hey, Perry. Of course. I didn't make the re-enactment this year. How did it go?'

'Well, it was a spectacle, as always.'

'Good. Good. Looks like you got a bum wheel there. This country's hard on tyres.'

'And other things.'

'Ha, well, I should be able to handle the tyre at least. Let me go put my pants on.'

He went into the trailer and re-emerged fully clothed, with a mug of coffee that he handed to Perry. 'Have a seat,' he said. 'This could take a few.' Perry sat on the porch and sipped at the hot coffee. It was still early and cool and the land seemed refreshed from yesterday's rain. There was a stack of fresh-cut lodge poles leaning up against the trailer wall and after he had finished his coffee Perry went over to take a closer look. He was running his hand over their smooth peeled surfaces when Ted came from the lean-to. 'Hey,' he said, 'you like my new poles? I just finished peeling those yesterday. Last time we went to the mountains and put up the lodge, I had two poles break in the middle of the night. You should have seen how pissed my old lady was when the whole thing came down on us and we had to sleep in the cab of the truck.'

'Well, you did a good job with these,' Perry said. 'They're smooth. I can't imagine doing it myself. I can't even peel a potato.'

'The secret's a sharp drawknife. And a light hand. And practice.' Ted patted one of the lodge poles and laughed. 'The good old tepee,' he said. Then he patted the side of his trailer and laughed again. 'And here's the new tepee. I got a leaky roof. Fuck me. Well, anyway, we got her patched – the tyre. A good-sized hole.'

'Thanks. It was the damndest thing. I had an arrow sticking out of it this morning.'

'An arrow? Like a good old Indian arrow?'

'Not exactly.'

Perry got the arrow and handed it to Ted who held it between two fingers as if it were something particularly distasteful.

'Whackmaster?' he said.

'I have no idea.'

'Well, you know what we need to do, Perry?'

'What?'

'Back in the old days if a warrior got hit by an arrow he had to break the shaft to make sure the guy who shot him didn't still have power over him. So his wound would heal.' Ted handed the arrow back to Perry.

'Really?'

'Sure. I'm an Indian. I know what I'm talking about when it comes to situations like this.'

'OK. How should I do it? Is there, like, a certain way it should be done?'

'I think just over the knee, like a piece of kindling for the fire.'

Perry brought the shaft down over his knee. The aluminium didn't break, but bent sharply. He looked up at Ted, who shrugged. Perry bent it back and forth a few times and eventually the shaft broke cleanly, like a paper clip.

'There,' said Ted. 'Now you keep that forever.' ∎

A BRIEF
HISTORY OF FIRE

Jennifer Vanderbes

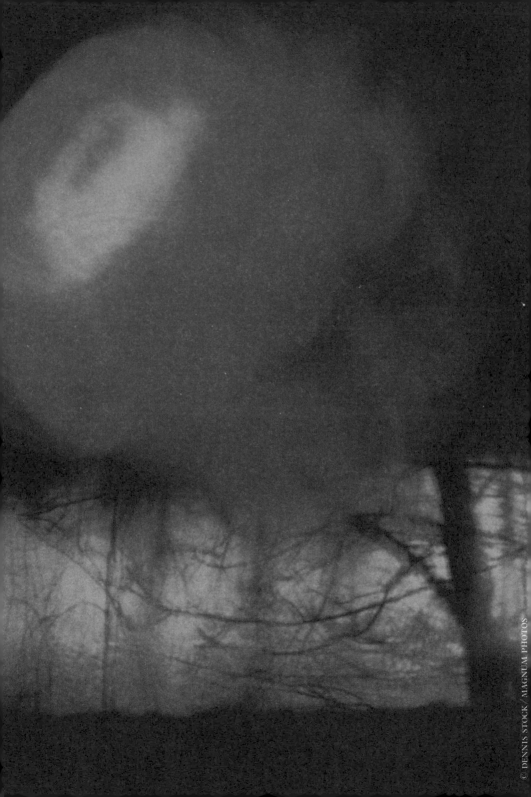

My name is Sarah. I live in the Gila Wilderness, in the mountains of south-western New Mexico, and I map fires. From the nearest road, by horse or mule, it's a day's journey here; few people pass through, only botanists and geologists, the occasional tree counter. In the rare event that one of these men is sent to discuss my data, they are surprised when I open my cabin door. I have neither the heft nor years to fit their image of a solitary outdoorswoman. I wear lipgloss. I French-braid my hair. Even in the late autumn, when I am in gloves all day, I still paint my fingernails. These men glance at my pyramid of firewood, the axe pitched in the stump; they study the fly rod leaning against the door frame, the line of trout drying in the sun.

'*You're* the lookout?' they ask, their heads shaking in disbelief.

They unload their bags in the small room provided for guests of the forest service and, through the open door, shout formalities: *studied forest patterns with Albert Popperly, concerned about mesquite and cottonwood regrowth.* Finally unpacked, they emerge with a fresh shirt and combed hair to share what wine or whiskey they have brought. I grill a trout and over dinner we discuss the land, the fires, the Indians who once roamed these mountains. As the sun sets, I light a fire, and, when the fire dies, we shimmy closer on the lumpy couch to share the large wool blanket that has borne witness to all of my wilderness couplings. The discussion continues, punctuated by probing silences, pauses that anticipate a kiss or a toppling of torsos, but I am, as always, unable to turn away from the embers. As I fight a yawn, the man declares that he loves his work but that all the travel has come at the expense of meeting the right woman. Don't I get lonely out here? I say that the spruce-firs and the ponderosa keep me company. In semi-surrender he smiles, and I stand to rake the ashes. But later, while I am showing him how to release the water valve on the sink so he can brush his teeth, I bury my face in the thick scent between his neck and shoulder, breathing him in, this stranger, as though it is the last scent in the world.

He lifts my chin. 'What on earth are you *doing* out here?' he whispers, kissing me before I can answer.

The next morning, he sets off up the mountain to get cell reception, and by sunset clomps breathlessly up the cabin steps, cheeks flushed. 'I lied to all of my superiors,' he boasts.

'Flu? Sprained ankle?'

'Snake bite.'

'And you're being tended by a nice forest ranger until you can resume your survey?'

'I think my recovery will take at least a week, don't you?'

'Well then. Would you like the grilled trout or the grilled trout tonight?'

For days we play house. We are honeymooners; we are an old couple reading side by side, wrapped snugly in our silence. In the morning, we drink coffee in our underwear. In the afternoon, sweaty from sex, he steps outside in Tevas only to retrieve firewood for the night. I try on his slippers, grow dizzy behind his reading glasses.

I harbour no illusion that I, in particular, have drawn him into this exchange. It is the wind rustling the ponderosa, the wingspread of a falcon traversing the evening sun, the scratch of bobcats on ancient rocks. We are a man and woman alone in the wilderness. We are Adam and Eve, or so he believes.

Splayed across the blanket on the floor, spooning condensed milk into my mouth, he asks, 'So you don't miss television?'

'Gah.'

'Newspapers?'

'No.'

'Baseball games? Telephones?'

'I miss draught beer,' I say. 'And oysters.'

'Nothing else?'

'Nothing else.'

'Come on, you're too young to be living out here like a hermit.'

I am thirty-two.

'I'm a hermit prodigy,' I say. 'I exhibited hermiting skills at age five so my parents entered me in a special programme.'

He reels in mock dismay, then growls and playfully smacks my thigh. 'God, look at that curve. Look at that delicious flesh.' He runs his hand along my side. 'Those are childbearing hips.'

He leans in to kiss me.

'Leave,' I say.

The Earth once existed without fire. Until 400 million years ago, primordial peat and reeds emerged from the sea, plants to feed the ravenous flames. Across the continents fire flashed and faded, sputtered and raged, a wild beast of heat and light roaming the forest until one day man tamed it.

Fire opened the night. Fire rendered animals edible. Brought together by their shared fire, early humans formed tribes, clans, families. For fire must be conceived, fed, disciplined, watched, put to bed, awakened. Fire is like a baby.

Here in the Gila Wilderness, walk a half-mile in any direction and you will come across a lightning-scarred tree. When a tree is struck, if the current runs just beneath the surface, the pressure blasts off a strip of bark.

If the current runs down the centre – *kaboom*.

Few fires in the world begin with lightning. Only one bolt in four reaches the ground, and most strike rock or water. There is hot lightning and cold lightning. Cold lightning will blast without burning. But hot lightning has the high amperage and low voltage to spark combustion.

Hot lightning loves these woods, and, at any given time of year, a half-dozen wild fires are burning here.

Apache, Aspen, Meason, Grouse . . .

Every fire is named, and mapped. From my lookout tower I
mark the hourly and daily changes in a fire's perimeters: one acre,
seventy-five acres. I note the wind speeds and air temperatures. In
the cabin lay seventy-five years' worth of fire maps, maps made by
my predecessors. These are used to overlay subsequent forest growth
maps. Sometimes, a tree counter will arrive and ask for a fire map
from 1962. A botanist will set up camp in my living room and for days
examine every fire map from the 1980s. Because present growth, or
lack thereof, means little without the record of destruction. I make
copies of these maps to send to the district office, indicating the basic
fire-data points so that it can all be computerized. But the originals
remain on site, and many are quite beautiful. The first man in this
cabin was named Everett Hodges, and he signed all of his maps with
a calligraphic drawing of bighorn sheep, though the bighorns had
already vanished from the landscape when he arrived. Perhaps he
spotted one, the last of its kind. Perhaps he imagined he did. These
woods are ancient; the past lingers. Everett Hodges also lived in this
wilderness alone. I am the only woman to have lived here. I have
made seventy maps. I have been here five years.

I once lived in another house, on another hillside, in northern
Arkansas. The house was a lofted wood cabin fronted by a wrap-
around porch with two rocking chairs from which you could see the
Ozark Mountains to the south and east. Sitting in those chairs as the
sun rose, you could watch the morning mail truck turn off the old
highway and slowly tackle the quarter-mile gravel road snaking up
to the house. Conversely – and this is important – from the bottom
of the same road, you could see the entirety of the front porch, even
the main door, above which hung the red wooden letters I had carved
and painted myself, spelling: The Lamberts.

The man who built this house was my husband, Luke.

Luke and I met in college. We ended up in the same corner of
a boring party together my sophomore year. I thought he was sexy

(a word I wasn't accustomed to applying to nineteen-year-olds), but as for what I said to him or what he said to me I can't recall. We were too young to think such details important. When, after too many tequila shots and a shared Marlboro Red, we made out on the hood of a car, we had no idea a significant era of our lives had begun.

Luke was the bass player in a band called the Skornflakes. He tried to teach me to play bass; in the name of higher education, he cracked my Indigo Girls cassettes in half and replaced them with Rage Against the Machine. He wore T-shirts, faded and ripped, hiking boots and dirt-smeared sneakers. The only time I ever saw Luke in a suit was at our lakeside wedding, a suit he peeled off at the night's end to dive from the dock and race his band's drummer across the lake.

We hadn't originally planned on getting married. After graduation, Luke went to work on a fishing boat in Alaska, and, for lack of a better idea, I had moved back to Boston where I worked as a receptionist at a law firm and in the evenings draped my floor with an old bed sheet and set up my easel. I had a few brief, disappointing flings, which always left me with the strange urge to confide in Luke. But I had no way of calling him. From the fishing boat, Luke wrote long letters that sometimes took weeks to arrive, the envelopes covered with ballpoint-pen drawings of king crabs, nautical knots, the crests of Pacific waves. He loved the ocean but did not like his job. The boat was a floating dictatorship, he wrote, and signed his letters Fletcher Christian, HMS *Bounty* Mutineer. He said he wanted to get home, to see me and to never look at another salmon again.

When Luke finally returned to the mainland, he learned his grandfather had died; he called to say that he was clearing out the house in Oregon and would drive his grandfather's truck across the country with some furniture, stopping along the way in Arkansas to see a plot of land his grandfather had left him, but that he would be at my doorstep in two weeks.

I told him I'd fly out and meet him in Arkansas, and we could drive the rest of the way back east together.

We never made it back east.

It was a spectacular piece of land. Situated on a hill near the town of Eureka Springs, the Ozarks rose above us, and below snaked the Buffalo River. That night, we pitched a tent, heated canned ravioli over an old camping stove, shared a warm beer and confessed that in our year apart we had each had some meaningless 'encounters'. Then we put on headlamps, lay side by side on our stomachs, and Luke showed me the photographs he'd taken in Alaska. He narrated each one, then laid out a row of six, edge to edge, that composed a full image of the horizon.

'*Muy* artsy,' I said, injecting Spanish into our conversation as we always did when we were alone, though we could never recall how this started.

'*De nada, señorita*,' he answered, collecting the photos. 'Now tell me about your paintings.'

I explained that I'd stopped painting landscapes because I could only work at night. I was painting still lifes instead, and to save money on canvases I'd buy old paintings from flea markets – some ten inches wide, some five feet wide.

'But you've got to have fresh canvases, Sarah. Won't your parents help?'

'I'm twenty-one. That's too old to live at home or ask for money. Besides, it's kind of interesting. Always painting over something else.'

He pushed the hair from my eyes and kissed me gently, almost nervously, and then slowly it eased into something more insistent, more urgent. Even though for weeks I'd imagined our passionate reunion, when we'd met at the airport it had felt strange to be near him again. For a year Luke had been jagged handwriting on worn paper; he'd been the perfect memory of young love, of sheet-tangled conversations about our parents and religion, talks that spiralled into dawn beside overflowing ashtrays. We'd shared every thought, every memory; I thought I knew him inside out. But he looked different now. His hair was longer and fastened in a ponytail. His left arm was sunburned from the drive and he looked – although I may only have imagined it – *salted*, or aged, from the sea. Before touching him I found myself needing to study every inch of him, and could sense him doing the same. So even though we'd never been shy around each other, it seemed proper to talk, to reacquaint ourselves before tossing aside our headlamps and kicking off our boots, then jeans, as we finally did then, toppling the pots from dinner.

'Do you still respect me?' I asked afterwards.

'Good God. I respect you even *more.*'

'Smart-ass.'

'I could live like this,' he said, pulling me close. 'This night sky, this air, that moon.'

My heart was still beating strongly. 'Me too.'

'I thought about you a lot when I was at sea.'

'You were on a boat full of men. Of course you thought about me.'

'Seriously.' Luke propped himself up on one elbow. 'Putting aside your shitty taste in music, you're the person I admire most in the world. You've got integrity. You'll eat beef jerky for dinner without complaint. You can drink me under the table. And, oh yeah, you're smokin' hot.'

I blushed. 'Well, what of it?'

'Grandpa Lambert was pretty generous. So I can buy you a ring, or I can build you a house. Right here.'

I lay back on a nylon sack stuffed with Luke's shirts. The sky above was dazzling. He laid his head beside mine and our ears touched, our jaws aligned.

'*Casa,*' I whispered.

It took seven months to build the house. We rented a garage apartment in town, and as Luke puzzled over blueprints at night, he looked older and more responsible than the bass player I'd met in college; for the first time I could imagine us one day being middle-aged, drinking wine together by a fireplace, studying the first faint furrows on each other's foreheads, joking about the reckless nights of our youth.

'Sarah, look at how you have to angle the ceiling beams to bear the weight of the roof.' Having majored in engineering, Luke harboured a deep respect for geometry and design. He decided to build me a painting studio with floor-to-ceiling windows and a skylight; it would be attached to the back of the house in order to share plumbing with the kitchen and have its own kitchenette and bathroom, but it would have its own entrance from the outside so that I could have some privacy.

This is also important.

His band mates came to set the timbers and frame. But Luke, alone, hammered in the siding, laid the roof, put up the Sheetrock. I helped with the plaster and sawed logs for the porch rails.

'You would have kicked ass on the frontier.'

'Luke, as far as my family is concerned, this *is* the frontier.'

The night we unpacked the last of our belongings – boxes of our college notebooks, ceramic bowls and vases I had made before abandoning pottery for painting, Luke's bass and speakers – we invited over the few local friends we'd made – the lumber merchant and hardware dealer, the contractor who installed the kitchen cabinetry and plumbing, the electrician – and their wives. Older people who were pink-faced from years in the Ozark sun, delighted to see a young couple setting up house.

'This, darlings, is a house you can grow into,' the lumber merchant's wife said with a wink.

Luke found work as a river guide, taking out canoes and kayaks for weekenders down from Kansas City or up from Little Rock, and I found a part-time receptionist job at a doctor's office, which left my afternoons free for painting. Before dinner, Luke would go for a long run, and sometimes I'd join him, and then we'd shower and sit on our front porch, feet propped on the log rail, our heads wet, drinking beer and watching the sun set above the mountains, amused and amazed that this was our life.

Most of our friends were in law school or medical school, or had headed west to join the dot-com boom. They worked long hours and regaled us over the phone with tales of their dating disasters. Luke and I had each other. We'd built a house.

Our lives felt full, settled, except that after our families came to visit that first year, we rarely had company. No one passed through

Eureka Springs. And so the downstairs guest room stood empty.

Luke could have set up his amp and bass in there, but he didn't. I hung some paintings on the wall, but my supplies remained in my cluttered studio. We put nothing in the dresser drawers, or the closets. The room, strangely, seemed to be waiting for something.

One night, as we were going to sleep, I studied my foil pack of birth-control pills.

'Luke –' I began.

He could see me struggling, and took the pack from my hand. We had been married two years.

'I say we flush these fuckers,' he said.

Derek arrives on my doorstep in mid-August with evacuation orders. He works in the Gila Wilderness on a saw team – the *sawyer* saws off unburned brush, then the *swamper* throws it across the fire line. Derek and his partner Mike used to swap jobs every time the saw needed a new tank of gas. Until one day, Mike, distracted by a fight he'd had with his wife, cut a tree with a hang point, not a hinge; it fell with a fast pivot and crushed Mike's ribcage before he could escape. While Derek held Mike's hand, waiting for the medic and talking to keep him conscious, the blood loss killed Mike. Derek has been grounded until the crew psychiatrist deems him fit to return to the fire zone. I know all the fire crew by name and speciality; I know their voices, but not their faces. In my lookout tower, I listen to them on their radios. The day Derek was with Mike, I heard him shout for the medic, talking Mike through his last breath, then weeping. This was three months ago.

'Macon is close,' Derek says. 'They told me they'd radioed your station but that you hadn't responded.'

'The winds are shifting,' I say. 'It won't come this far.'

He looks up at the sky. He is short and stocky; he has the build of a boxer. 'You're probably right. But I've got nothing better to do than get you out of here. I can give you thirty minutes to pack up your valuables, then we hit the trail.'

'There's nothing to pack.'

He stares at me, then walks back to his horse and mounts the saddle. 'Hop on.'

We ride silently through the woods, watching smoke rise in the distance. The air is hot and dry. Two miles from the cabin, we stop at the stream to water the animal.

'I hear you've been out here a few years,' he said.

'Going on six.'

'And that you don't much leave the park. Lost your taste for humanity?'

'Just strip malls and traffic jams.'

'Can't argue that.' He sits on a rock and pulls out an apple and knife. He quarters it and hands me a slice, then offers one to the horse. 'It's the going back and forth that always gets me. Sometimes we don't sleep for days, don't shower. We breathe smoke all day and hike right into the thick of a fire. Can't really finish up and wander Kmart on the weekend. Like trying to re-enter the atmosphere; the skin just wants to jump from your face.'

'It's been an active season,' I say.

He nods, and then his gaze settles on his boots. I regret my remark. He is thinking of Mike.

'Are you from these parts originally?' I ask.

'Phoenix. My grandmother was Apache. Chiricahua. She lived in a wickiup with a big domed straw roof. All anyone is supposed to want in life is a roof over their head. I hate roofs.' He turns and strokes his horse's face, nodding to the animal as though they have discussed the matter many times. 'Roofs literally make me sick. Perforated ulcer. There's a doctor in Albuquerque wants to study me.'

'You like being up in the trees.'

'Even if there's fire right below. My wife said I must have been a monkey in a former life. Before she decided I was an ass in this one.'

I laugh, and look at his ring finger.

'She gave you the boot?'

He smiles. 'With a steel toe.'

'I'm sure you deserved it.'

'Well, she wanted a roof over her head.' He looks up at the sky. The wind has shifted. 'There goes Macon, running the other way now, just like you said.'

'Then I can go home now.' I stand and head for the horse.

He watches me, without moving. 'You're not scared of the fires?' he asks.

'Not scared,' I say. 'Terrified.'

According to the Cherokee, Grandmother Water Spider spun a bowl and placed it on her back to steal fire from the land of Thunders and Light. It was the Rabbit, claim the Algonquin, who pilfered fire from an old man and his daughters. The Apache say it was the Fox who stole fire from the fireflies, tying bark to his tail to catch their flame, then running away, igniting brush and wood along his path, spreading fire across the Earth.

The record of mankind was written with fire. Prehistoric hearths scorched cave roofs, leaving traces of human habitation for millennia; the charred remains of rabbits and bison settled in the earth, awaiting the shovels of palaeontologists.

Fire is history.

'I'm here to evacuate you again.'

'No you're not. Nothing's burning within twenty miles of here.' Derek stands on my front porch; it is a week later. He is clean-shaven. His black hair gleams with some kind of gel.

'An unofficial evacuation,' he says.

'You've gone rogue?'

'There's somewhere I'd like to visit. Call it a destination evacuation.'

I can see the determination in his face; I can see how this mission, this small adventure, has for the time being subsumed his grief.

'Aren't you supposed to be on leave? Or working the station?'

'They've already grounded me.'

'Well, where do you want to go?'

He is already walking back to his horse, mounting the saddle. A cooler is tied to the horse's flank. 'You coming?'

The sun sits low in the sky as we slowly descend the hill; when the ground levels and the trees clear, Derek gives the horse a kick and the animal tears loose across the grass. The wind is warm on our faces. As we pass a fire site from two years ago, Derek halts the horse to examine a field of black stumps. 'This one . . .' he says, his silence conjuring a momentary sea of flames.

By the time we arrive at the monument entrance, the gates have closed. 'Hold on.' Derek urges the horse into a run and then a long jump. The cooler rumbles. I am briefly lifted from the saddle, and I don't want to lose my balance but avoid lingering in a hug. I'm grateful when we slow for the approach to the cliffs. In five years I have never been here, but I know what we are looking at. Almost a thousand years ago, the Mogollon people roamed this wilderness, taking shelter in the cliff-side caves. With stone axes they felled pines to use as roof beams. Dozens of ceremonial rooms and homes were built into the cliffs.

Derek ties up the horse and we approach on foot. He rests the cooler on his shoulder. The landscape is silent but for the sound of the rocks beneath our boots.

We pass a pictograph – a red stick figure of a man walking – and examine it silently. It looks like a child's drawing.

'Take your pick,' he says. 'Cave one through five.'

'Three.'

We duck and enter sideways. Then we are standing in a massive stone room, looking up at ancient beams.

I put my hand on my hip. 'I thought you hated roofs.'

He smiles and from the cooler tosses me a beer. He sits and opens a can for himself, then cuts a salami in thick slices and lays them on pieces of bread. He cubes a chunk of pimiento cheese and lays it on a bandanna between us. The view from inside the cliff is somehow more stirring than looking at it from the outside. I can imagine living here one thousand years ago, looking out at these wilds every night, hiding from the wind. I wonder what version of myself would have emerged if I had lived then; would I have had more courage?

'You're not from around here,' Derek says.

'Boston. Born and raised.'

'Are your people still there?'

I like this phrasing: *your people*. Family, friends, distant cousins, tribes. I say, 'Yes,' and do not need to elaborate.

Soon we have finished the salami and the cheese and the bread. He pulls two more beers from the cooler, and when he hands mine over, he clears away the bandanna with the pimiento scraps and repositions himself closer to me.

He thinks it would be wrong to make a pass; I see him struggling with this. He is, technically, supposed to be protecting me. But I like him. So I lean against his arm, and he seems pleased.

'They found bodies here, you know,' he whispers.

'Is this the time of night when you try to scare the girl with a ghost story?'

'Scout's honour. They were mummies. They're gone now, of course. A hundred years ago, they found the mummy of an infant in one of the caves. They named him Zeke. That's how this place got famous.'

I try to calm my breathing, and Derek mistakes the meaning of my silence.

'*It's true*,' he insists.

I consider how Derek flaunts honesty, as if it is a badge permitting entry into the darkest of stories.

I close my eyes and rest my head on his chest; he kisses my scalp and soon my mouth is searching his. In the warmth and tangle of our bodies, my mind releases its hold on all memory, like a shoe kicked to the corner of the room.

Derek pulls himself up from me. 'I don't have anything. But it would look pretty bad if I carried rubbers when heading off to fight fires.'

'Agreed.'

'Should I stop?'

'Don't worry. I'm tied up.'

He looks taken aback, but says nothing.

In winter, halfway to the hospital in Little Rock, Emily Anne Lambert was born.

The first months were like a fever dream; days slid into the swirl of night; my body was her captive. At the slightest cry from across the room, milk rushed my breasts. She latched on to me, gasping, in a fit of madness, then drank greedily; afterwards, conquered, spellbound, I gazed at her red-lipped face. Leaning in to smell her breath – sweet and sour – I'd press my mouth to hers.

My happiness was so deep I was afraid to speak of it.

Luke offered to watch her so that I could leave the house and glimpse the real world, but I refused. I wrapped us in blankets and in the grey afternoon light she nursed on the porch; day after day we watched the winter days slowly lengthen, until, in March, I put her in the car seat for the first time and we went for groceries.

The world looked different; in every face I passed – the man slicing ham at the deli counter, the distracted cashier, the boy who wheeled abandoned carts across the parking lot – I imagined the babies they had once been. At the post office, the sight of an old man hobbling on a cane, struggling to open the door, struck a blow to my heart. He is all alone, I thought. He is looking for his mother.

As my body healed from the birth and the awkwardness of pregnancy withdrew into memory, I began to doubt that I had ever *made* Emily. She giggled when I sneezed or coughed, grinned at pictures of dogs; with Luke she batted her eyes and tugged at his ear lobes, squealing when he entered the room. She was a *person*. And I couldn't help but think that she must have always existed; perhaps, I told myself, she'd been waiting to join the world and thought Luke and I seemed a good arrangement.

Like old furniture making way for a grand piano, Luke and I shifted our former selves around Emily. Cigarettes and sleeping in were abandoned. Luke swapped his amp for headphones, and took up cooking. He grilled eggplants, zucchinis, slices of tomato sprinkled with Parmesan. I set aside my canvases and threw what energy I had into painting murals in her room; with balsa wood I built a mobile of Matisse's dancers. The baseboards of the house became a sea-blue horizon of turtles and sea horses and zebra fish. Luke bought her a baby drum set. A baby guitar. A baby bass.

My days were filled with the scent of apples baking for her lunch; the juice of mashed blueberries stained my fingertips. I pinched bananas and slid pieces onto her tongue, watching her eyes widen and her legs kick with excitement. Everything was new for her; each day held a first.

At night, when she had finally surrendered to sleep, I would lie awake wondering what her world must seem like. Did the chairs and tables she zigzagged through hold meaning? While she lay in her crib, did she dream of the living room? Did she recall, like a trip once taken to Paris, the night we roused her from sleep and carried her outside for the meteor shower? Did she fear the staircase? Long for the porch? Did she know there was a world beyond our house?

I, certainly, was forgetting.

'Diapers, bottles, soiled blankets – I don't know. None of it bothers me,' I told Luke. 'Betty Friedan would be appalled.'

'You're in the honeymoon phase. You'll miss your work soon enough.'

I didn't, but during Emily's long naps I set up the baby monitor and forced myself to wander into my studio and prop up a canvas. For weeks I stared at the blank surface, while household tasks – *boil and purée peas, buy more diaper wipes* – crept into my head. Fearing I'd never again concentrate, I resorted to my freshman method, taping a landscape postcard to my easel – one that Luke had sent from Alaska years earlier – so that I could finally begin putting down colour.

Within weeks, this daily struggle had transformed into an obsessive escape, the perfect counterpoint to the chores of parenting, and by the time Emily turned one, I was painting better than ever. The deep reserve of emotion that motherhood had brought me now spilled onto my canvases faster than I could understand. The process was exhilarating, and exhausting. Often, I curled up on my cot and slept.

So there was nothing particularly notable about the Tuesday afternoon in October when I put Emily down for her nap, then carried a cup of tea outside, sat on the porch for a few minutes, and headed drowsily into my studio. I hung the usual white shoelace from my studio doorknob, a signal to Luke that I was napping.

He had phoned that day to say he would head home early, as he often did when he had no afternoon boat rentals. He said he'd go for a run and then wake Emily and get dinner started. I could relax.

On the cot I flipped through a magazine – I don't recall which one – until I drifted off.

What I now know was an hour later, I awoke choking on smoke.

We are in my cabin, on the bed. It is midday, overcast; the sky has been grey for hours. It is one of those days where dusk swallows dawn.

We have been talking about movies, and old-time movie stars. Derek has never heard of Greer Garson, my favourite, so I am listing her films. He shakes his head. 'Sorry,' he says. 'You're dealing with a hick. I know Marilyn Monroe, and the one who was in *Go West, Young Man.*'

'Mae West,' I said. 'You know the ones with big boobs.'

I have lost track of how many days we have spent like this. I know only that we have begun to run out of banter; our bodies are too exhausted to fill the silences. We lie naked in an awkward limbo, each wondering if we should say goodbye, or ask something that matters.

'Wait a second,' he says. '*Breakfast at Tiffany's*. Audrey . . . Hepburn. Flat as a wall!'

'Brute.' I kick the sheet at him.

He clasps my toes, lifts my foot, then holds his breath in deep concentration.

'I know these scars,' he finally says. 'The way the skin regrows.

You have no footprint. Just like I –' he shows me his palm, '– have no handprints. The lines never come back. They never told me that when I had the graft. Those whorls and swirls. We lose the very thing that's supposed to always identify us.'

'Now you can burgle without fear.'

Derek smiles, but I feel his grip on my foot tighten, ever so slightly. 'I opened a door. I was nineteen, and eager to prove myself. You?'

I suddenly wish it were night-time, and pitch dark. I gaze out the window. 'I *didn't* open a door.'

'This stuff . . . it's hard to talk about.' He lifts my bare foot and, as if it is the most delicate of birds, rests the sole gently on his shoulder. 'I hated working the engine. House fires. Buildings with people. Out here it's different. Just me and the flames. No bystanders. Or that's what I thought.'

I remember listening to the radio the day his partner died and he called for the medic: *Get here, just fucking come help, I can't do anything.* His voice had the heightened pitch of a child's.

I stare at the muscled slope of his shoulder, the hairy breadth of his arm. I cannot, or perhaps refuse to, imagine that voice coming from him.

'So did you prove yourself?' I ask. 'When you were nineteen?'

'I went in for an old lady who decided to jump out the window rather than wait for me to get upstairs.'

'She was scared.'

'She should have been scared of the concrete.'

'She died?'

'She died.'

I pull my foot from his shoulder, slide it under the blanket, and then he carefully arranges the blanket around my foot, as though putting it to sleep. He scoots towards me, presses his chest to my back and whispers into my hair, 'Sarah . . . It started in the basement, yes?'

I can speak of every fire, except one.

My pregnancy had been uneventful but for some minor insomnia. Through my eighth month, I went kayaking and hiking; every day I ate spinach and broccoli and sardines; I didn't once touch alcohol. I felt entirely ready for the birthing process.

Luke had made me a mix CD – classic rock for active labour, heavy metal for pushing. And as my due date approached, we bought scented candles, an exercise ball; we loaded our camera with film, packed a bag with baby clothing and placed bets on when I would go into labour, how many hours it would take.

What happened was this: my water broke in the middle of the night, but labour did not begin. So we lazed around the house, eating scrambled eggs, waiting for my contractions. We called friends, family, laughing at the anticlimax of it all, we watched morning television, cooking shows and small-claims-courtroom disputes; we took photographs of me supine, balancing the labour bag on my belly. Then at noon our midwife called and recommended I drink some castor oil to avoid being induced at the hospital.

This, too, was done with a good deal of silliness – Luke pouring the castor oil into a Martini shaker with grapefruit juice and ice. He served it to me in a sugar-rimmed glass, putting Marvin Gaye on the stereo. Within an hour, though, I was crawling the floor. The pain – like being bludgeoned from the inside – overwhelmed me, and nothing Luke said could make me look at him. He hovered nearby with cups of tea, glasses of coconut water, crackers. Like a dying animal, I curled up in the corner of the bathroom and moaned.

I had imagined labour as a process of endurance, like climbing a mountain; something that required strength; instead, it was trauma. I had difficulty thinking. As water leaked from me and the contractions strengthened, I lost my grip on memory and intention. It was as if *I* were being born, a terrified and weakened version of myself.

'I don't think I can do this,' I cried.

'We're going to the hospital right now,' said Luke, a look of terror on his face.

I hobbled into the back seat of the truck, writhing as we drove, trying to assure Luke, between gulps of air, that I was OK, until I felt my skin tear. I reached down and felt the baby's head. Luke pulled over to climb into the back seat as the midwife and ambulance raced our way. He poured water into my mouth, held my hand as I whimpered.

Once the medics arrived, I pushed for an hour while Luke and the midwife held my legs. I closed my eyes, at times stopped pushing because the pain dizzied me. I wanted to sleep; I wanted it all to end.

'You did it,' Luke finally said, as he held Emily to his chest.

'What choice did I have?'

Later, when I had rested and recovered, I said to Luke, 'I never thought pain could scare me so much.'

'She was ten pounds,' said Luke. 'Go easy on yourself.'

'You don't understand. I never felt pain like that. I had no idea that part of me existed.'

'Well,' he said, kissing my forehead, 'it only existed for a few hours.'

I remember thick smoke; I remember tripping over my shoes. I remember air so hot my eyes felt singed. Fire eats oxygen and sucks the air from your lungs. It strangles you. I swung my arms around, knocking down easels, gasping and trying to find my way out.

The door was a rectangle of flame. I stopped moving, trapped, until the heat began to eat my skin. I stepped back and prayed to anything and everything and kicked at the door. It fell forward, and I stumbled onto the flaming wood. I didn't feel the pain on my feet until I stepped out onto the cool ground beyond, toppled over and vomited. The cuff of my jeans was on fire, and I rolled until the flame died.

Behind me, the entire house thundered and crackled. I scrambled along the grass to the front porch, grabbed a rail and pulled myself up. My feet stuck to the wood, skin peeling off as I mounted each step. I stood before the front door and heard the splintering of wooden beams. Glass shattered in the window to my right and flames leapt out. Emily's room.

I opened the door and a blast of air seared my face. Throughout the living room, columns of flame spiralled upwards. Between them, a thick black smoke, lit with embers, churned scraps of wood and glass.

I could not move.

I called her name. I must have, right? I must have at least done this. Then I closed the door and stumbled away.

'Object permanence' was coined by Jean Piaget to describe a child's understanding that objects and people exist when not seen.

Watch a baby in its early months, and it shows little concern when things disappear. Hide its favourite toy, and there is no protest. A baby won't even cry when its mother leaves.

But somewhere between eight and twelve months, infants realize that things exist when out of sight. A baby that age will understand that its mother is in the next room, down the hall, outside the door. A baby that age, in distress, wants her mother to come back.

When the fire truck arrived, I was lying on a blanket in the back of our truck, having passed out from smoke inhalation. Luke, bare-chested in running shorts, stood beside our neighbour Max, both spraying kitchen-sized fire extinguishers into Emily's flaming window, to no avail, then tossing in heavy wool blankets.

From the bottom of the hill, coming back from his run, Luke had seen smoke rising from the house. He had seen me on the porch, had seen me, as he ran faster than ever to reach the top of the hill, pull closed the front door.

Doubled over, he looked up at my blackened face.

'Tell me she isn't in there.'

I wanted to tell him she wasn't in there.

'Sarah!' He shook me hard, as though to loosen words.

It took the firefighters almost two hours to extinguish the blaze; I learned this later in the hospital, where I was treated for my burns. I lay silently in the bed, as a stream of nurses and doctors and friends came to offer their shock and condolences.

'She tried to go back in,' Luke would say, hugging his legs in a chair by the window. 'She kept trying to get back in to save Emily.'

'Stop it, Luke,' I said when we were finally alone, the words garbled by my oxygen mask. My eyes, with what strength they had left, reminded him that I knew he'd seen me close the door.

'It's OK,' Luke said, tears in his eyes. 'She was already gone.' He pulled his chair close and searched for a part of me that wasn't singed, some piece of my former self, his wife, that was left intact, that he could still grab hold of. He rested his hands in the crook of my elbow and set his forehead on his hands.

I did not tell him that Emily wasn't already gone. Because through the door, beneath the roar of the fire, I heard her calling for me.

It is getting dark, and with each exchange, with each detail spoken, I find myself putting on an article of clothing. I wear socks, my underwear, and I'm clutching a grey cardigan at the waist. Derek remains naked beneath the sheet, but I stand and cross the room and find his jeans. I hand them to him, coins falling to the floor in a noisy rattle.

'A mother is supposed to do anything for her child,' I say.

'You'd have been caught in the flashover. You would have burned to death.'

I slowly pick up each of the coins.

'People jump out of windows rather than walk through fire,' he continues, setting the jeans down. 'Maybe you can walk through fire – once. And then you know what it feels like. Once you've known that pain, you can't make yourself face it again.'

'Yes, of course. You're right.'

'Sarah.'

'I'll forgive myself; I'll start a new life. I'll have more children and make it all better.'

'Sarah, come on.'

'You should go.'

He steps into one leg of his jeans, then looks up. 'Survivor's guilt, Sarah. I know it back and forth.'

I want to tell Derek that in ancient Rome, while Romulus ruled and Tacitus wrote and Horatius stood alone on a bridge against the

Etruscans, an order of vestal priestesses, all virgins, guarded a single flame for a thousand years.

I want to tell Derek that the Earth itself is filled with hidden flames that can never stop burning.

The Baba Gurgur in Iraq has been aflame for thousands of years. In Turkey and Taiwan, in New York and Washington, fires smoulder – small and controlled – which can never be extinguished. In Australia, a single coal seam has burned for 6,000 years.

'Derek,' I say. 'I didn't survive.'

At night, I lie in bed, alone, and think of her. She would be six. She would be in school. She would tell me about her day – her friends, her art class, a pet turtle that her class adopted. She would ask questions about rainbows and rivers, she would demand to know *why* about everything, the way children do, and I would have answers.

Instead, I have questions.

After everything I have learned about fire, I do not understand this: Why is it that one day a wire in the basement overheats? And why are you asleep when it happens? Why is it that you are in the same house as your child, but your husband, in kindness, has built you a separate entrance, so that to get to her you must walk through two walls of flame? And why is it that, despite your love, despite everything you ever believed about yourself, you can't?

You shake your head: *You* would have raced in, you think. Walked through the flames, carried her out in your arms. You would never let that happen to your child.

I am here to tell you: you don't know. ■

GRANTA

SAFETY CATCH

Lauren Wilkinson

I

Her mother left them the year before and went back to Martinique. Her daddy's name is William and he served in Korea. He risked his life for his country, was stationed in Biloxi where they made him sit at the back of the city bus when he left the base, still in his crisp air-force uniform. He's a hero and as far as Marie's concerned no other man is as brave or as handsome.

They live in a yellow house out in Queens Village. John Ali and Albert Taylor, two of her father's old army buddies, are waiting for him by the front door, both of them wearing hats. She watches her father put on his coat and say I love you to her older sister Hélène.

William is a beat cop in Hell's Kitchen; he does his best to keep order but it's the Westies who run the neighbourhood. He tells his girls about the time he saw Mickey Spillane himself, damn near respectable now on account of marrying rich Maureen McManus, with his foot up on a hydrant. 'Pulling up his sock. And he looked up at me smiling and said you want something from me, niggercop? Grinning like he'd won a foot race. But still, New York isn't so bad as Mississippi. Or Vegas. Those are the two most racist-ass places I ever been to in my life.'

William is learning the basics about wine while he's on duty, from a sommelier on 25th Street. At home he tells his girls to remember you can never go wrong ordering a Pinot.

On Christmas Day he tries to take their picture, the whole family. Marie is eight. Hélène is thirteen and trying to keep their Airedale Rajah still and the Santa cap on his head. Their father fiddles with the camera on its tripod. He's wearing a fishing cap, a polo sweatshirt and boat shoes; his duty gun is in its holster over his jeans because you never can be too safe. The first photo is a failure. Rajah is a brown blur; Hélène is looking at the dog in open-mouthed frustration; Marie is rubbing one eye; their father doesn't get into the frame in time and his shadow falls over both girls. But later, the picture makes it into Hélène's photo album anyway.

Her father reads books by Basil Davidson because he's interested in Diaspora. He likes to make reminder lists on his typewriter and tape them up around the house. On the wall above the toilet:

COUNTRIES TO VISIT
1. Brazil
2. South Africa
3. France
4. Ghana
5. Egypt

On the wall by a light switch in the kitchen:

PAINT JOB FOR *SWEET AND LOVELY*'S HULL
1. Solvent
2. Epoxy filler
3. Soft rags
4. Rust-Oleum marine paint (red)
5. Small can for topside coating (black)

GUN RULES
1. Your girls are as curious about guns as boys would be. Don't be mysterious about your firearms or hide them. Be the one to teach them gun safety so they'll learn under competent supervision
2. Teach your girls to touch a trigger only when they're ready for the gun to go off

3. Show them what a gun can do; impress them with the power of a firearm
4. Muzzles point up, down or down-range only
5. Eye and ear protection are essential

He takes the girls to his gun club, which is just a five-minute drive away. Because he's a cop and has been going there for years, they bend their rules about minors for him. He wears his boat shoes to the range. He rents a .22 and, leaning on the wooden counter, tells the girl behind it, 'I swear to God, Denise, if I were fifteen years younger I'd give you a fit.' Denise smiles like she's heard it before.

There's a knothole in the wooden counter and Marie puts her eye to it hoping to spy on a new little world of something or at least through to the other side and to Denise's bottom half. But there's just shallow black space inside. Denise leans over the counter towards her. 'Such a pretty little girl! Try and keep your daddy out of trouble, huh?'

In October he takes the girls deer-hunting upstate. The car still smells like crayons from when Marie left a box of them on the seat and they melted in the heat of the summer.

Arriving at Daddy's favourite hunting spot, they find it empty. The spot is near a deer trail and has a wide stump in it. Marie sits on the ground and leans her back against it.

They wait for a long time. She is nearly asleep when Daddy taps Hélène's shoulder and gestures towards the deer trail.

'Go,' he mouths.

Hélène lifts the .30-06 into position. 'Can he see us?'

Daddy puts his finger to his lips and shakes his head no.

'Is it gonna kick?' Hélène whispers.

He shakes his head.

'It's gonna hurt my shoulder,' she says, louder now, but still the buck doesn't look up from its low shrub. Hélène takes a deep breath and, pulling the trigger, manages to hit the buck right in the neck. It drops to the leafy forest floor, feet still moving like it got the notion to run away a second too late.

'Unbelievable eye, kid!' he says and claps his hands once. 'Did it kick?'

'If it did, I couldn't feel it,' Hélène says in a soft voice.

Daddy makes Hélène straddle the buck and hold its head up by the antlers. There's blood on its black nose, pooling in its open mouth, dripping down to the white fur beneath its straight, white, almost-human teeth. Daddy takes photo after photo of unsmiling Hélène until she says, 'Can I get off it please?'

Marie tugs on his hand. 'Can I try the big rifle too?'

'In a couple years, Pumpkin.' He puts his camera away and gets his knife out. Turning the buck on its back, he presses the knife into its belly and says, 'Your first cut is here, where the white fur starts. You pull up to the top of the sternum –'

'I'll be in the car,' Hélène says.

'And then what?' Marie asks. 'What cut do you do next?'

On the drive to a butcher he knows upstate, Hélène throws up in the back seat. She says it's only because the car smells like melted crayons, she swears to God that's the only reason she feels sick.

Marie is lying on the living-room carpet watching TV when John Ali, Albert Taylor and her father come into the house, bringing the cold in too. Mr Ali takes off his wool coat, unwraps his scarf and falls back on the sofa, stone drunk. He pulls his hat down over his face. Still in his coat, Mr Taylor takes the reclining chair. She finds her father in the kitchen gulping water from a glass.

'You should be in bed,' he says, pouring two more glasses. 'Take these in to them, would you?'

She taps Mr Ali's shoulder and he lifts his hat, smiles, taking the glass. 'You're a pretty girl, Marie, and nice. I tell you, we need some nicer girls working for the Bureau, don't we, Al? The one who used to answer my phones was mean as a snake.'

In February, two days after Marie turns ten, Malcolm X is shot. Daddy comes home and says he saw Betty Shabazz with his own eyes; she was pregnant and looked exhausted. He says she told the police no white cops near Brother Malcolm's body and because

Daddy is the only black cop in his precinct he gets to be an honorary pall-bearer at the funeral.

Hélène is making dinner and Marie is watching TV. During the evening news she tells her sister to come quick because their father is standing beside an easel spray of what must be red and white carnations arranged to look like the Nation of Islam flag. He looks nervous and solemn in his uniform. Then John Ali is talking at a podium, and as the news goes on, Marie comes to understand that he doesn't only work for the Bureau. He's the Nation of Islam's secretary too.

For days after the funeral William talks about communism. 'Your mother was sympathetic to communists, did you know that? She was a beatnik and that's why she just up and left us.' He uses the past tense like she's dead.

The girls grow up. Hélène enlists and is sent to Long Binh. She's away for a year and, after her first tour, returns safely to the USA. Then dies in a head-on collision while driving back home from the Oakland Army base.

Marie finds her father in the kitchen with his forehead down on the table and assumes he's drunk until she hears his voice. He says, 'She flew halfway across the world just to die on US soil because of some boozer in Las fucking Vegas, that son-of-a-bitch city! It all gets me, but that gets me the most.'

Marie's mother shows up for the funeral and William refuses to speak to her. Marlène is only in her early fifties but looks much older, frail. Wandering back down the aisle from the coffin she looks like Hélène's ghost.

On the Saturday after the funeral, Marie gives her mother a ride back to LaGuardia. At the airport they pay their dimes and go up to the observation deck. There aren't too many other people up there, just a handful of businessmen. A redhead in a grey suit is watching the taxiing planes through a binocular machine. Marlène leans against the guard rail looking out towards Co-op City and pulling hard on her cigarette.

Maman's back. The same black A-line dress she wore to the funeral and a dark-brown wig to hide her natural hair. What if she said, right now, I won't go. You've got to have someone here to take care of you, Marie.

Marlène turns to face her and says something Marie can't hear over the plane engines screaming out on the tarmac. Marie moves to the guard rail.

'Feel that,' her mother says again in French, taking Marie's hand and putting it on the rail. 'The engines are making it vibrate. Because sound is just energy, you know? That's all anything is. All we are. Nothing dies because you can't destroy energy.'

Marie nods and, without saying goodbye, begins walking towards the stairs. She's hurt by what her mother has said. Her mother, who should be able to understand her grief, who should be feeling as bad – worse – should know better than to talk about the universe or whatever hippy bullshit it was that she was trying to drive at.

In the parking lot she sits in her father's car for a while with her eyes closed. Thinking: she doesn't know me. And: she didn't know Hélène. She feels let down by this and so exhausted by everything else that she briefly considers taking a nap, but opens her eyes instead and puts the key in the ignition, thinking: I'm eighteen now. I'm an adult and I can't just sit here in a goddamn parking lot all day long.

2

John Ali dies under suspicious circumstances – his brakes fail one day while he's out driving.

Marie enrols in the ROTC at Queens College. The army keeps her in Texas for five years, then she gets the runaround trying to apply for a job as an officer at the CIA. When she complains about it to her father he says, sounding unsympathetic, 'I told you it was a good ol' boys club over there.'

'But that don't make no damn sense, Daddy,' she says, frustrated, pacing the blue shag carpet in her father's living room. 'They only want to send white boys to China?'

'I just know they don't want to send black girls from Queens.' He scratches the back of his salt-and-pepper head and looks at her. 'Look, I'm not saying you give up on it just yet. But why not go talk to Al and see what he can do for you?'

'Maybe I should've joined the navy instead,' Marie is telling Albert Taylor as she sits across from him in his office. 'I would've seen more. Different people, different places.'

'If you want to join the CIA 'cause you want to work overseas, you should know we also send agents abroad. The way I see it, the FBI is the better fit for you. Or the USSS; I've got friends over there who'd look out for you.'

She nods, standing.

He walks her out to the elevator and hugs her goodbye. Holding her out at arm's length he says, smiling, 'Shoot, still pretty as all get out. Why law enforcement at all, Marie? Why not go out to Hollywood and learn to act?'

She applies for several positions at the Bureau and despite Albert Taylor's recommendation still has to endure a six-month background check before she's cleared to head to Quantico, Virginia, for the twenty-one-week training.

Her Behavioural Science instructor, Stewart Reid, a ruddy fair-haired man whom she suspects is an alcoholic, holds her back after class one day to tell her she's got an aptitude for the subject. He asks her out for a drink later, to talk more, he says. But she turns him down.

She works for a couple of years in the New York field office, as an agent in the foreign counter-intelligence division. Occasionally she goes out to lunch with Al Taylor, who works in the same office. He always pays and lets her fantasize out loud about working abroad some day.

She lives alone in a tan tenement building on 127th Street and Lenox. She dates plenty of boring men and sometimes lets one come home with her.

In March of 1984 a man named Alan Johnson contacts her. He claims to be from the CIA, but because he asks to meet with her in the Mid-Manhattan Library, she assumes he's lying. She agrees to go anyway out of curiosity. He says she'll find him by the microfiche readers.

When she gets up to the fourth floor she sees a man who must be Johnson: bald and with a walrus moustache, wearing khakis and a white polo. He nods towards the chair beside him. 'Take a seat. We're waiting for someone. He didn't go far, just to the restroom.'

She sits. Two readers over is a man in a green cardigan, wearing two pairs of eyeglasses on his face. Johnson tries making small talk until finally Marie's former instructor, Stewart Reid, appears. Reid's wrist is wrapped in a bandage and there are deep circles under his blue eyes. He looks somewhat startled.

'What's the matter with you?' Johnson says.

'A man was shaving his head in there. He told me not to stare at him.'

All at once, Marie realizes she's amused. She asks Reid, maybe a little incredulous, '*You're* CIA?'

As the three of them stroll among the reference shelves Johnson tells her that, based on Reid's recommendation, she's being considered as a candidate for a special training programme. Eventually, he says, she'd be able to come work for the agency full time. But for now she'd be a specialist.

She requests a leave of absence from the FBI and goes to Camp Peary for a nine-month-long CIA training. She is one of a half-dozen female contractors from different branches of law enforcement. Two drop out after the first week and another is told to leave at the end of the month.

She is taught several methods of execution, about sniping and poisoning, about shooting a man at point-blank range and the accompanying psychological fallout.

LOOKING FOR MORE?

Have *Granta* delivered to your door
four times a year and save up
to 38% on the cover price.

Subscribe now by completing the form overleaf, visiting granta.com
or calling UK free phone 0500 004 033

UK
£36.00 | £32.00 by Direct Debit

EUROPE
£42.00

REST OF THE WORLD*
£46.00

*Not for readers in US, Canada or Latin America

'An indispensable part
of the intellectual landscape'
— *Observer*

GRANTA.COM

GRANTA

THE MAGAZINE OF NEW WRITING

SUBSCRIPTION FORM FOR UK, EUROPE AND REST OF THE WORLD

Yes, I would like to take out a subscription to *Granta*.

GUARANTEE: If I am ever dissatisfied with my *Granta* subscription, I will simply notify you, and you will send me a complete refund or credit my credit card, as applicable, for all un-mailed issues.

YOUR DETAILS

MR/MISS/MRS/DR ....

NAME ....

ADDRESS ....

....

POSTCODE ....

EMAIL ....

☐ Please tick this box if you do not wish to receive special offers from *Granta*
☐ Please tick this box if you do not wish to receive offers from organizations selected by *Granta*

YOUR PAYMENT DETAILS

1) ☐ Pay £32.00 (saving £20) by Direct Debit
   To pay by Direct Debit please complete the mandate and return to the address shown below.

2) Pay by cheque or credit/debit card. Please complete below:

   1 year subscription: ☐ UK: £36.00   ☐ Europe: £42.00   ☐ Rest of World: £46.00

   3 year subscription: ☐ UK: £99.00   ☐ Europe: £108.00   ☐ Rest of World: £126.00

   I wish to pay by   ☐ CHEQUE   ☐ CREDIT/DEBIT CARD
   Cheque enclosed for £——————— made payable to *Granta*.

   Please charge £ ——————— to my: ☐ Visa   ☐ MasterCard   ☐ Amex   ☐ Switch/Maestro

   Card No. ☐☐☐☐☐☐☐☐☐☐☐☐☐☐☐☐☐☐☐

   Valid from *(if applicable)* ☐☐☐☐   Expiry Date ☐☐☐☐   Issue No. ☐☐

   Security No. ☐☐☐

SIGNATURE .... DATE ....

Instructions to your Bank or Building Society to pay by Direct Debit

BANK NAME ....

BANK ADDRESS ....

POSTCODE ....

ACCOUNT IN THE NAMES(S) OF: ....

SIGNED ....

DATE ....

DIRECT Debit

Instructions to your Bank or Building Society: Please pay Granta Publications direct debits from the account detailed on this instruction subject to the safeguards assured by the direct debit guarantee. I understand that this instruction may remain with Granta and, if so, details will be passed electronically to my bank/building society. Banks and building societies may not accept direct debit instructions from some types of account.

Bank/building society account number

☐☐☐☐☐☐☐☐

Sort Code

☐☐☐☐☐☐

Originator's Identification

9 1 3 1 3 3

Please mail this order form with payment instructions to:

Granta Publications
12 Addison Avenue
London, W11 4QR
Or call 0500 004 033
or visit GRANTA.COM

Each woman is given a different target. Hers is Thierry Bernard, a New York-based French national who's both a private arms broker and an engineer. When she first sees a picture of him she says to Johnson, 'He looks like a college professor.'

'Bernard is a genius, which makes him an asset to several powerful governments. But the fact that he has access to a lot of sensitive defence information also makes him a liability. Unfortunately for us he's in the bad habit of revealing our secrets to our enemies, if the price is right.'

Towards the end of her training, she begins having the same anxiety dream again and again. She has just left her apartment to kill Bernard; she's on her stoop patting her pockets in a panic, realizing that she's forgotten the scope for her sniper rifle. When she goes back up to her apartment to try and find it – for some reason she suspects it's in her closet hidden in a shoe – suddenly there is Bernard sitting on the edge of her bed, tapping his watch and looking very impatient.

By the end of her training Marie is sleep-deprived and knows she's performing poorly because of it. So when Johnson calls a meeting with her she assumes it's to reprimand her or to dismiss her from the programme. Instead, he informs her that the target has been terminated.

'What do you mean?' she says from out of her haze, not quite understanding him.

'He's dead. Shot three times in the head when he went to answer his front door. It looks like Mossad were behind it.'

Although she receives a lot of money for her specialist training, she doesn't hear any more about moving into a formal position at the CIA. She continues to work for the FBI and is not sure if she'll ever hear from Johnson again.

In February of 1987, she does. At their meeting place in the Mid-Manhattan Library, he says, 'Your next target, Thomas Sankara, the president of Upper Volta – Burkina Faso – is scheduled to speak up here in New York. I want you to attend the rally and get a sense of who he is before you go to his country.'

At the rally, she stands towards the back. First a hulking man in a loud polyester shirt takes the stage; Sankara's translator. He introduces President Sankara, who's sitting in the front row of the audience, and calls him to the stage. Sankara wears a military uniform, a red beret and a dainty moustache. At the podium he raises a clenched fist.

'*L'impérialisme!*' he says into the microphone.

'*À bas!*' the French speakers in the crowd return.

'*Le néocolonialisme!*' he shouts.

'*À bas!*'

'*Le racisme!*' he shouts.

'*À bas!*' the crowd says.

Marie says it too each time. It feels odd to be so energized by what she knows to be propaganda.

Sankara is undeniably magnetic.

After his speech, he goes into the crowd. As he moves in her direction, she starts a mental list of his crimes. He's letting the Soviets build a base in his country. He's purchased hundreds of thousands of artillery shells and is instigating war with Ivory Coast – but still, when she shakes his hand, she holds it for maybe a little too long.

Two months later, on the evening before her flight to Burkina Faso, she spends the night at her father's house. In the morning, she sees his wallet on the kitchen table and starts flipping through it before she even knows what she's doing. Inside she finds a list, typed up and laminated, that makes her laugh:

10 WOMEN NOT TO DATE
1. Friends' Wives
2. Wife's Friends
3. Friends' Daughters
4. Daughters' Friends
5. Girls Younger than my Oldest
6. Family members
7. Ex-cons

8. Ex-Christians
9. White girls
10. Substance abusers

She is living in Ouagadougou and working at the US Embassy, posing as an FBI legal attaché, ostensibly helping to track a US fugitive who's fled to West Africa.

A private birthday party is held at the embassy for Jean Compaoré, the assistant minister of security. She works closely with Jean. She doesn't have much respect for him. And yet, he's the only person she's met in Ouaga who is suspicious of her motives for being in the country. Maybe he understands her because he's also hiding in plain sight – the better she gets to know him the more she suspects that his politics aren't revolutionary at all.

Influential people attend the party, including Blaise Compaoré, Jean's first cousin, whom Jean introduces as *Le Capitaine*.Compaoré is also President Sankara's deputy and his oldest friend. He is a tall, lanky man with boyish features. His eyes turn down at the corners when he smiles, which she likes, and his face seems wide open and trustworthy.

Near the end of the night, Sankara himself appears. From across the room he seems small, flanked by two bodyguards much bigger than he is. And he's wearing a tracksuit, which she thinks looks a bit goofy on him.

Jean introduces Marie to Sankara and the three of them discuss imperialism and food aid. Sankara talks a little bit about music and tells her what she already knows, that he plays guitar in a band called Tout-à-Coup Jazz. A bored Jean steps away and Sankara tells his bodyguards that they don't need to stay either. He says, 'I think I'm mostly in the company of friends here.'

Although he's easy-going and chatty, talking to the president makes her jumpy. They argue about the situation in Ethiopia. He tells her about his anti-desertification campaign and about impatience – 'People are always telling me I expect things to get done too quickly,' he says.

Other partygoers float towards them, join their conversation and drift away. They talk about his plans for his own birthday: in two weeks he'll be thirty-six and far away from home, in Addis Ababa for a conference. He talks about whether or not a united Africa is possible. He's funny and he communicates well, like a woman she thinks, *he expresses himself as well as a woman might.*

Later, standing in front of the embassy building, she watches Sankara slip a leg over his motorbike. His wife approaches. Marie watches as he takes her by the wrist and kisses it. But she doesn't get on the back of the bike. Instead she and her driver walk towards a government car and speed off.

Sankara lifts a hand and smiles at Marie, waves her over. When she goes to him, he starts his engine and says, 'I'll take you home.'

CDRs, Committees for the Defence of the Revolution, are cropping up rapidly throughout the country. Thomas imported the idea of the committees after visiting Cuba. CDRs are supposed to be democratically run organizations through which the Burkinabé can exert power in their own communities. CDRs do things like organize the construction of schools and clinics.

'But the secondary function of Fidel's CDRs is spying; the head of each one keeps a file on everyone in their neighbourhood. And Burkinabé CDR heads are starting to act like spies too. Always listening. Watching. I don't like it. Neighbours spying on neighbours, *les murs ont des oreilles.*'

He explains all of this to her as they lie in her bed together, her legs wrapped around his.

In the morning, sitting with her back propped up against the headboard, she watches Thomas get dressed. Outside it's pouring; it was the sound of rain battering the corrugated roof that woke them. As he paces the room looking for his beret, she asks to see his pistol. Without hesitating he removes it from the holster and hands it to her. He sits on the edge of the bed with his back to her and begins wrestling a boot onto his foot.

The handle is made of mother-of-pearl. She says, 'It's beautiful.'
'Don't shoot,' he jokes, leaning over to tie his shoes.

Mostly they meet at her home; she pays her guard, Youssouf, well to encourage his silence. Occasionally they meet in the cities and villages where he speaks at public assemblies. She is always careful about how she regards him in public and never asks him about his sons.

A regular schedule would be impossible; it is more like he steals the time that he can to be with her. When Marie's phone rings at three in the morning, it can only be Thomas. He is at her house before the sun is up. He has his guitar and looks angry. She lets him in and asks, 'Have you had breakfast?'

He hasn't. She begins preparing *bouillie de mil*. It's lucky that his favourite food is so easy to make, especially since she can buy the millet pre-prepared in a plastic baggie from the grocery store. If she had to pound it herself, she'd be in trouble.

She stirs the millet porridge and he begins playing around on his guitar.

Marie is waiting for Jean Compaoré to pick her up from in front of the embassy; when a Renault pulls up instead of his Mercedes she is surprised. When she gets into the back seat beside Jean, the driver greets her in heavily accented French, instead of Mòoré, which she takes as a subtle reminder of how conspicuously foreign she is. Her clothes and her complexion, even the way she walks, all mark her.

She says, 'Nice car. Why the downgrade?'

'Sankara sold my other one,' Jean complains, kissing her on both cheeks like a Parisian. 'He sold the entire government fleet. Now we're all stuck with these cheap pieces of shit. Even the top ministers. Even Blaise.'

'Why do you even need a car? Why not learn to ride a motorbike like Sankara?' she says, teasing him.

'That asshole and his motorcycle. He thinks he's Che.'

As Jean often does when upset about something, he blows his nose into his handkerchief. She sees a glimpse of red on it before he folds it up, not blood, but the red Sahel dirt of the road that gets in her nose too when the windows are down in her car or whenever she takes one of the intercity buses. They turn onto rue 213, where traffic is at a standstill. The driver shuts down the engine and they wait to move forward. Jean grabs her hand and she grudgingly lets him hold it.

She looks out to the yellow-painted wood shack nearby, a food stand. Men are standing around it eating and laughing. A woman with a metal bowl on her head passes through the middle of the wide road, weaving around the cars. She stops the woman and buys one of the small plastic bags of water from her bowl.

As she is struggling to rip open a corner of the bag with her teeth, Marie sees the first of the cows. A herd of white cattle stream past the car on both sides, a white river pouring through the red dirt road, beautiful. She puts her hand out the window and pats one on its hump. A Fulani herdsman races to the front of the herd on his speckled horse – she watches through the back window as he drives them around the corner, a bend in the river, and out of sight. Once the herd is gone, traffic begins to move again. The driver starts the car. Jean takes out a pack of Gauloises and starts speaking sharply to him, telling him in Mòoré that he's a fool for taking this road.

When they arrive at her home Youssouf pulls open the tall gate and lets them into the property.

In her living room, they talk idly about the national football team and then she goes to her room and returns with the sum of money they'd agreed upon. She considers Jean her most valuable informant. He looks pleased as he tucks the envelope into his suit jacket.

'What have you heard?' Marie says.

'The French, the DGSE, are funnelling money to Blaise. There's going to be a coup within the next six months.'

'That's *it*?' She is annoyed. This rumour has been floating around

Ouaga for months; anyone with any sense at all knows what Blaise is up to.

He shakes his head no and, smiling, takes her hand again and kisses it. Perhaps he is feeling excited by the information, or maybe unburdened by revealing it; he moves closer and kisses her on the mouth. She lets him, staring at the wall behind his head until it is over. Then, going to her door, she calls to Youssouf who's standing in the yard. 'Open the gate,' she says. 'Jean is leaving now.'

Two weeks later, she is relieved when she gets her order from Johnson: *Let the French do what they've already set in motion. No need to get involved.*

Thomas spends one last night with her before she leaves Ouaga. When she wakes up he is already half dressed. When he notices she's awake, he sits on the edge of the bed beside her. He kisses her and puts his hand on her cheek.

'You know you can't trust the people around you,' she says. 'Not any more.'

He nods. 'My circle of friends is getting smaller.'

'Blaise should be in jail.'

He shakes his head. 'Blaise is my oldest friend.'

She considers telling him to go into exile and to save himself, but there would be no point in saying that. He would never desert Burkina Faso.

'Take care,' he says and kisses her again, *bisous*, goodbye.

She leaves Burkina Faso, not for New York but for Martinique. Her mother lives with her great-uncle, her *tonton* Alexandre, on a steer farm in the country. Tonton Alexandre is an odd, quiet man who always seems to be fiddling with something. She can understand why he's never been married.

She formally resigns from the FBI and is paid the rest of the money she is owed from Johnson.

She is on the farm a month before she is able to work up the courage to call her father. She's still as afraid to disappoint him as when she was a child. She suspects that, by now, Al Taylor has told him about her resignation.

She stands at the yellow phone on the kitchen wall, while her mother sits at the table for moral support. When William gets on the line she starts talking fast: she tells him where she is and that she won't be coming back for a while, then hangs up before he can respond. She sits at the table.

There is silence for a long time. Then Marlène says, 'I know he can be hard to talk to.'

Marie is angry with herself for being a coward. Taking it out on her mother, she answers, her voice full of spite, 'So that's why you left? I finally get an answer after all this time. 'Cause he was hard to talk to?'

Marlène stays quiet.

'I want to know,' Marie presses. 'I mean it. Lately, I've been thinking a lot about what it takes to be a mother. I want you to make me understand how you could just leave us.'

'There was just something that was, like, thick in the air,' her mother begins in her languid, spaced-out English. 'All his cronies were cops or spies. It was this feeling like –' Her hands start creeping up to her neck. 'And so, like, the whole scene with your father was just too *heavy*.'

The pure incomprehensibility of her mother's answer, and the fact that she has waited so long to hear what amounts to nonsense, makes Marie wildly, disproportionately angry.

She goes to the kitchen door, off the porch, and follows the pale dirt path to the end of property. There is feral sugar cane growing on the other side of the main road and she goes blindly into the green stalks, knowing she'll probably get lost.

She walks for a long while. The shushing of the cane as she moves through it pleases her, calms her down. When she stops walking it is suddenly very quiet. She likes the intensity of the silence, being alone in sugar cane is quiet like being alone in snow is quiet.

She starts again and walks until the air begins to stink, which makes her realize that she must be near Chamoiseau's chicken farm. The smell is so overpowering that she has to turn back.

At six months pregnant she's so large she considers the possibility of giving birth to another species altogether – a giraffe baby perhaps, or some kind of bison. The babies ride low, so low that it seems they're going to tumble out of her at any second. She is scared and wishes she had someone to help her. Hélène. She thinks about how Hélène would've spoiled her children rotten.

The twins are born at the hospital just outside Fort-de-France. Later they are brought out into the sunny courtyard because they have jaundice. Sleeping in their hospital bassinets in the courtyard, right from day one, they look just like Thomas to her.

She helps her *tonton* Alexandre care for the cows. She finds breaking up bales meditative; even mucking out the stalls doesn't bother her. On the day she hears that he is dead, that Blaise Compaoré has murdered Thomas Sankara and is the new president, she finds a steer dead behind the barn. She squats beside it and cries, wiping her tears away with the back of her arm and swatting away the flies dancing around the animal's huge and cloudy eyeball.

When the boys are three, she reads an interesting story in the newspaper. Someone has blown the whistle on a CIA deputy director named George Clark, who was running a secret assassination programme. The last lines of the article are:

LIONEL ROSS, THE CIA'S DIRECTOR, HAS INFORMED CONGRESS OF THE PROGRAMME AND CALLED FOR ITS IMMEDIATE SUSPENSION. CLARK IS BEING INDICTED FOR VIOLATING THE PROHIBITION ON NON-WARTIME ASSASSINATIONS.

There is an official head shot of Clark alongside the article; he is wearing a suit and there's an American flag in the background. George Clark is the man Marie recognizes as Alan Johnson.

3

Now she lives in a Connecticut suburb with her seven-year-old twins. Their tiny single-storey house is white and has an attached garage. So far she's only told her boys that their daddy died before they were born, that his name was Thomas and that she loved him.

Her twins are close with their grandfather. Lately, William has been talking about taking them out to teach them how to hunt. Sooner rather than later, he says, 'because I won't live forever'.

She doesn't want them to go out with him. She likes Connecticut and feels safe there. Without knowing how, she's stumbled into a life she wants and she doesn't want her boys out with her father, learning to shoot. She feels like that might somehow ruin things.

Mostly she works at home, translating for several small companies in the city. She works at a desk in her bedroom. The bottom drawer is filled with mementos: her sister's old photo album, a letter from her mother, a newspaper clipping about Thomas on the fifth anniversary of his death.

Her most vivid memory is of the last time she saw him speak at a public assembly.

She'd been late and so was sitting impossibly far back from the front of the room, beside a man in a suit who was either asleep or dead from heat exhaustion. Thomas was at the far left of a long table of seated government officials and during the question-and-answer period he was asked to comment on his future plans for Burkina Faso.

She remembers him leaning slowly towards the silver table mic and remaining quiet for a moment as he looked out at the crowded convention hall. Then he looked to his left, to where Blaise was sitting and although she couldn't see it, she is sure that he was looking Blaise directly in the eye as he said, *En tant qu'individus les révolutionnaires peuvent être tués, mais vous ne pouvez pas tuer les idées*: While individual revolutionaries can be killed, you can't kill ideas.

He leaned back in the chair and didn't say anything else.

Blaise made no acknowledgement that he understood the message. Instead, he stood and began the applause for Thomas's answer, banging his hands together for longer and louder than anyone else in the room.

She isn't new to her neighbourhood but is only on friendly terms with the woman who lives right next door, Shirley Ferris.

'Marie,' Shirley starts in on her one day over coffee, 'there's no point in keeping yourself up on the shelf like the goddamn good china.'

Shirley's kitchen looks like it was at the height of modernity during the 1960s. She dyes her thinning hair blonde and talks freely about the hatchet-job abortion she had in the forties, an operation that made it impossible for her to have children. Shirley mentions a guard at the museum in the city where she volunteers. 'He wants to meet you. He said, "Marie was my great-aunt's name. I'd love to meet her."'

At home that evening she's boiling water in a saucepan. Billy's sitting dainty and cross-legged on the floor, drawing something that might be a cow or maybe a gingerbread man. Poochini, who's part German shepherd, is pacing from her to Billy to Thomas and back again. Thomas is leaning against the threshold to the hallway, fastidiously piling X-Men cards in some sort of order that will never make any sense to her. Her boys are identical but Billy is effeminate and it gets him picked on at school.

'Would you two sit at the table?'

'I like the floor,' Billy says.

She asks him to go out to the garage to get some juice boxes for them but he doesn't want go alone because he's afraid of the freezer. He thinks it looks like a coffin.

'It's just a fridge,' she says, breaking uncooked spaghetti in half and putting it in the water. She calls over to Thomas, 'You go with him.'

He pretends not to have heard.

'Thomas, you go too or I won't take you to that Magic Dungeon place this weekend. Or whatever it's called.'

That gets him moving. He's been begging to go to this store in Bridgeport for far longer than she'd suspected he could manage to maintain interest in a hobby. She wonders about this special card he wants to buy, convinced that there will either be an enormous gun or an enormous set of breasts on it.

All week she's been using the trip as a way to extort good behaviour from him. She worries that a better mother would feel guilty for doing this. For being a little cruel. But on the other hand, he's never been so well behaved in his life. 'I think they're a waste of money, those cards,' she says as he climbs to his feet.

After dinner and some television with the boys, she gets in the shower. As she's towelling off, there's a small rap on the door. She says, 'Billy, I'm in here.'

'How'd you know it was me?' his lispy, husky voice asks.

'Billy, I'm in here. Tell me what you want.'

'Tell Thomas you got them juice boxes for me too. He got some more out of the garage and is drinking all the juice boxes.'

'I bought them for the both of you. You go tell Thomas yourself.'

She hears Billy's muffled voice shouting at his brother, then something clatters to the floor in the living room. There's another thump and more yelling, then heavy pounding on the bathroom door.

'Thomas, I'm in here.'

'Billy bit me!'

She buttons up her jeans, pulls her shirt on and opens the door. 'What is it with you guys? Can't I just have one second to myself in here?'

Thomas holds out his arm to reveal the dotted circle of Billy's bite-mark on his forearm.

'You tell Billy I'm going to be out there to talk to him in a second.'

'She says you're in big trouble!' he shouts across the hall into the living room. And just behind him, because of Thomas's raised voice, Poochini has his snout in the air and is dancing in excited circles.

At the A&P she takes boxes of sugar cereal off the shelf for herself and for Thomas to share and gets Billy his favourite, Raisin Bran of all things, because he loves the ad with the California Raisins.

She turns and notices a good-looking white guy, about her age, in the aisle just behind her. She watches as he takes a box from the shelf. As she pushes her cart down the aisle, a ridiculous image of a different life, of a man like him playing catch with her sons, floats up into her head. Or inviting him over to dinner for pepperoni pizza with her and her boys.

But in reality that'd be a disaster. She's only had a date or two since they moved to Connecticut and each time she was out the boys were awful to the sitter. Last time one of them, or maybe it was both, shaved long strips of fur from Poochini's back.

As she's deciding on a brand of potato chips, a young redhead stocks cookies on a nearby shelf. A man with a smoker's voice approaches and in a stage whisper tells him that a woman in the next aisle is shoplifting frozen dinners. 'She's sort of old and wearing big, big glasses.'

Instead of waiting for the redhead to respond he continues down the aisle. Then calls back, 'I just thought you should know.'

The redhead shrugs, continues stocking the cookies, and as Marie passes he says to her, 'What does he want me to do about it? I don't even work here. I work for Keebler.'

In the cosmetics aisle Marie picks out some eyeliner. She opens a lipstick and tests the colour on the back of her hand, something she's done a million times before. She's not sure the colour suits her. But then suddenly, inexplicably, she feels so guilty for having used it without paying that she puts it into the cart.

She packs her groceries in the trunk, uses her vanity mirror to put on the lipstick then drives to the school. The boys usually take the bus, but she thought it'd be a nice Friday-afternoon surprise to give them a ride home. She honks when she sees Billy and he gallops to the car. It looks like he's pretending to be a dog. Poochini maybe.

'Hi, puppy.'

He whines and pants.

'Where's your brother?'

'Ah-ru-roh,' he says and pants some more.

When Thomas exits the school he's the nucleus of a small pack of boys trading X-Men cards. She calls his name out of the open window and waves. Billy calls him too and when he gets in the back of the jeep, Billy pretends to lick his brother. Thomas pretends to hate it. She turns to them. 'We ready to go? Everyone wearing seat belts?'

'Your lipstick's pretty,' Billy says, clicking his belt into place. She smiles up at him in the rear-view mirror. He's the only seven-year-old whose opinion she'd ever trust about make-up. She sees that Thomas has his finger in his nose.

'Don't do that,' she tells him and he laughs at being caught.

Shirley Ferris is on their porch as Marie pulls up to the house. She cuts the engine and the boys tumble out of the car.

'I was just leaving you a note,' Shirley calls. 'When are you free to come over for coffee?'

'Is tomorrow OK with you?' she says as she struggles with getting the grocery bags out of the car. Then she shouts across the lawn to the boys, 'I need some help with these.'

Billy is still being a dog and running in tight circles on the grass, and Thomas is heading behind the house to the giant hole he's digging back there. To China, he says. She's hoping he'll get bored with it soon.

'How's noon?' Shirley says, and she says that sounds fine.

When the bell rings at a little before noon the next day, Poochini, as he always does, goes nuts barking. She goes to the door thinking she was sure they'd agreed to meet over at Shirley's house. She pulls Poochini back by the collar so she can open the door and is surprised to find, standing on the porch on the other side of the screen, the handsome man from the grocery store.

He's got black stubble on his chin and blue eyes and he's taller then she remembers. Up close she realizes how muscular he is. He's wearing a dark-blue cap with two wavy light-blue lines, like water, next to the initials C.T.W. Poochini settles down. Then barks once more, like he's asking a question.

'Hello?' she says.

'Ms Mitchell?' he asks and he sounds like he's from down South. 'I'm from the water company. How are you doing today?'

She nods to mean she's doing fine.

'I'm reading everyone's meters this afternoon. Yours looks like it's inside? Maybe in the basement? I didn't see it at the side of the house. Mind if I come in and take a look?'

She steps out onto the porch, still holding Poochini by the collar, and clicks the door shut behind her.

'Now isn't a good time,' she says. 'I was just heading to my neighbour's house. See her there spying on us?' He turns to look and from her kitchen window Shirley waves at them. Not at all embarrassed at being caught.

'You should seduce the man I just saw you talking to,' Shirley says when she lets Marie in the house. Marie laughs as she follows her into the kitchen. Shirley puts some coffee on and Poochini paces her kitchen with his nose glued to the floor.

'Who's kidding around, Marie? Shoot, if you don't I will.'

'Not interested.'

'But aren't you just bored to death out here? Going out with a nice bit of beef like that would be fun.'

'I'm not so bored. And it's too much work, trying to find one that's halfway decent. You have any milk?'

'Sure.' Shirley goes to fridge and puts the carton on the table. 'Who was he anyway?'

'Wanted to check the water meter.'

'Oh yeah? Maybe I'll get him to come by here.' She grins. 'I've got a meter that needs checking.'

Marie is using a safety pin to work the string of Thomas's pyjama pants back through the hole. He asks for permission to go play a video game in his room, one where he runs around a military base murdering everyone he sees with some kind of huge gun that shoots white acid. The Freudian implications of his video games astound her.

'But keep the noise down. Billy is sleeping; his stomach hurts.'

Thomas nods and runs out. After a moment she hears the game's start-up music. Bored, she goes to the bathroom to try her new lipstick. She puts on mascara too and the eyeliner. A little foundation. Not half bad, she decides, appraising herself in the mirror.

The bathroom window is open and from outside she thinks she hears something. It sounds like – it might be – footsteps shushing through the leaves behind the garage. Then it's quiet again.

'Hello?' she says out the window and is greeted by the sound of nothing but the distant noise of cars on the expressway. She closes the window and locks it.

When the boys are asleep, she gets her old duty Glock out from the safe in her bedroom. She doesn't like handling the gun again.

She's sure she's just being paranoid, but stays up all night in the living room with the TV on, occasionally getting up to check on the boys.

D inner time. Poochini's tail thumps the kitchen floor as he looks up at their plates. Billy dabs at his mouth with a paper napkin and lifts his pinkie in the air as he sips from his juice box. She wonders if he's picked up these flourishes from some television show and smiles down at her plate, happy. She loves both her boys equally but feels guilty for liking Billy just a little bit more.

I t's the afternoon and she's at her desk, working at translating a brochure, when Poochini gets off her bed, goes into the bathroom and begins to growl. Through the wall she hears him bark once. She closes her dictionary and turns off the radio. Sits totally still at her desk to listen. Nothing. She goes to the phone to call the police, but hesitates with the receiver to her ear then puts it down. Really, she's not sure why she's scared. There's no one here. She's seen no one.

N ear midnight. Marie takes her gun with her to the bathroom. On the toilet she hums a little to herself then flushes. She leaves the Glock on the tank as she washes her hands. Then picks it up, shuts out the bathroom light and leaves.

In the hall she hears Poochini, closed in the bedroom with the boys, scratching at the door and whining.

She waits for a long time in the hall, pressed up against the wall, not sure what she's waiting for. She's about to head back to her room when she hears a familiar noise, amplified in the night silence. The shower-curtain rings moving against the metal rod. The curtain was closed, she realizes.

The bathroom door opens slowly. Quietly. The dense dark of a man's silhouette appears in the looser dark of the hallway and comes towards her. She tries to flatten her body against the wall but still he stumbles into her in the dark. He makes a small, surprised sound and she feels a hot blast of his breath on her forehead before she pulls the trigger. The sound of the shot explodes through the quiet house and the man's silhouette collapses to the floor.

'Mommy?' a scared voice calls out.

'Stay in there!' she shouts. 'Don't you dare open that door!'

She turns on the light. The man is easing onto his back from his side. She sees the top of his shaved head and that his feet are just inches from the boys' room. Poochini is barking hysterically, jumping up against the door and making it shudder.

She goes to the man, crouches at his side. The man from the grocery store. He looks stunned and is hyperventilating. She hit him in the left thigh; blood soaks through his jeans. A lot of it. She's terrified the bullet has hit his femoral artery and that he'll bleed to death right there at the threshold to the boys' room.

The phone starts ringing. She guesses Shirley heard the gunshot. The man is still gasping. She's overwhelmed by the absurd desire to take it back, to pluck the bullet out of him like magic, to fix all the tissue she's destroyed. She says, 'Hey. Don't you die here, all right?'

He nods almost imperceptibly, puts his head back against the floor and closes his eyes.

'Mom? Was that a gun? Mommy?' She looks up. Half of Billy's face right above her, peering out from behind his door and looking scared.

'Close it! Close it right now!' Her voice sounds rough in her own ears and panicked. He closes the door.

The man passes out. She doesn't want the boys to see him, doesn't trust that they'll stay in their room. So she takes him by the hands and drags him into the bathroom, where there's barely enough space for his body on the floor. She reaches out to the door, pulls it closed and locks it.

She hears Billy's voice: 'Don't, Thomas! She said not to.'

There is banging, loud and heavy, on the bathroom door. She says as calmly as she can, 'Thomas, I'm in the bathroom just this second.' Under the sink, beside the bathroom cleaner, are rubber gloves, which she puts on. 'I'm in here.'

'Mommy, there's blood. Did you get hurt?'

She smiles, the old trick of smiling to make your voice sound cheerful. Catching a reflection of her face in the mirror she sees that she looks ghastly. 'I'm fine. I'm OK. Is your brother OK? Is he scared?'

'He's OK, I think.'

'Thomas? Can you please do something for me?' She clears her voice and starts again, louder. 'Thomas, can you do me a favour?'

'Can I come in?'

'Call the police for me, please? Would you?'

She hears his footsteps run across the hall to the living room. But already there's the distant sound of police sirens.

Gloves on, she checks his unconscious body. She feels a gun in the holster at his waist and takes it. His pockets are empty.

She looks at his face. He's still breathing. There's something about his bearing that makes her think he is, or was, in the military. She wonders whom he works for. He's been watching her. She wonders for how long and feels sick and exposed.

'Mommy?' Billy says softly. He's right outside the door. She looks down at the man. He must've known the kids were in the house and the thought makes her angry at him for the first time.

'Billy? Are you scared?'

He hesitates. She can hear him starting to cry. 'No!'

'I'm OK in here. Don't worry. How are you?'

She hears him sit down by the door. 'Fine.'

When the doorbell rings she shouts out, 'Only open it if it's the police!'

She hears heavy boots come down the hall. There's a knock on the bathroom door. Poochini is barking and a man's voice tells him to be quiet. Then it says, 'Ma'am? It's the police.' And he too sounds like he's from down South.

'I think he's alive,' she says back. 'Just make sure the boys can't see in here, OK? Tell them to wait in their room. Boys, go back to your room!'

Billy starts screaming. He says to someone, 'Don't! Don't do that. Stop it!'

'Are you all right?' she shouts at him through the door. There's no answer.

She picks up her gun, afraid now that these men aren't the police. Could they have arrived so fast even if Shirley had called them? Yes. Maybe. She doesn't know. Her heart is still racing.

'Ma'am, my partner took them to their room. OK?'

'Why was he shouting? What's going on?' She gets up on the tub again and reaches for the door, ready to go out. She's got her gun. She's got to protect her boys. Keep them safe.

'Nothing. He just, um, was talking to his brother. It's just me out here, now. Open the door, OK?'

'Is he all right?'

'He's fine, I swear it. But, Ms Mitchell, you've got to do something for me now. You've got to open up the door, OK? You've got to open up and let me see what's going on in there.' ■

What We Talk About When We Talk About Anne Frank by *Nathan Englander*

From the critically acclaimed young American writer comes a masterful collection of short stories that has already received rave reviews from many of the most prominent writers working today. Some of these stories are comic masterpieces, some embody as dark a vision of the universe as you are likely to encounter and all of them showcase a writer grappling with the great questions of modern life.
Phoenix £7.99 | **PB**

Ambit Magazine

Ambit Magazine // 96 pages quarterly // poetry, prose and art // founded 1959 // put together entirely from unsolicited submissions // newcomers alongside established names // past contributors: J.G. Ballard, Eduardo Paolozzi, William Burroughs, Carol Anne Duffy, David Hockney // '. . . a surreptitious peek inside a private world. Without it such vital sparks of inspiration could well be lost for ever.' – Ralph Steadman
Ambit Magazine | £10 for a single issue, £30 for an annual subscription. www.ambitmagazine.co.uk

Climates by *André Maurois*

A beautiful and heartbreaking novel of two marriages and the fractures endured by both, which was published in 1928 and became a best-seller in France and throughout Europe. The *New York Times* exclaimed, '*Climates* . . . proves for all time André Maurois's mastery as a novelist.' In this new translation, its penetrating examination of the psychology of love is made vivid for a new generation.
Other Press $15.95 | **PB**

Kind One by *Laird Hunt*

'Opening with a prologue in the form of an extraordinarily beautiful meditation on loss, Hunt's writing deepens into allegory, symbolism and metaphor, all while spinning forth a dark tale of abuse, incest and corruption reminiscent of Faulkner . . . Profoundly imaginative, strikingly original, deeply moving.' – *Kirkus*, starred review
'[A]n unforgettable tale of the savagery of antebellum America . . . Hunt deftly maintains an unsettling tone and a compelling narrative that will linger with readers long after the last page.' – *Publishers Weekly*
Coffee House Press $14.95 | **PB**

FLOWERS APPEAR ON THE EARTH

Samantha Harvey

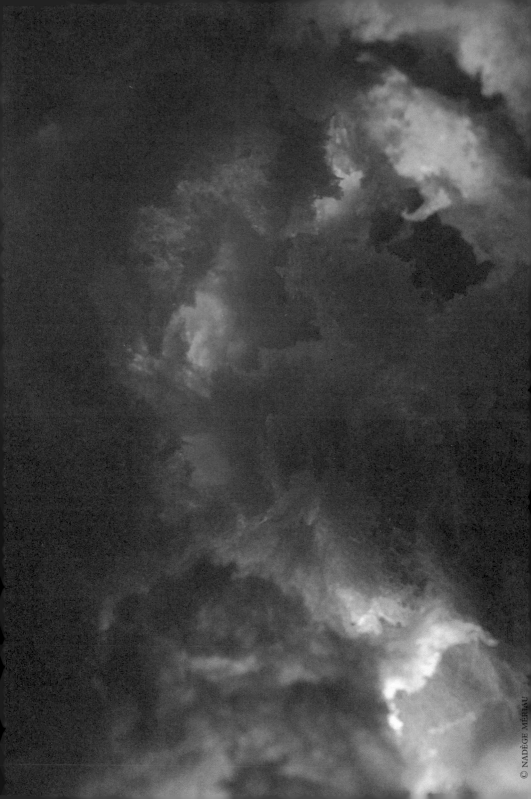

Five weeks after the disaster, at the end of July, the islanders trooped from the church of St Helene to the eastern promontory. At the front of the cortège was the vicar and those carrying urns. These men and women tucked the urns in the crooks of their arms, or held them with both hands, solicitous and anxious, or clasped them to their chests. Behind those the rest of the islanders, who carried bouquets and spades. At the back, the small party of cameramen and journalists from the mainland for whom the island's acrid smell was new and who could be seen now and again flinching where it collected in sheltered dips. Their track followed a gentle descent along the southern edge of the island, bordered by rhododendron bushes on one side and a low unbroken wall of bracken on the other, and to the front a wide blue vista of sea, waves furling and unfurling on its surface.

As they neared the site of the old factory, the track became a tarmac road which led to gates and barbed-wire fencing, and the smell seemed to catch at the air – a chemical smell, almost stinging, though nobody could pin down exactly what it was like. Something burning, no, something melting or rancid, noxious, rasping, corrosive, miserly. At first it had made the throat sore, though lately not so much, now that the body had adapted. When they reached the site, those with urns put them down and a group of men and women began to dig, one grave for each urn, where the small polished wooden crosses marked a spot. Blackened, friable, the earth gave easily. The seams of dried dye that ran through it might have been mistaken for something naturally occurring, like the striking pigments of fossil moths in oil shale, the beautiful greens, purples and blues. In their deepest sorrow the islanders buried the ashes of their forty-six dead, pushed them back into the ground as if these two finished forces, the earth and the ashes, might find comfort in each other.

How discreet the journalists were in their recording of the scene. What could have been crass was made reverent by their light-footedness and silence, and the tender advances of their cameras towards the bent heads of the diggers, an almost maternal care in the way the lenses attended to the greatest concentrations of pain and anguish. There was a feeling of safety and recognition among the islanders, whose eastward gaze naturally enough turned out from time to time towards the faint heathery scrim of colour that was England's most south-westerly tip; our motherland, they thought, even those who'd usually have spoken proudly for Tre's independence.

Although affliction cometh not forth of the dust, neither doth trouble spring out of the ground. Yet man is born unto trouble, as the sparks fly upward.

The vicar stood facing east into the wind, and his reading voice was compromised by his own grief. *God does marvellous things without number. To set up on high those that be low; that those which mourn may be exalted to safety.*

On the first anniversary, the boats came in. Two of them had gone and two were returning, just as the new tradition had it. There was a quiet wait at the head of the jetty where the islanders grouped, tight-jawed and protective of their children, and then two dark specks expanded into form: there's the prow, the mainsail, there's the mizzenmast. When the ketches came into view the islanders stood if they hadn't been standing already and straightened their backs and anticipated some kind of salvation.

The boats quivered back into the harbour on a soft June wind with their flags and festoons rippling. The larger of the boats was called *Xanthippe* and the smaller *Lamprocles*, mother and son, in service of all those child–parent bonds that had been broken a year before. After the disaster it was agreed that to commemorate the dead the boats should be sent out to the mainland the day before the anniversary, where an English dignitary of some sort would greet them and lay flowers on the decks. The boats would moor at Penzance overnight, a meal would be shared between the islanders and the dignitaries, and the next morning the islanders would take the thirty-mile crossing back.

So it was, and on the first anniversary the dignitary was no less than the Leader of the Opposition himself, bowing his head empathetically all the way through dinner. I lost my brother recently, he said, my heart goes out to all your families, a waste, a terrible misfortune. He had to leave before dessert, but not before he'd confessed a love of sailing vessels and asked the three islanders about the magnificent ketches in the harbour. On the boats' return, the people of Tre collected from the decks the forty-six wreaths of roses and lilies from England and made their way to the burial site. There were still tracks between the crosses where the media had first worn their tiptoed routes, slinking under the weight of cameras; like sheep tracks, somebody remarked – sheep tracks cutting across ground in search of something to chew on. For the anniversary a small number of journalists had come to photograph the laying of the flowers and the raw ceremony was conducted – as had been most of Tre's events over the last year – under the lens.

Although affliction cometh not forth of the dust, neither doth trouble spring out of the ground.

He is giving the same reading as last year, one or two of the islanders remarked to themselves as they laid their flowers. *God does marvellous things without number.* He must be busy doing these marvellous things in England then – went the thinking – because He hasn't been doing them here. Perhaps the vicar protests too much, perhaps he's lost his faith. The vicar rounded the graves with a blessing for each and when the sun was falling low enough to make the shadows yearn across the ground, he and his community made their way back from the eastern end of the island to the harbour at the south, to the pub, where for the most part they drank one toast and then went home.

The national news reported it with grim diligence at first, and pictures of a beautiful island rendered hellish were splayed across Britain's living rooms. Uproar hit the nation and for two years afterwards tourism even increased; people wanted to see what a chemical explosion does to houses, trees and beaches, which, extrapolated, meant that they wanted to measure the wingspan of evil in more general terms – how resilient is good to ill? Are creation and destruction equal opponents, in other words, are we locked in a fair battle, us humans; can creation win, can good win? Those tourists were disappointed to find that two years on, the score wasn't settled. Some of Tre was rebuilt, some was still gnarled and sunken. Good was winning here, evil there, the battle was fought in fits and starts. Then the rest of the world lost interest and Tre was left to its own spoils.

Then malaise. The island had lost a quarter of its people – men, mostly, so that what the survivors seemed to suffer was post-war in miniature. Forty-six people had died and several more had left the island to return to the mainland to find work. The remaining islanders looked hopefully towards Britain. Britain looked sympathetically back. Compensation cheques began to arrive, which for the most part were banked and left untouched for lack of any idea of how such money could be spent; those who had to spend theirs to make up for lost livelihoods did so with parsimony and regret, which became reluctance, which became bitterness.

The normally rinsed and glowing island fell into a state of shabbiness – the hanging baskets outside the shop weren't watered, the model ketch that welcomed visitors at the harbour grew a damp covering of mould through the winter. The wall that bordered the dramatic drop from the pub garden to the sea became encrusted with gull droppings; so too did the coin-operated telescope at the same site, its eye trained on England – it was even difficult to put your twenty pence in and set the mechanism to work. Services at the church of St Helene gained vehemence as they lost attendance, and in response to his shrinking congregations the vicar began to read more from the Old Testament, declaring those vigorous and spectacular passages in a raised voice that was as relentless as winter waves crashing at granite. One day he realized he was almost shouting, and to a near-empty room at that, and in shame and sudden self-dawning he sat and prayed, and from then on delivered lacklustre sermons that spoke of patience and fortitude and asked for the strength to bear what had to be borne.

It was the rattling, most of them had said, the rattling and shaking as if in an earthquake, and the way their living rooms had seemed to lurch as if startled from sleep. The cat fell off the bed, the doors fell off the cupboards, the glass shot like shrapnel from the windows. It had happened on a Friday evening when fewer than usual people were working at the plant; over half had gone home. A fire broke out and vat after vat of dimethylaniline subsequently exploded: one of those situations – so the British government liked to say at least – in which both everybody and nobody was to blame, and where the knife of blame is in any case soon blunted by being driven repeatedly at an impermeable body of grief.

The plant made dyes – acid, acid chrome, reactive, direct, dye intermediates – producing a bounty of colours: Orange S, Copper Blue 2B, Scarlet 4BS, Fast Black G, Turquoise Blue SE-2R. It exported colour to the rest of the world. It had, at the island's insistence, high environmental standards, higher than average pay for its staff at all levels, very good general staff welfare.

The mushroom cloud produced a curiously perfect circle of smoke and debris that could be seen from the mainland, and every house on the island had its foundations rattled by the blast; most lost windows or doors or roofs, and fourteen of the forty-six killed were not employees at all – just people blown from their bikes or armchairs. Because the plant was situated on the eastern edge of the island, and because of the strong easterly winds that day, the firefighters – who had been trained especially to deal with chemical fires – could not get upwind of the flames to put them out. It took five days to extinguish the inferno completely, which flaunted tropical, beautiful flames where it fed on the dye, and when the fires were gone a deeply hued hell was left where the plant had been, veins of astonishing pigments forking through the blackened ground.

When the plant was built, Tre's population more than doubled, a coterie of chemists, colour technicians, engineers and administrators relocating with their families. With a population of around a hundred, the island's genealogy had long been a small stagnating pool, everybody related, the young forced to go elsewhere if they didn't want to marry their own cousin. This haemorrhaging of youth aged the island in every respect, which further shrank the population. With an economy based largely on farming fruits, vegetables, dairy and flowers, the ageing, shrinking population was struggling to maintain any profitable industry. Skills, money and motivation began to disappear from the islanders' list of assets.

With the plant came money in generous subsidies, and with the young people and the families came energy, with money and energy some excess resources that manifested as creative pursuits, so that Tre regained, from decades long lost, a reputation for the arts, which deflected attention from the pure hard task of survival. That softer focus brought small numbers of tourists – not enough to fuel an industry, but that was all right, Tre now had an industry, and the island was big enough to accommodate the plant without too much loss of its natural bounty, so the tourists came and went satisfied. The older islanders, who had once farmed and now couldn't, instead opened up bed and breakfasts from their homes, or ran improvised tea shops in the summer from their gardens.

Yes, there was a fondness for the chemical plant, not just because it brought large subsidies to the island from Britain, but because sometimes, often, the plant really did look almost majestic poised on the easternmost cliff edge glowing orange as it reflected the rays of the setting sun. It had the air of empire, with the cargo ships sailing in and out every week destined for Asia. The resonant chord was upbeat, a zing of enthusiasm at the island's undiscovered and unspoiled beauty, a bubble that expanded with each week of the plant's operation. Even an abstract delight in Tre's new commodity: colour. Colour breaking out in chemical reactions: benzanthrone into dibenzanthrone by alkali fusion, and out streams blue. Sodium hypochlorite added to Yellow 4, and out streams a brighter, mood-lifting yellow that looks sunlit. Something godly about the ability to make colour and send it forth across the oceans.

A year passed and another. For the second anniversary sailing, an MP had come to the Penzance commemorations; for the third, it had been an opposition MP. The day before the boats left for the fourth anniversary, the islanders gathered in the boathouse. After their noon meeting they migrated from the southern harbour and went inland, through fields in which nothing much grew, past the skeletons of old farm machinery and outbuildings collapsed into the churlish soil and couch grass. They dispersed into groups and surveyed the land, tried to assess its condition, tried out rudimentary calculations. When the boats came back two days later, the islanders took the forty-six wreaths, bequeathed this time by the Mayor of Penzance, not to the buried urns at the old chemical site but to the church of St Helene, where they were all but forgotten and where the roses held long onto a papery life preserved by darkness and coolness.

What people seemed to forget – what the islanders themselves had forgotten those recent solemn years – was that there'd been industry at Tre before the dye factory, that Tre had prospered in other ways and could prosper again. It had tried shipbuilding in the nineteenth century, a little smuggling, tin mining. In between the collapse of each of these industries the island went back to its trusted dependence on the land and sea – fishing, kelp harvesting, flower farming, grape growing. Flung thirty miles out to the south-west of England on a huge heft of mostly submerged granite, the island lies low and constantly negotiates its boundaries with the ocean. Each incoming tide goes out again with some of Tre's geology, never to return it. All its granite neighbours have long since drowned. Each onslaught of Atlantic wind hacks back at the protective gorse that covers the westernmost end of the island, and bends the trees a little more eastward; and this is perhaps to say: if the sea doesn't drown you, we the winds will push you back to England. Either way you will lose yourself.

A quarter of our population is gone and what do we get in return? one of the older islanders had asked in the boathouse. Flowers. Once a year, flowers. With all due respect, Britain can keep its flowers. That's one thing we could grow ourselves. We've asked if perhaps one year the dignitaries could come to Tre's shores for the commemorations, instead of us going there. Show them the graves, show them our community. But no, always this yawning indifference from the mainland, this recumbent slump it assumes while it clicks its fingers and beckons its lessers to come running. They say they're too busy, there's Afghanistan, there's trouble in the Gulf, there's a disaster in Bangladesh. *We* are British, yet the country carries on as if we're nothing to do with them.

What we should really ask is this: instead of wreaths, which die every year out in the sun and winds on the corrupted ground where our dead are buried, might we have our compensation claims reassessed? Might we not be entitled to a little more than these paltry, token sums that have already run out – can't we look again at the contracts that were signed when the government agreed Tre would have the plant? Might we not re-examine the evidence we were given when we were told the plant was safe?

What the listeners realized as this speech was made was that Tre's acquiescence to Britain's ways had become, over the years, more an act of apostasy than of homage. The expedition to the mainland was less an exercise in national goodwill and more a defiant act of proof that Tre still existed; and if the festooned boats sailed into Penzance with a cheery serenity it belied only anger. They give us flowers! We will show them a thing or two about flowers. The people set to work. The former factory engineers who'd stayed on Tre, and the men who were good with their hands, went about fixing the broken tractors and farm machinery; they retrieved ploughs from part-burial and went to work on cleaning up the main frames, the skimmers, the disc coulters, checking the hydraulics, fitting them to the tractors to try out a piece of ground, estimating the furrow size, testing the extent of pulverization. Others who had knowledge of farming, or who were business-minded, went about calculating how many bulbs and seeds could be planted in how much soil, what yield, which flowers would grow in Tre's warm but wet conditions, how many greenhouses they would need, how much irrigation, what potential profit, what possible risk.

Export subsidies were requested from Britain so that Tre could compete with the flower industries of Europe, and each request was gently rejected. At the next anniversary dinner with the dignitary – once again the Mayor – the island representatives asked again. If we have no subsidies we can have no industry. We are all set, we have business plans, we have expertise and farming is our heritage. If only we have the word from Britain we can go ahead and plant. May we count on Britain's support, do you think? We are, after all, a part of Britain – at least you take our taxes as if we were; we are British ourselves. The Mayor had looked down at his girlish, hairless hands and the piece of hake collapsing on his fork and had asked cautiously, Flowers? Yes, flowers, he'd been told. Subsidies? Yes, subsidies. It isn't for me to say, answered the Mayor, I do Remembrance Day ceremonies, I open bus stations. Well, to be fair, Mr Mayor, Your Worship, we used to have dinner with an MP, we once had the Leader of the Opposition – now it's you representing Britain. What do you say? I will have words, he said.

The answer remained no. Tre's plight was understood with great sympathy, but flowers were not a priority in the UK's commercial plans. Nor was a further inquest into safety at the chemical plant seen to be necessary; the explosion had been found to be an unfortunate accident, the risk of which had always been inherent to such an industry, no matter what lengthy precautions are taken. Everybody should rest assured that all precautions *had* been taken.

As for the flowers, at the commemorative dinner next year, the sixth year, they would send along a more senior dignitary and one of the government's business advisers who would willingly take away with him accounts, business plans, profit and loss forecasts, and perhaps then, once Tre's ideas had had a couple of years to mature, they could reassess. Meanwhile, if the island did manage to produce any flowers, Britain would, as a gesture of goodwill, pledge to buy from Tre some 70 per cent of the national quota of flowers for official state events, a business deal that they hoped Tre would regard as an honour.

And every year there were the forty-six wreaths, which went to St Helene's where they passed indecipherably from life to death next to a wall carving of the *Confessions of St Augustine*. They were cheap Dutch freesias and carnations, and the over-scented lilies that stained the nose with rust-coloured pollen when one went in for a smell and whose sweet heady vapours filled the sinuses with a thick wooziness that began to feel provocative, mocking, even when dampened by the stone in the church.

The islanders marked out, ploughed and fertilized the fifteen square miles of available land, ordered 400 greenhouses, 10,000 metres of irrigation pipe, 5,000 metres of horticultural fleece, a million daffodil bulbs in forty different varieties, a million each of tulips, freesia, lilies, amaryllis, a 100,000 ragged robin, anemones and iris, 12,000 rose bushes and 40,000 chrysanthemum cuttings, which then cruised in on ships from the mainland over the course of the next few weeks, the islanders waiting at the harbour with sleeves rolled up, ready to take delivery of their goods.

Here it is, a slab of granite bordered by white beaches of finely ground shells, and atop it strips of colour that blow in the wind, flanked by sweating, sweet-scented greenhouses. The sun glimmers off the glass and weaves rainbows through the water from the irrigators, and picks up the sparkles in the sea. The sea moves with seals. Where the bulb fields are idle for the summer, corn marigolds grow in a joyous upsurge of yellow that falls down to the cliff edges.

From the air it is the most beautiful sight. Colour colour colour, no longer stored in vats and shipped invisibly away, but rising from the ground like an ensign for the first birds migrating back to Europe for the winter.

Flowers everywhere, except at either end of the island. At the western end, bashed by the winds that have built strength all the way from America, nothing but trees, gorse and bracken will grow. At the eastern end, where the winds are broken by Tre's highest hill, a patch of slightly blackened uncultivated land where the chemical plant used to stand, with its rectangle of little crosses. About thirty-five of the islanders leave the pub one Saturday lunchtime to get spades from their sheds and farms, and then they converge back at the harbour. The summer's morning tilts into an afternoon of rain-flecked wind and, almost without words, and with spades shouldered, they head towards the little nub of land at the island's far east.

Fog, one of them remarks, and from the north they see it begin to roll in and dissolve the bright day. The island fogs are infamous and when they come Tre is alone for the duration – nothing comes, nothing goes; no post, no excursions to or fro, no imports of food and goods. They are quite prepared for it, and when the fog appears now they lift their heads to the damp chill that precedes it and welcome its enveloping. The road that leads up to the site of the old chemical plant is potholed and yielding to weeds. They pass the fallen barbed wire fencing that nobody has removed, perhaps because nobody has wanted to take away that one last defence between themselves and what happened. With the fence there the old site is like a sick animal kept in quarantine.

Among the islanders is the vicar who is aware he's fallen to the back, no longer the shepherd but the sheep, spade in hand, hoping his poor over-curved lumbar will hold out for the afternoon. The crosses are serried on this piece of slowly recovering land and the tracks between them have healed, so that you'd never know this was once a place of great interest to anybody outside of Tre's bounds. Even the islanders no longer come much now; over the years more permanent and personalized granite memorials have been scattered around the island – three benches at the southern foreland, another nine at the western end to catch the sunsets, some in families' gardens, a cube of stone tucked within a clump of gorse where it could enjoy the long season of almond-scented petals, one piece of granite hewn into a heart, inscribed and placed on a cairn at the island's highest point, a little set of carved circular table and stools in the school playground for the two children who died.

Who in their right mind would have chosen to bury their husbands, sons, sisters, mothers in stained and barren ground? Why did we not scatter them out to sea where they could be free of all this? the islanders ask themselves as they take up their spades. They have come to agree that they were coerced into doing so in the name of drama, so that the news channels could put on a good show – of course not openly coerced, but steered in the time of their greatest weakness when the comfort of another's arm in yours, leading the way, is enough to take away the worst of the pain for a moment or two. They agree that it's enough, they've been weak, and now they should stand up for themselves.

They feel no irreverence at digging up the urns; they only wonder why it's taken them so long. The past is full of turning points. The present is just a matter of one foot in front of the other. It curves and veers, but it doesn't navigate. Yet the past, when looked back on, is mapped, is itself a process of conscious mapping. This afternoon, the present takes on the characteristics of the past and becomes full of panoramic purpose. As the islanders dig they can feel a rare significance in their action as if, finally, they are lifting themselves from a pit. Enshrouded by the fallen fog, and a spadeful at a time, they free the earth until metal hits metal. *For lo*, the vicar speaks as they dig, *the winter is past, the rain is over and gone; the flowers appear on the earth; the time of the singing of birds is come, and the voice of the turtle is heard in our land.* They exhume the ashes of their loved ones with hands that shake with bitterness and hope. ■

ABINGDON SQUARE

André Aciman

Her emails, when I look back, still show how fragile everything was. Brisk and lightly crafted, they were no different from everyone else's, except for that one, overly effusive word that burst on my screen and aroused me each time. *Dearest.* It's how she called me, how she started every email, how she said goodnight. *Dearest.*

For a second I'd forget how disappointingly brief each of her emails was, or how deceptive straight talk can be at times. In her attempt to reach out and say something real and close to the heart, she was simultaneously eliding the one thing I craved to hear the most. She wasn't curt, or shifty, or chatty – that wasn't her style at all – nor was there anything bland or tame in her emails. Her style was bold. But there never was a hint of *something else* in what she wrote, no subtext, no unspoken sideline, no allusion, no Freudian slip asking to be mulled over and dissected, no nickel inadvertently dropped on the table for you to raise in what could have been a long-standing game of email poker. Perhaps her tone wasn't troubled, wasn't needy or awkward enough. Perhaps she really was the happy, untrammelled sort who dropped into your life as easily as she sprang out of it, no baggage, no promises, no hard feelings. And perhaps the normal mix of anxiety and irony, which trips so many of us when we meet someone new, was so thoroughly airbrushed that her emails had the breezy good cheer of summer-camp letters to distant relatives who like to receive notes in the post but seldom read them closely enough to notice that the unusually large script is there not to help with their failing eyesight but to fill the gaping blank spots in otherwise perfunctory bulletins.

Her emails looked like letters but were really text messages running out of breath. She respected capitals, punctuated with fussy correctness and never used abbreviations – yet everything had an unmistakable air of suppressed haste, meaning: *I could say more, much more, but why bore you with details?* the flip side of which was: *I have to run but for you I'll always make time,* the whole thing capped and fluffed with a heady *Dearest* to keep me from seeing that the *something else* I kept waiting for was not coming this time either. There was *nothing else.*

I had read one of her articles and knew how complicated her mind was; I liked her complicated mind. Her prose reminded me of a warren of arcane, sporadic lanes in the West Village that take swift, sudden turns and are perennially ahead of you. On email, however, she spoke the polished language of the tree-lined *grands boulevards* of Paris, all clarity and transparency, no hidden corners, no false trails, no dead ends. Never *anything else.* You could always choose to over-interpret the meaning of so much clarity, but then you'd be reading your own pulse, not hers.

It was the Lower Manhattan that I liked in her – the way she'd sit with me over coffee and confide the intricate patterns in her life and then, on impulse, change her mind, turn the tables on herself, and say that patterns made for good stories but rarely meant anything – there were no patterns, we shouldn't look for patterns, patterns were for regular people, not for us, we're different, you and I, aren't we? Then, as if she'd taken a wrong alley, she'd back up and say that her analyst disagreed with her. Perhaps he'd figured her out long before she could – which wouldn't be the first time. I'm totally off track about myself, she'd add, throwing in unexpected zingers of self-deprecation that made me like her even more each time she brought herself down a peg, because it made her more vulnerable, because I loved the way she'd say one thing then sidle up to its opposite, because this unabashed tossing and turning with herself promised spellbinding fireside chats in some beloved, cosy corner of our invention.

This was the young writer whose article on opera I had turned down months earlier. Yet I had picked up an inflection in her prose that was at once wry and brooding and, in my two-page, single-spaced rejection letter, had outlined the strengths and weaknesses of her piece. She shot back an email, saying she needed to see me right away. I replied just as quickly: I wasn't in the habit of meeting people simply because I had turned down their work; in any event, I'd have very little to add to what I'd already written in my letter. All right, thank you. I wished her luck. Many thanks. Our tit for tat was over and done with in a fraction of a minute.

Two months later, she wrote back to tell me that her piece had been accepted by a major magazine. She'd taken my advice and used all my edits. Now would I see her? Yes, I would see her. She bought me coffee in a place on Abingdon Square, *across from the little park*, she said, *and not too far from my office*. Both of us sat with our winter coats on. It had started to rain outside, and we ended up staying much longer than we'd planned, talking for almost two hours about Maria Malibran, the nineteenth-century mezzo-soprano. As we were saying goodbye and she was getting ready to light a cigarette, she said we should do this again, maybe real soon.

We should do this again, maybe real soon stayed with me as I rode the train to Brooklyn that evening: bold and feisty yet unambiguously sweet. Was she asking me, *Maybe real soon?* Or was it a deft, roundabout way of saying *No need to wait two months to meet over coffee next time?* I felt like someone who's been promised a Christmas present in June.

I tried to nip the flurry of joy by reminding myself that her *maybe real soon* might easily be one of those open-ended deferrals thrown in to cover up an awkward leave-taking between people who already know they'll probably never meet again.

Or was it trickier than I thought? Was there perhaps a touch of affected diffidence in her implied *next time?* Had she already guessed that I'd say *Absolutely yes!* the moment she asked but wanted me to think she wasn't sure I would?

I never asked why I spent so much time mulling over her sentence on the train. Nor did I ask why I reread her piece first thing the next morning at the office or when catching myself thinking about her that night. But I knew I'd been 100 per cent right about her: a woman with that sort of a pen, spirited and glum in the same breath, just had to be very beautiful. I knew where this was going. I'd known it the moment I'd spotted her.

On the same evening after we met, an email arrived. *Dearest*, it started. Not *Dear*. Suddenly I was someone's *dearest*. No one had called me *dearest* in years. I loved it. I knew of course that I wasn't her dearest. The line of men her age or a few years older with a better claim to the title was surely very long. Everything about her told me she was well aware of this. *Dearest* was also her way of thanking me for meeting her on such short notice, for helping her with her piece, for coffee, for talking to her about her next article on Malibran. *Dearest* for being so friendly. There was something so practised and easy, so sure-fire in her gratitude that I couldn't help thinking there were many who had helped her in exactly the same way and who had become *dearest* because they'd given so selflessly – at first, to draw her closer, later when they were up to their knees in friendship and couldn't step back to ask for anything else. *Dearest* was how she spelled the terms of your induction, how she kept you in tow.

In her email that evening she told me it thrilled her to think that only .0000001 per cent of humanity knew who Maria Malibran was, and yet we'd managed to find each other, at this tiny cafe in, of all places, Abingdon Square – and with our coats on for two whole hours, she added.

I was smitten. I loved *And with our coats on for two whole hours*, thrown in as an afterthought. So she too had noticed that awkward detail about our coats. Perhaps neither of us had wished to show we wanted coffee to last longer than fifteen minutes, which is why we sat with our coats on, neither daring to alter anything for fear of reminding the other that time was flying. Perhaps we'd kept them on so as not to show we were actually enjoying this and were hoping it might last a little longer provided we behaved as though it might at any moment come to an end. Or was this her way of telling me that we'd both noticed the same thing and that if we finally ordered two refills each it was because we were still wearing our winter coats, which gave us an alleged out in case we'd overstayed our time?

Dearest. It instantly brought back how she looked at me and returned my gaze as though nothing else mattered in that small cafe. *Dearest*: how she made no secret of having read up on me. *Dearest*: the flattering barrage of questions – what was I working on now, what were my hopes, where did I see myself in five years, what next, why, how, since when, how come – questions I'd stopped asking myself but that were being now hammered at me with the reckless, searching whimsy of youth, tying knots in my stomach each time she drew closer to the truth, which I loved. Then there was her smile, her lips, her skin. I remembered watching the skin of her wrists, of her hands – it glistened in the early-evening light. Even her fingers glistened. When was the last time I'd had coffee with someone so beautiful who had things to say I couldn't wait to hear and seemed totally riveted by what I'd said? The answer scared me: never.

Not to be easily taken in, I forced myself to reconsider *Dearest*. It probably signified zero interest. It was the kind of over-the-top formula she would never have used on someone her age, and certainly not immediately after meeting him the first time. One used it with friends of one's parents or with the parents of one's friends when they became quasi-avuncular figures – an endearment, not a come-on.

From Germany early the next morning came my friend Raùl's email: *Stop it. Learn to take things at face value.* This was his response to my email where I'd managed to wring every conceivable twisted reading of what *Dearest* could mean. With no one to confide in, I'd reached out to someone who was far away enough not to ask more questions than I was eager to ask myself.

That morning I wrote to her and said we should meet exactly a week later.

Where? flashed her speedy reply. Same place, I said. Same place, same time it is then – on Abingdon Square. On Abingdon Square, I repeated.

She arrived before me again and had already ordered tea for herself and the same double cappuccino I'd ordered the last time for me. I stared at the cup waiting for me on my side of the same table by the window. What if I'd arrived late or had to cancel? 'You didn't and you wouldn't have.' 'How could you tell?' 'It's so good to see you,' she said, standing to kiss me on both cheeks, nipping the flirtatious banter I'd attempted. Had I gotten lost this time? she asked. No, not this time. Found the place easily enough. But I didn't tell her that I missed wandering through the streets as I'd done the first time, that I was hoping to get lost again, if only to play back all that preceded our last two hours together. Would our meeting be the same this time as well? Or was I setting myself up for disappointment?

Coffee lasted longer than either of us expected. Outside, she took out a cigarette. Obviously two-plus hours without smoking was difficult for her. On the way to where we had separated the first time, we were stopped by two individuals speaking into walkie-talkies. They were part of a film crew. They asked all those on our side of the sidewalk to wait and remain very quiet. This was like a fire drill, she said. She hated fire drills. I liked the pretext of hanging out together a while longer in this kind of induced suspension. It gave our walk a dreamlike quality, as though we too belonged in a film. I asked one of the crew members what they were filming. Something from a 1940s novel. Old hotel sign fixed to a building blinking away – the Miramar – couple arguing on the deserted sidewalk, vintage Citroën parked aslant on the gleaming slate kerb. At a given signal, there was a sudden downpour of rain. All of us stepped back. Applause seemed called for, but no one dared.

The director wasn't pleased. They were going to have to shoot the scene all over again. *Thank you for your cooperation.* We were allowed to cross the street and go on our way.

Did I want to go? she asked. Not really. Watching them shoot the same scene again was just another way of staying together a while longer. So we stood and waited for the cameraman to start filming again. Blinking Miramar sign, couple arguing, black old Citroën with its passenger door flung open, everyone waiting for the sudden downpour in this twilit film-noir setting that made me feel we'd stepped into John Sloan's portrait of the West Village.

When we separated it was almost eight o'clock. Next time we'll have drinks instead, I said. You're right; it's way too late for coffee.

*D*earest, she wrote. She had started work on her essay on Malibran. I told her I'd once seen a long-out-of-print volume containing Da Ponte's letters to the young Malibran. She should try to find it. Besides having been Mozart's beloved librettist, the much older Da Ponte, living in New York in the early years of the nineteenth century, had helped launch the operatic career of the young Maria Garcia. In New York, Maria would marry the Frenchman Malibran, twenty-eight years her senior. She kept his name but then left to find fame in Paris. The parallel thrilled me.

Our third coffee was no different. She was already waiting at the same table by the window with my double cappuccino. We watched the snow begin to fall on Abingdon Square. This was a gift, I kept telling myself. *So learn to be grateful and avoid asking too many questions*, spoke my inner Raùl. Just take what is given, be in the moment, ask for nothing more, there may be nothing more. Part of me, though, couldn't help but take sneaky peeks at what was waiting around the corner. 'Maybe, if the weather changes, we'll pick a day and visit Da Ponte's grave in Queens,' I finally said.

Fancy Mozart's librettist buried in Queens, she said.

And in a Christian cemetery too, I replied. He was born Jewish but then converted. Maria Garcia's family was not really of Gypsy origin, but more than likely of Converso descent, I said.

She knew a woman who claimed to be of Converso descent.

Out came the story of an old, rather pious Catholic woman who on days coinciding with the Jewish high holidays each year made sure all the Christian images and icons in her house were turned to face the wall. I pictured an old, shrivelled *abuelita* dressed in perpetual black with gnarled, arthritic fingers. No, the woman held an important post at the State Department and was, I realized when told her age, not exactly that old.

'When do you think we should go?'

'Go where?' I asked.

'To the cemetery. Really!' meaning, *Where else?*

Could things be so easy, I thought, or was I missing something?

I'd let her know, I said. I'd meant to say something like *Some of us have jobs, we're not all freelancers*, but then suppressed it. Maybe early next week – but I avoided saying this too. I would have had to check my cellphone's calendar and I didn't want the formality of the gesture to cast a chill over what had all the makings of a spontaneous outing to Maspeth, Queens.

But the silence and the time it took to say *I'll let you know* had already cast a shadow over us. The unasked, the unspoken sat between us. Her bewildered look was the question, my silence the answer.

When she continued to stare at me with that bold, confiding gaze that lingered on me as though she had more warmth in her heart than she wished to show, I knew that what had rippled between us was a disquieting instant of awkwardness and of opportunity lost. Perhaps we should have talked about it right then and there. Perhaps it needed bringing up. Neither of us said anything.

We had met three times already and never once spoken or enquired about the other's life. We had exchanged cellphone numbers, but we never called. Telephones were off-limits it seemed, and contact, other than through email, taboo. That we didn't even mention this and preferred to glide over it in silence gave our meetings a guarded, tacit, over-the-transom but under-the-radar air. Her name never figured on my calendar, and mine, I sensed, never entered hers – though most likely for different reasons.

Ours were the cobbled lanes; major arteries we steered clear of. On Abingdon Square the snow kept piling up and made me wish we could spend endless hours together in our coffee shop, do nothing but sit there and hope that neither made the slightest effort to lift the spell. Provided we stayed put, and provided it snowed, we could manage to meet like this next week, and the week after, and the week after that as well – she and I together at this same corner table by the window, with our coats bunched up on a third chair, knowing how lucky I was to be there, because I had never before had the chance to sit face to face with one of the most beautiful and most intelligent women I'd met in my life. And now it was given to me, and if neither had yet mentioned the drinks we said we'd have instead of coffee, and if neither brought up others in our lives, it was because we didn't wish to alter anything or abandon this tiny, safe islet we'd found for ourselves. For me, it was the rarest thing on earth. For her? I couldn't begin to know. One day I'd have to ask. And that day might be the last.

Tread softly. Do nothing. Spoil nothing.

Two days later my resolution gave out. Did she want to have drinks?

My dearest, I'd love to. Let me get a couple of things out of the way. I'll let you know.

Early the next morning – what a good sign this was: *I'm free tonight.*

Yes, but tonight isn't entirely mine, I emailed back. I can do drinks but then I have a dinner to go to. How about six?

Let's make it five thirty.

Fine, I wrote back, there's a bar off Abingdon, not far from our cafe.

So it's ours now?

On Bethune. All right? I ducked her humour but hoped that my abrupt reply told her that her meaning had pleased me and wasn't lost on me.

On Bethune it is, my dear.

Seldom in my life had anyone been so wilful and acquiescent at one and the same time. Was this a sign? Or was she just the accommodating sort?

When we met yet again a week later we ordered two Hendrick's gins. 'The rest of this week is not going to be good for me,' she said. 'Actually it's going to be pretty awful.'

Well, I thought, finally something's coming out.

The week wasn't so hot for me either. I alleged dinners and cocktail parties that were excruciatingly boring, give or take a few people.

'Give or take?'

I shrugged my shoulders. Was she teasing me? Why was her week going to be so dreadful?

'I'm going to have to break up with my boyfriend.'

I looked at her, trying not to show how startled I was. Most people throw in *the boyfriend* to tell you they're taken.

I never knew she had a boyfriend. Was he that terrible?

No, not terrible. They'd outgrown each other, that's all, she said. 'I met him at a writers' colony last summer, we did what everyone does in these places. But once we were back in the city, it dragged – we fell into a rut.'

Is it that hopeless?

Why was I playing friend-analyst? And why the disappointed inflection in the word 'hopeless', as though the news pained me?

'Let's say it's just me. Plus –'

She hesitated.

Plus?

'Plus I've met someone else.'

I thought for a moment.

Well, in that case, maybe you should definitely break up and clear the air between you. Does he know?

'Actually, neither of them knows.'

She levelled her eyes at me with a resigned, semi-rueful shrug of the shoulder that meant something like: *Life. Can't be helped. You know how it is.*

Why wasn't I asking more prodding questions? Why was I refusing to pick up the hint? What hint? Why let her drop this bombshell and pretend I wasn't even fazed? All I could say was: I am sure things will work themselves out.

'I know. They always do,' she replied, at once grateful that I'd left things vague enough and yet sorry, perhaps, that I'd dropped the matter a bit sooner than she might have wished.

At seven she reminded me I had to be at a dinner party to dine with my *give or take* friends.

I wished I could bring her along to such dinner parties. She'd have them eating out of her hand, women included. As we stood outside the bar, I stared at her, hoping she'd see how sorry I was that we were separating so early in the evening. She reached over to kiss me as she always did, on both cheeks. Without thinking, I found myself kissing her forehead, then hugging her. I felt the spur of arousal. This was not just in my head. And she had hugged me back.

As I walked her to what had become the undeclared spot where we'd say goodbye, something told me that she should have asked about the dinner party. I had railed too much against dinner parties for her not to have made a passing comment. But she hadn't shown the slightest interest even in asking where it was being held – for the same reason, perhaps, that I hadn't asked a single question about the new boyfriend. Perhaps, like me, she too didn't want to appear interested. On Abingdon Square, we took everything that had anything to do with the rest of our lives and turned its face to the wall. My life, her life, like everything that didn't really bear on why we kept meeting here, we simply staved off, never brought up, put a padlock on. On Abingdon Square we led a spare, hypothetical life, a life apart, set between Hudson and Bleecker, between five thirty and seven.

After saying goodbye to her that evening, I watched her walk downtown and, for a few moments, lingered on the square, thinking to myself that I could easily stop taking the Brooklyn train, move in somewhere not far from here, start a new life right next to the bar, take her to the movies on weekday evenings, find other things to do in life, and, if this worked, watch her become famous, more beautiful, have children, until the day she'd step into my study and say we'd fallen in a rut and had basically outgrown each other – *Life. Can't be helped. You know how it is*, she'd say, and, *FYI, I'm moving to Paris.* Even this didn't scare me. The vision of this alternate life was outlined on the large glass pane of the bar where she and I could easily spend so many more hours together. When she looked back at me after crossing the street, I liked being caught standing there, watching her go her way. I liked that she had turned around. I liked the sudden arousal that had made me hug her and, for the first time since we'd met, allowed me to think of her naked. It had come unbidden.

That Saturday evening, in a crowded movie theatre, I watched a young couple ask those seated in our row to move one seat over. You could tell they were on their first date by the tentative way they took their seats and then hesitated on how to go about sharing their bag of popcorn. I envied them, envied their awkwardness, envied their back-and-forth questions and answers. I wished she and I were together in this very same movie theatre. With a bag of popcorn. Or waiting in line outside with our coats on, eager for our show to begin. I wanted to see *Last Year at Marienbad* with her, take her to hear *The Art of the Fugue*, listen to the Shostakovich Piano with Trumpet Concerto together and wonder who of us two was the piano and who the trumpet, she or I, trumpet and piano as we'd sit and read St John of the Cross on quiet Sundays and I'd hear her say things I'd never known about Maria Malibran, and then, on impulse, throw on a few layers and head out together to see something really stupid, because a stupid movie with super-moronic special effects can work wonders on drab Sunday evenings. The vision grew and began to touch the other corners of my life: dinner with friends, short trips to the Cape, longer trips abroad, Salzburg, Cinque Terre, Corfu, new friends, old friends, her friends would become my friends, as my friends would become hers if they wished to remain my friends. The weekends we'd go away and on Sundays would come back from the country with lots of dirty laundry, but first a bottle of wine, then something on TV.

There had been a moment while I helped her with her coat when I could have said something. I'm falling for you, you know I am. The dinner thing with my *give or take* friends tonight can go to hell. Just about everything else can go to hell too. All you have to do is make one crack about my life, say one word about the unspoken, and everything I have goes up in smoke. But I knew, as I watched her make her way through the crowd, that she was as grateful for my silence as I was for hers. High-tide avowals are all very good but they mustn't break the surface. This works. What we have works. We could be doing this for months, years even. One day I asked her which she'd like to be, the piano or the trumpet. The piano is blithe and spirited, she told me; the trumpet wails; which did I think I was?

A mantra from my friend Raùl: *What you need is less scepticism and more courage.* Courage, he said, comes from what we want, which is why we take; scepticism from the price we'll pay, which is why we fail. *What you need is to spend some time with her, not in a cafe, not in a bar. Take it to the next step. She's not sixteen. If it doesn't work, well, you'll be disappointed, but you'll move on, and that'll be the end of that.* When I told him that my scepticism was hardly misplaced, considering she already had someone waiting in the wings, his reply couldn't have been more heartening. *That someone is you. And if it's not, only knowing it might be can move mountains. This woman is all real.*

I tried to find a way to pry open the lockage between us. She wanted me as I wanted her, and everything else was just nonsense and speculation. But the more I saw how much I wanted her, the more the idea of her new beau began to muddy my thinking, the more her blandished *dearests* began to irk me. Everything I liked about her, everything she wrote and said had the ring of hollow appeasements thrown around to prevent me from drawing closer. There was nothing upfront about her. I became more guarded and oblique.

T wenty-four hours after our gins, I wrote saying I wished I'd stayed and had dinner with her in *our neighbourhood* rather than go to that dumb dinner party.

Dearest, did you have as terrible a time as all that? What about the give or take *friends you like so much?*

I liked sarcasm. Wish I had brought you along with me – would have livened the company, thawed winter, dusted off their old bookshelves, made me so happy.

I remembered dinner in my friends' carpeted dining room, all of us talking about someone we knew who had cheated on his wife but had chosen to stay with her because he couldn't think of life without her, or of that other friend who had left his wife for a man twenty years younger than he, claiming that all he wanted was *just another go*. One look from her across the table, had she been present that night, and we would have burst out laughing together, repeating *just another go* on the sidewalk as we were heading back to Abingdon Square.

We were neither friends, nor strangers, nor quite lovers either, simply wavering, as I wavered, as I wished to think she wavered, each grateful for the other's silence as we watched the evening drift into night on this tiny park that was neither on Hudson, nor on Bleecker, nor on Eighth Avenue, but a tangent to all three, as we ourselves were, perhaps, nothing more than tangents in each other's lives. In a blizzard, we'd be the first to go; we'd have nowhere to go.

Two days later, past midnight: *My dearest, I haven't been happy once this week. It's been very rough. And the worst isn't over. I want you to think of me.*

Think of you? I'm always thinking of you, I wrote as soon as I was up at five thirty the next morning.

Later that same day: *My dearest, let's have drinks soon.*

Done.

'I wish I could do something to help. Have you told him where he stands?' was my tentative foot forward.

'I've already told him everything. I'm not afraid of telling people the truth.'

I wish I knew how to tell people the truth.

I wanted her to say something like: But I thought you did tell the truth. You turned down my article when you didn't like it, didn't you? You've always told me the truth.

I wasn't talking about that kind of truth.

Then, what kind? she'd have asked, and I'd have told her. All I needed was an opening.

'I don't always like being straightforward,' she said, 'but I always tell the truth when it matters,' she added. I loved when she snuggled in tightly between two opposites.

She had sidestepped my flimsy little trap.

A few days later she wrote saying a family emergency was taking her to DC. Meanwhile she had finished her piece on Malibran.

How many words?

Too many.

I'd love to see it.

But you know I can't publish it with you.

I know that. I don't care who runs your story. But I care about everything you do, write, think, say, eat, drink, everything, can't you tell?

This was as straightforward as I could be. If my meaning wasn't clear, then obviously she wasn't eager to know it.

Dearest, your feelings for me touch me deeply. I too listen to everything you say. Surely, you know this. I just hope I'm worthy of you. I'll email the manuscript as soon as I've revised it for the nth time. Your loyal and devoted me.

From Raùl in Germany a word of caution: *Stop talking shop with her. This is not about work.*

What he didn't see was that, as she and I continued to write to each other, my emails were becoming ever more cryptic: too many smoke signals and plenty of allusions. I was speaking in irked nudges, she with syrupy shrugs. I didn't even know what I kept hinting at; what mattered was for her to know I was hinting, that hinting had become my language, my only language. I wanted her to see, to imagine, to intercept, and ultimately to invent the undisclosed script behind everything I hadn't said, couldn't say, was never going to say, because I didn't need to say it – because she already knew and if she knew and wasn't saying anything, then she was already saying plenty enough.

Peeved by her inability to respond in a manner less oblique than my own, I didn't write for three days.

Dearest, is something wrong?

I could almost feel the smooch you give grumpy grandaddies when they want to seem hurt.

Raùl: *You've been seeing each other far too many times to assume she doesn't already know. She wouldn't have met you a second, certainly not a third time if she didn't already want what you want. No man in my world spends more than a minute with another man without knowing they both want the same thing. She likes you; she doesn't like the twenty- or thirty-something idiots who surround her. If anything, she's probably no less puzzled or hampered than you are. Just cut the coffee face-to-face interviews and sleep with her.*

The following Friday we decided to have dinner. I'd found a restaurant on West 4th and made reservations for six thirty. That early? she quipped back. I knew exactly why she was smiling and what she was asking. The place gets overcrowded, I explained. *Overcrowded,* she replied, echoing my own word to mean *Understood.* Tart and snide. At least this much is clear between us, I thought. Knowing that she saw through everything was an irresistible turn-on. A woman who knows what you're thinking must be thinking what you're thinking.

If the weather didn't change, it might snow again, and the snow would slow things down and put a halo on an ordinary dinner date and give our evening the lustre and magic that snow always casts on otherwise drab evenings in this part of the city.

What bothered me was the strange suspicion that she wasn't coming to dinner willingly but had consented to it, was playing along – who knows why. This was goodwill, not desire. Perhaps I'd made her uneasy and she had relented. We were face-to-face-coffee people. In-between people. Not strangers, not lovers, not friends. In a blizzard, she'd be the first to go.

And yet, on the walk to the restaurant I already knew I'd never forget the sequence of streets as I took my time on West 4th Street. First Horatio, then Jane, then West 12th, then Bank Street, Perry, Charles and then West 10th. The picturesque buildings with their tiny picturesque high-end stores, the people heading home in the cold, the old lamp posts shedding their scant light on the cobbled streets. I caught myself envying young lovers living in their tiny apartments here, all the while reminding myself: *You do know what you're doing, you know where this is likely to go tonight* ... I loved every minute of the walk. *She knows what this is about. She knows and she's telling you she knows.* The worst that could happen at this point was being invited upstairs after dinner and explaining that I could stay but couldn't spend the night. No, I corrected myself, the worst was walking back along these same streets a few hours from now after making love to her and wondering whether I was any happier than I'd been before dinner, now that I had left her and was crossing Charles, Perry, Bank, West 12th in reverse order, as though nothing had happened between us.

Then it hit me. The very worst would be walking back these selfsame streets without having spoken or come close to speaking. The worst was watching nothing change, that nothing ever changes – which is when I'd feel the stab of delayed irony puncturing my makeshift defences. For somewhere along that walk to the train I'd recall rehearsing my deft little exit line for when I'd have to tell her that I'd sleep with her but couldn't spend the night. It would have to come out sounding natural, I'd told myself, not the kind of thing one rehearses and still fumbles. Silence is worse than fumbling, said my inner Raùl, but fumble if you must.

She was wearing high heels when she showed up, looking much taller than I remembered. She had dressed up and was wearing jewellery. When she came to my table after negotiating her way through the crowded bar area, I told her how ravishing she looked. We kissed on both cheeks and I on her forehead, as we always did. Everyone was staring. Any doubts about what we meant to each other were instantly banished. This moment of clarity between us thrilled me and dispelled my inhibitions. How silly of me to have even considered taking my time getting here.

I ordered two Hendrick's gins. Did she like the place? 'Feels decadent but quite, quite wonderful,' she said. She removed her shawl and for the first time I saw her arms – same glistening skin, same tone as her hands; slim, but not delicate; the merest sight of her underarms stirred me and reminded me that none of this was a mistake, that I wasn't making any of it up, that if I couldn't find it in me to attempt a pass, just the sight of her underarms at the table when she sat and stared at me would prod my courage.

The menu seemed to confuse her. She didn't feel like ordering.

I didn't quite believe her. But I loved what she was doing and couldn't resist: 'I know exactly what you'll like. I'll order for you?'

'Please!' She seemed relieved. She shut the menu, put it down and continued staring at me.

She let me order the wine too.

The way she scraped her mussels made me hope she'd take her time and keep eating and finish none of it, ever. You're staring at me, she said. I'm staring at you, I said. She wasn't displeased.

Of course, there was no way to avoid Maria Malibran. I asked if she knew that Pauline Viardot, Maria's sister, was an opera singer as well. Yes, she knew that Maria's sister was an opera singer. Somehow, it didn't seem to interest her. Did she know that Ivan Turgenev was madly in love with her sister for years? A lifelong love, she said, yes, she knew that Ivan Turgenev . . . 'Now tell me about you. You never say anything about you.'

It was true. I seldom spoke about me. 'Everything there is to say is more or less already out there.' A moment of silence.

'Well, then tell me what's in there,' she replied, pointing to her chest to mean mine.

For a moment I was about to tell her that the one and only thing going on *in there* for weeks could easily be summed up by *I think of you all the time. I keep seeing you everywhere. I want you everywhere in my life.* But perhaps she hadn't meant the question this way at all. Perhaps she simply wanted to know more about the part of me involved in the arts. A friendship question, an I-listen-to-everything-you-say question.

'Do you really want me to answer this now?' I didn't mean it to sound wistful, cagey or give her request a sinister inflection. What I meant was: I'll answer this question later, once we leave the restaurant and are on our way to your home. I want you to ask me again what's going on *in there* when we're past the film crew, which I hope will be out there tonight and which I pray will stop us from crossing the street as fake rain pours down. Let the gofers manning their cellphones and eating donuts tell us to be very, very quiet, because I want to walk and talk and walk till we reach your door, where you'll ask me to come upstairs, and we'll go upstairs, and you'll open the door, and say: This is my place. I want to see where you live, how you live, how you look when you take your clothes off. I want to see your cat spring on you and snuggle in your bare arms, I want to smell the cat litter in your stairwell, I want to see where you sit and write. I want to know everything. That's what's happening *in there*.

Instead, I ended up by saying: 'A restaurant may not be the best place.'

The girl who had written about Maria Malibran and who knew all about crypto-Jews who for centuries had been living with their identities turned in would easily have read what I was saying in my crypto-lover's speech. If she picks up on it, she's telling you something. If she lets it slide, she is telling you something too.

Raùl: *You're giving her an out.*

Me: *Yes, I am.*

Raùl: *Not fair. Not fair to you. Not fair to her.*

I remembered his latest email after I'd told him of our plan for dinner tonight. *If she invites you to her home, don't hesitate; don't ever let her think you're rejecting her.*

I know when to put the moves on, thankyouverymuch. I can read signs.

Your problem is not that you misread signs; it's that you see them everywhere.

And yet, as we lapsed into a moment of silence during dinner, how very, very far from sleeping together all this seemed. Dinner still felt like a concession I'd wrenched from her – and yet such a godsend, such a gift, her arms, her skin, even *dearest* began to seem real, plausible, thrilling. All she had to do was expose her armpit, tell me something sweet, almost promise she'd repeat the exact same words with a *dearest* thrown in, and I was ready to believe that things could go anywhere tonight. Just looking at the other women in the restaurant and the way they cast fleeting glimpses in our direction told me I was being watched, was being talked about, envied. So why not just tell her that this was exactly what was going on *in there* right now? I want nothing to go wrong tonight. Yet, the silence that had crept between us wasn't relenting.

I knew exactly what was happening: one more second of this and she'd put something on the table, say something that would chase away the illusion of the godsend and the dream. And I knew that what she was about to say was not what I wanted, that her arms, her hand, her fingers, which seemed to beg me to reach out across the table and touch them, would, within seconds of what she'd say, turn into stone and take back the dream. She chose silence instead.

'We should plan to see the Da Ponte tombstone,' I finally said. Shop talk better than no talk.

'Maybe this weekend,' she said.

Her comeback was too quick, snappy, almost intentional.

'This weekend is difficult.'

She stared at me.

'Dinner and things?'

What a sharp and twisted mind she had.

'*Dinner and things*,' I replied.

Any other woman would have scorned *dinner and things* and held it against me. Instead, she let it slide. In anyone else this silence would have meant *I don't want to cause trouble*. In her it felt different. *Dinner and things* worked for her too – which is why I began to feel something rise within me akin to anger, though it might have been despair, or, worse yet, just sorrow. I couldn't begin to tell them apart.

More talk of Lorenzo Da Ponte. How I hated shop talk. And

yet, one of the reasons I liked her so much was because talk of Da Ponte with her came so naturally. Such a mind, such a woman, why hadn't I met women like her earlier in my life? *Because you never tried to. Because you never trusted*, Raùl would have written. Because you wouldn't know how to go about doing anything unless she took the first step, because you still haven't learned and will never learn that women make the first move or never move at all, because, my dearest, it wasn't given to you to meet a woman like her, and when you finally did meet such a woman you were little more than a tangent in her life. Not a stranger, not a lover, not a friend even – a tangent.

'Pauline Viardot became friends with everyone who was anyone: Chopin, Tchaikovsky, Liszt, Sand, Gounod, Berlioz, Saint-Saëns, Brahms.' Then, not knowing what else to add, I couldn't help myself. 'So tell me about this new man in your life.' Was I being jealous? Or was I trying to show that I wasn't?

'The new man?' she said, musing for a moment. 'I don't want to talk about him yet.'

'Doesn't want to talk about him,' I echoed, trying to be jovial.

'Doesn't.'

Her mood had changed. I couldn't tell why. Our conversation was losing its footing. We were both groping for strings.

Towards the end of dinner, I said I knew of a small place nearby for dessert and coffee. I was hoping she'd counter with an offer of coffee at her place. Sounds like a good idea, she said.

We walked out. This, I knew, was the moment when years ago I'd have put a hand on her cheek and kissed her right then and there, on the sidewalk, in full view of the other diners. I took my time putting on my coat while she was looking for her cigarettes. In the end she produced one out of her pocket but, considering its bent shape, called it a cripple. I said I used to smoke two packs a day once. How long ago had I quit? 'I'm not going to answer this.'

'Why?' she asked. 'Because you cheat, or because you are afraid to claim you quit?'

'Do you really want me to answer?'

'I asked, didn't I? You're dying to tell me, anyway.' She had regained her spunk it seemed.

My answer, after so much hesitation, might give everything away and underscore why I'd avoided the subject.

'I quit the year you were born,' I finally said. 'Does that say enough?'

She looked at the ground as though taking her time to examine her boots. She had lit her cigarette, and was either deep in thought or was inhaling for the first time in more than two hours.

'Do you still miss them?'

'Cigarettes? Are we really talking about cigarettes?'

'I thought we were –' she paused – 'but I guess we're not.'

'I don't miss cigarettes, but I miss who I was before quitting.'

This was by way of both compromise and evasion.

She must have sensed, from my hardscrabble confession, why I wasn't comfortable being clearer.

'Has this been bothering you?'

Was she still speaking about cigarettes? Or about the years separating us?

I wanted to scream. When I'm with you, I feel I can take what others call my life and turn its face away from the wall. My entire life faces the wall except when I'm with you. I stare at my life and want to undo every mistake, every deceit, turn a new leaf, turn the table, turn the clock. I want to put a real face on my life. So why can't I speak to you now?

All I said was that no one likes watching time go by. That was abstract and safe enough, perhaps too abstract and safe for the likes of Raùl.

She made light of the whole thing. 'So, while I'm kicking about in my mommy's tummy, you're smoking away in some nameless cafe in Paris. I'm learning to say *dada*, and you're busy reading up on Dada. Is that what's been bothering you, dear?'

'There's more to it than just that,' I said, 'as I'm sure you know.'

'I do know.' She said nothing more.

'My dearest.' I knew she'd come out at so critical a moment and throw in a *dearest*.

She looked at the ground again and began shaking her head ever so slightly. At first I thought she meant: 'You'll never let yourself go, and what a pity that is.' Then I thought she meant something a touch more hopeful, even exasperated, as in: 'What am I ever going to do with you?' Finally I made out what the shaking was about: *I don't want to hurt you*.

'What?' I finally asked.

She continued to shake her head in silence. Then she looked up and I could feel the tension almost explode in my temples. 'Walk me to my building?' she asked.

'I'll walk you to your building,' I said.

We were, I assumed, nixing the idea of coffee and dessert. A good sign. Or a very bad sign. I did not say anything. I was trying to keep pace with her as we made our way down Bleecker. Why was she walking fast, why the chill between us, why the mounting fear of saying goodbye the closer we neared her building?

Before I knew it, we were already there. She stopped right at the street corner, not even before her stoop. We were obviously going to say goodbye. She kissed me on one cheek, I kissed her, then she turned to go away, but then came back and gave me a second kiss on the other cheek. I didn't have time to hold her, nor did she perform what had become a ritual suggestion of a hug or a kiss on her forehead. I watched her walk away towards her house. I thought she looked downcast and deep in thought – dejected almost. She did not look back this time.

Why hadn't we spoken? Had I perhaps rejected her as Raùl had warned me not to? Had I missed my cue? There was no cue.

As I walked away towards the West 4th station, I had an image of her entering her apartment, dropping her keys somewhere on her desk and finally giving out a yelp of relief. She'd acquitted herself of dinner, it wasn't even ten o'clock, and she was free to do as she pleased, take off her clothes, lounge in jeans, call her beau: Yes, dinner's over, thank God he's gone, it's the weekend, let's just go out and see something really, really stupid tonight!

Bold and rakish, like the piano, while I, the trumpet, was plangent and lost.

I had meant to take her to my favourite pastry shop after dinner. I'd known happiness there once, or maybe not happiness, but the vision of it. I wanted to see whether the place had changed at all, or whether I had changed, or whether, by sitting with her I could make up for the loves I'd gotten so close to but had never been bold enough to seize and, in the course of things, lost. Always got so very close, always turned my back when the time came. Hadn't I learned a thing about love, or about people, or about life and how to live it? My life, my real life, hadn't started yet, and all this was rehearsal still. I hadn't changed; the years had changed. Tonight, I thought, relishing Joyce's words and feeling exquisitely sorry for myself, the time has come for me to set out on my journey westward. St Augustine's words sprung to me. '*Sero te amavi!*' Late have I loved you!

So here I was making my way back through the streets just as I had feared a few hours before, remembering now with a cruel chuckle that I'd gone so far as to rehearse an exit line.

As soon as I got home, I opened my email and started typing something very short: We'll have dessert another time. I had just pressed the 'send' button when her email arrived: *Dearest, I forgot to thank you for the wonderful conversation, a great meal, a truly lovely evening.* A few seconds later, another email from her: *I'd like that.*

She's thinking of me.

No, she's scrambling to say something nice.

No, she's thinking of me. She's trying to stay in touch and not break the evening's spell. Perhaps she was trying to tease something out of me, get me to say those extra few words that I'd been trying to coax out of her and had frequently blamed her for not saying, or myself for not helping her say. Perhaps she was reopening a window I thought she'd closed the moment we'd said goodbye.

So I ventured something light: Work hard. Listen to the Shostakovich. And have coffee with me tomorrow.

She did not reply.

On Monday she wrote back. She'd been out with friends all day Saturday and Sunday. And Sunday night, dearest, was just too horrific for words. *But let's definitely have coffee soon.* She wasn't playing coy, and her deferral, we both knew, was no longer about coffee.

Monday evening I couldn't resist. I wrote what I considered a layered email about Maria Malibran and her sister: It turns out that Casanova had known Da Ponte in Venice and that he too, like Maria's father, is alleged to have had Gypsy origins. Could it be, do you think, that Casanova too . . . ? Then, quite unexpectedly, as though it had occurred to me right then and there: We should go out for dinner again. It was good to be with you. But I don't mean to crowd you. I'm leaving things in your hands.

Not crowding me in the slightest, she replied, eventually.

In the days that followed I didn't know how to reach out to her without sounding either desperate or peevish. In discussing Turgenev's hopeless love for Maria's sister, Pauline, I finally let myself go: 'I understand him completely, I wish I could hold you again.' I had nothing to lose, and like all those who know they've lost already, I was firing my last salvo, no ammunition left, no backup, no water in my gourd. The feckless sputters in my sentence said I had shot my wad.

The silence that followed was more than a simple omission to respond yet less than a gloved rebuke. She had lost interest, and I was losing her.

I would wait another half a day, maybe even a few days, but a week was certainly pushing it. Still, I'd have to struggle to avoid drowning in this. I'd never allowed myself to sink in too deeply for her – that much was good – though I did like her, liked her very much. Liked her on the day she ordered coffee for me. Liked that we had kindred souls. Already knew I liked her when I sent her my two-page, single-spaced rejection letter. Liked her. Liked the sheen on her skin. Liked everything. I even liked the spot of eczema under her right elbow

which she showed me on that night at the restaurant once she'd
removed her dark blue cardigan with the rounded mother of pearl
buttons and could tell I was admiring every inch of her. 'See this?' she
said pointing at her elbow. 'It's new. Do you think it could be cancer?
I've always had good skin.'

'I know,' I said. She knew I knew, every man knew. 'Probably just
eczema,' I replied. 'Nothing but dry skin,' I added. 'Do you have a
dermatologist?' I asked.

'Nope' – as if to mean, Why should I? At my age?

'Want the name of one?'

'Nope. Maybe. Don't like doctors.'

'Want me to go with you?'

'Maybe. No. Yes.'

'Maybe. No. Yes?' I asked.

'Yes,' she replied.

There was nothing I wanted more at that very moment than to
put my arms around her, or reach over and hold her hand and say:
'Put on your coat, I'm taking you to the dermatologist. He's a . . . *give
or take* friend, he'll see you if I ask him.' No sooner said than once
we'd stepped outside on the kerb I would have changed plans, taken
matters in my own hands and said: 'We're going to your place instead.'

I opened the window of my study and let in the cold air. *We're
going to your place instead.* My unspoken words rang like a promise of
bliss that I'd failed to seize but that continued to throb like a dream
and a vision long after we'd woken up and drunk coffee.

I liked the cold air. A few nights ago, I had faced the same street,
the same view, the same neighbours' lights across my building and
asked myself whether I'd ever miss this street some day. I remembered
the young couple I'd seen at the movie theatre a month earlier; they
couldn't even eat popcorn together. Yet, they were going to see plays
together, have children together, hang out on rainy Sundays and
listen to the Shostakovich and hold their breath when they heard how
the bold piano and the soulful trumpet sang each to each of newborn
loves and mended lives. Later, they'd head out to eat somewhere in

the neighbourhood and then loiter their way into one of those large bookstores where people always end up buying books, when they sometimes don't mean to, the way I'd bought Da Ponte's libretto one Saturday night after a movie, unsure whether I was buying it for her or for me, yet almost certain that it would make her happy because everyone likes a gift, because she'd love the book, because it came from me, I thought. I remembered her hand across the table, how doleful it looked as it seemed to beg me to hold it, just hold me, it seemed to say, even if the arm it belongs to has eczema, just touch me. Now, how far did Abingdon Square feel, as though it and she and the restaurant, and Da Ponte, and Maria Malibran, and the rainfall by the flickering lights of Hotel Miramar, belonged to another life, a life unlived, a life I already knew had turned its back to me and was being nailed to the wall.

I would survive this, of course, and grow indifferent, and soon learn to squelch every access of regret. For heartache, like love, like the longing to reach out and touch a hand across the table, is easy enough to live down. There were sure to be more emails with more *dearests* – I knew this – and my heart would skip a beat and catch itself hoping each time her name floated across my screen, which meant I was still going to be vulnerable, which meant I could still feel these things, which was a good thing – even losing and aching for her was a good thing.

What was sad was knowing she was most likely the last reminder that I'd missed out on so many things and that, perhaps, there was not, had never been, and might never be *another go.* We would still communicate, and we might still meet for coffee, but the dream was gone, the hand across the table was gone, the square itself was gone. And I knew this because for the first time ever that evening, after shutting my window and turning my computer off, I walked into the living room and told my wife of a brilliant new piece that was soon to be published about a nineteenth-century diva called Maria Malibran. Had she ever heard of Maria Malibran? I asked. No she hadn't.

'But obviously you're dying to tell me,' she said. ∎

GRANTA

Award-winning non-fiction
from Granta and Portobello Books

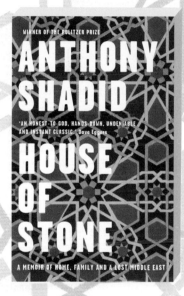

'*House of Stone* takes the reader to the heart of the Middle East and all its conflicts: the core question of what gives people a sense of who they are and what they are.' *Newsweek*

'A page-turner with a gripping human story, this is essential reading for anyone interested in the real India.' Jonathan Foreman, *Mail on Sunday*

JULIE

Darcy Padilla

1993- I was working on a project about urban poverty. Every Thursday, I met with a doctor, a social worker and a nurse, who cared for the Aids patients at the Ambassador Hotel, an SRO flophouse in a neighbourhood littered with crackheads and soup kitchens. One morning, I met Julie, standing in the lobby with a newborn baby in her arms, trousers half zipped, her then-partner Jack at her side. They said Rachael gave them 'a reason to live'.

Julie said yes to being in the project. I hoped that she would let me get closer.

When I knocked on Julie's door, sometimes she would answer and other times she would say, 'Not today, bitch.' Jack was happy being a speed freak. Julie did not want to lose Rachael, so she left him. We would sit on the floor in the lobby or hallway of the hotel and talk about Rachael, Julie's past boyfriends; she would ask me questions about myself. I wondered if she was lonely, wondered why she was letting me into her life.

Rachael didn't crawl until she was two, because there was no room on the floor. She was a sweet baby, didn't cry much. Julie read to her, loved her. I can't forget Rachael sitting on the soiled, stained carpet in the lobby of the West Hotel when Julie slapped her across the face, leaving her handprint on the baby's cheek. I took the photo. Felt like shit for doing so. Rachael cried and Julie clenched her teeth, started to pull her hand back to slap Rachael again. I said to Julie, take a timeout and I will deal with Rachael. I tried to calm her. Julie walked away.

Julie did the best she could with what she knew. Her first memory of her own mother was getting drunk with her at six; then there were years of being sexually abused by her stepfather. They lived in an SRO, blocks from where Julie lived now, in a room divided by a sheet on a string.

1996- Julie gave birth to Tommy. The father wanted nothing to do with them. The next Christmas, she met a man named Paul at the Salvation Army. She moved out with Tommy and Rachael to be with him, to live in the suburbs. I thought the story was going to end here.

1998- In January, I got a phone call. Julie was in the hospital when the cops came and told her that Paul had abused Tommy. He was found with adult bite marks on his torso and legs, covered in vomit and blood. Tommy and Rachael were taken away.

1998- Jack died of Aids. Julie visited him before the end. I wondered if she knew this would be her fate too. We never talked about it.

That same year she met Jason and became pregnant with Jordan. Julie had tested positive for drugs and, afraid the baby would be taken away, she and Jason kidnapped her from the hospital. I told her that she shouldn't run. Julie and Jason got nine months in jail. They would have two more sons, Ryan and Jason Jr, taken away at birth.

2005- I found a posting on the Internet by someone looking for a 'Julie Baird, born 10/10/73'. It was her father who had been looking for her for thirty-one years. I told Julie to call. Julie and Jason moved to Alaska to be with him. Weeks later Julie was in intensive care. Mr Baird met me at the airport. We hugged. He was thankful and the tears in his eyes looked like they had been there for years.

Julie's father thought she looked like a crackhead but 'loved her just the same'. For two years Julie had a positive family experience before her father passed away on an Easter Sunday. He died knowing his daughter, finally able to let go of the hurt that had haunted him for years.

Months later Julie called to say she was pregnant with Elyssa.

'I don't think you should have the baby, it could kill you,' I told her. I said that I was 'sad but happy for her'.

Around the same time, a woman named Karen called me after finding my website. Karen had adopted Julie's son Zach (also called Jason Jr) whom Julie and Jason had not seen since birth. That summer Karen, Zach and I made the journey to Alaska. After Zach left, I was doing a video interview and Julie was giving canned answers. I asked her if this was what she wanted her children to remember. We started again. Julie fell apart, her hands trembled and tears that had been trapped for years escaped. I cried.

2009- The last couple of years were the hardest. I watched Julie fade. Her weight was dropping off and her legs could barely hold her. Jason, Julie and Elyssa moved into the wilds of Alaska, near her uncle Mike. To save money, they lived in a small trailer, with no running water or electricity. They lived off the grid in the beautiful wilderness, in a yard littered with broken-down cars and appliances.

Things were bad. Julie was taking thirty-five pills a day. She could not hold Elyssa any more. We sat in the yard and she started to get angry, saying that she did not want a child to see her die, but Jason had just wanted one he could bring home. Julie knew she was dying.

I drove to see her one last time. Every minute seemed like an hour. When I walked in, we held each other. My eyes fought like hers to hold back the tears. I started to speak but she stopped me. 'You have been in my life the longest and you can do whatever you want.' All I could say was thank you. I brought Julie pictures from her life, ones I thought she would like, for her to hold, to see.

Days ended up being weeks. I watched her sleep, tanked up on morphine so she would not feel pain, waiting to die. I sat with her for hours and days. Not wanting her to be scared when she saw people in the room who were not there. Not wanting her to be alone. Each night I left in the darkness, alone on the road. Falling asleep, all I would see was Julie gasping for air.

I try to remember her and all I see are my photos in my head. ▪

1993

1994

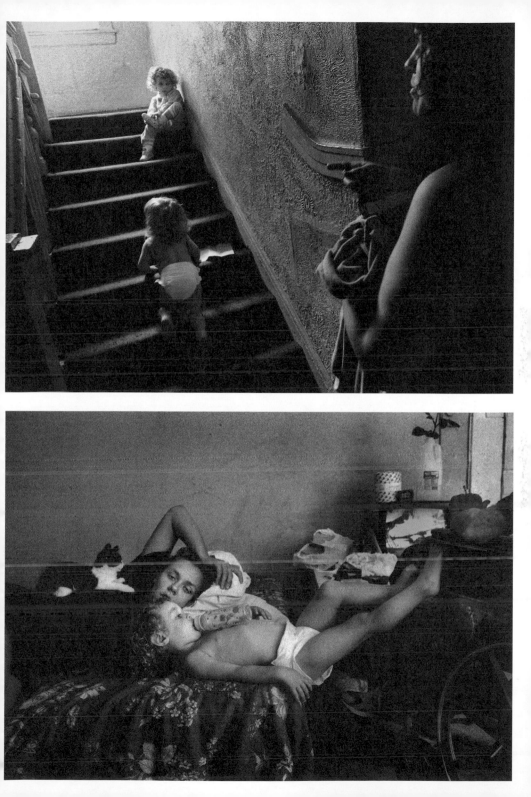

1998

1998

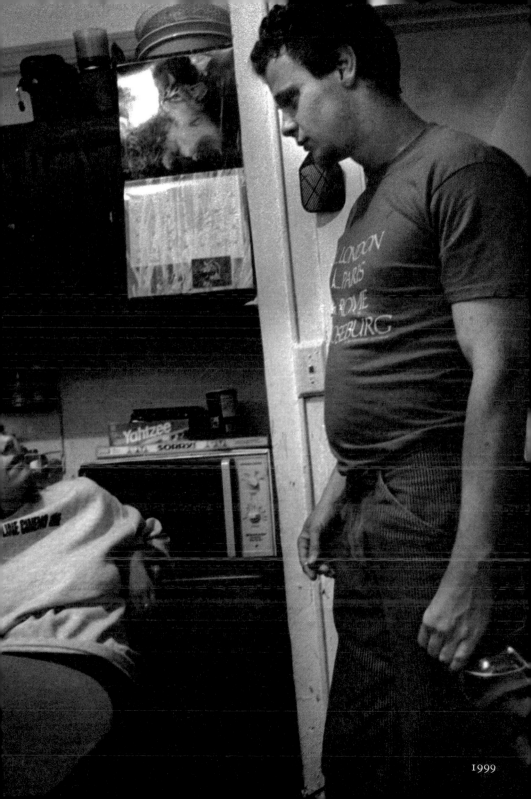

1999

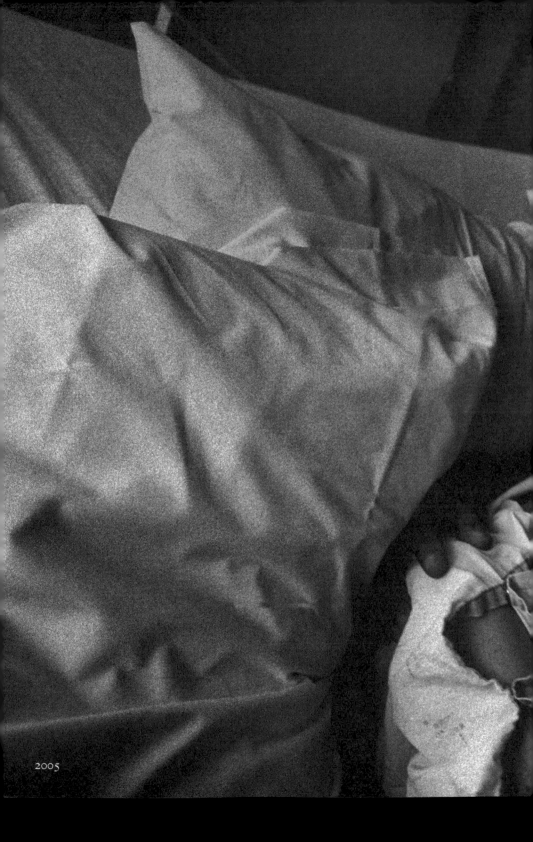

2005

2007

2008

2008

2008

2009

CAMEL

2010

2010

2010

GRANTA
THE MAGAZINE OF NEW WRITING

SUBSCRIPTION FORM FOR US, CANADA AND LATIN AMERICA

Yes, I would like to take out a subscription to *Granta*.

GUARANTEE: If I am ever dissatisfied with my *Granta* subscription, I will simply notify you, and you will send me a complete refund or credit my credit card, as applicable, for all un-mailed issues.

YOUR DETAILS

MR / MISS / MRS / DR ....

NAME ....

ADDRESS ....

....

CITY... STATE ....

ZIP CODE .... COUNTRY ....

EMAIL ....

☐ Please check this box if you do not wish to receive special offers from *Granta*

☐ Please check this box if you do not wish to receive offers from organizations selected by *Granta*

YOUR PAYMENT DETAILS

1 year subscription: ☐ US: $48.00   ☐ Canada: $56.00   ☐ Latin America: $68.00

3 year subscription: ☐ US: $120.00   ☐ Canada: $144.00   ☐ Latin America: $180.00

Enclosed is my check for $ _____ made payable to *Granta*.

Please charge my: ☐ Visa   ☐ MasterCard   ☐ Amex

Card No. ☐☐☐☐☐☐☐☐☐☐☐☐☐☐☐☐

Exp. ☐☐☐☐

Security Code ☐☐☐

SIGNATURE .... DATE ....

Please mail this order form with your payment instructions to:

Granta Publications
PO Box 359
Congers NY 10920-0359

Or call toll free 1-866-438-6150
Or visit GRANTA.COM for details

Source code: BUS122PM

PADDLEBALL

Colin Robinson

Named for an Irish immigrant, a pioneering surgeon who was a leader of the women's suffrage movement, the Dr Gertrude B. Kelly Playground is located in downtown Manhattan just west of Eighth Avenue. The park is surrounded by high buildings and, in the summer at least, when it is shaded by a canopy of mature plane trees, receives very little sunlight. The few straggling shrubs that survive the gloom are overwhelmed by tarmac pathways and ball courts, a concrete water play area and a children's playground. At the centre of the park, which at just over half an acre is not large, stands a disproportionately tall flagpole flying the American, New York State and Parks Department flags.

The park is not a salubrious spot. The air is regularly freighted with the diverse smells of cooking from local restaurants; one day it is fish and chips, on another curry and, on yet another, the sweet, sickly smell of wok-seared noodles will saturate the breeze. The office tower across 16th Street emanates a ceaseless low growl that, though not loud enough to impair conversation, reminds one of the park's pressing urban environs.

Rats are a persistent problem, brazenly scurrying across the paths at dusk. One evening, dismayed at spotting several large rodents under the climbing apparatus and slides in the children's area, I called 311, the New York City helpline set up by Mayor Bloomberg. It took considerable time and patience to register a complaint to the ostentatiously uninterested woman at the other end of the phone. But I persevered and on my next visit found warnings posted on several trees concerning the presence of poison.

This is not a playground much frequented by the middle-class residents of Chelsea who predominate elsewhere in the neighbourhood. Though located immediately behind the newly restored Maritime Hotel, with its elegant dining terrace, and just a couple of blocks away from the galloping gentrification of the Meatpacking District, home to Soho House and Stella McCartney's boutique, the park draws a quite different crowd. Just to its north are several blocks of housing projects and it's the working-class residents of these densely packed and foreboding towers who constitute the overwhelming majority of the park's patrons. On a warm evening the benches will be occupied by elderly African Americans dozing or reading the newspaper, Puerto Rican youngsters will be laughing on the slides and the playgrounds will be filled with teenagers wearing extravagantly capacious jeans and T-shirts. A couple of boom boxes will be blaring in competition with each other and someone will likely be inspecting the contents of the rubbish bins for collectable tin cans.

My brother and I can't help but stand out in such a gritty locale. We'll arrive on our bicycles, elderly sit-up-and-beg models, with rucksacks on our backs and hand towels around our necks. Having propped up the bikes against the inside of the fence that surrounds the hardball area, we will take seats on the adjacent bench to change into our spotless trainers. In summer we will be wearing shorts, probably linen and recently purchased at the nearby branch of Banana Republic, and ankle socks, grey in my brother's case, white in mine.

Our attire, to say nothing of our physical appearance as white men in advanced middle age, separates us sharply from the other regulars at the playground. So, too, does our purpose for being there. We visit the park specifically to play paddleball, our adopted sport or, perhaps I should say, adapted sport, because we have rewritten the rules of the game substantially so that it more closely resembles tennis, which we played regularly when we were in England. The standard paddleball game is played by four players in teams of two and involves hitting a small rubber ball fast and low against a wall with a bat that is switched from one hand to the other depending on the shot. In the special

'Robinson' variation that A. and I have developed, there are just two players, the bat is held in only the right hand and the trajectory of the ball is often an arcing loop, which deposits the ball, with depressing regularity, and at no little cost because it cannot be retrieved, over the twenty-foot-high wall of the court and into a neighbouring backyard.

Only very rarely have we seen anyone else playing paddleball at the park, even in its conventional form. The preferred game here is handball, an older and more widely played sport that requires no bats, but does demand tough hands and a high pain threshold in order to thwack ball against wall with an unprotected palm. Paddleball, as recounted in a history of the game by 'Maury the K', president of the One Wall Paddleball Association, was derived from its more popular sister game by a man named Beale in upstate New York over half a century ago. According to Maury, 'The winter of 1940 was brutally cold and Mr Beale's hands became too brittle and painful to continue playing handball. [He] substituted a Wooden Paddle with no holes and a taped handle to start the game of ONE WALL PADDLEBALL.' Subsequent leading practitioners of the sport, according to this account, include Marcel 'Hoppy' Hopkins, Arroyo 'Shotgun' Louie and the number-one player of all time, Robert 'The Ice Man' Sostre, also known as 'The Kid'.

There are three adjacent courts, without separating fences, at the Gertrude B. Kelly. It's unusual to have to wait for any length of time for one to come free but a number of regulars are often there. A group of Puerto Rican teenagers, all bling and biceps, can often be found playing handball or standing around smoking, sometimes both at the same time, an achievement I've always admired. A favourite game involves pushing one of their group against the wall and having the others throw the ball directly at him, as hard as possible. Gusts of laughter mark every direct hit.

A distinguished-looking man in his sixties often sits on the bench at the side of the ball area, his hands stuffed in the pockets of a blue anorak and his shoulders hunched, in a manner that signals deep contemplation. He watches whoever happens to be playing with a vapid expression and a fixed, beatific smile that suggests perhaps he's not all there. Should the ball roll over in his direction he'll jump up and retrieve it with the exaggerated nimbleness of someone who remembers what running is but can no longer manage it instinctively.

And then there's Jimmy. Jimmy is a loner, a young, athletic black man with pale skin and sad eyes that look as though they're ringed with mascara, like Charlie Chaplin's little tramp. He's often at the court slapping a ball against the wall, over and over, always on his own. Despite his evident shyness, he gives a silent nod in our direction when we arrive and on one occasion, when we lost our ball, insisted on giving us his, saying he was about to leave and didn't need it any longer.

Jimmy is unusual in paying A. and me any heed at all. For the most part, despite our starkly evident differences with the regular crowd, scant attention is directed towards us, and often none at all. When picking up our ball if it strays onto another court (which, given the unpredictability of our game, is quite often), those sharing the courts will sometimes scrutinize it with the curiosity of an archaeologist studying a fragment of ancient pottery, before throwing it back to us with a supple-wristed flick that I've concluded must be a baseball throw for it is never seen in Britain. They'll shout 'Hey, mister!' or 'Sir!' if they want their own ball back. And on occasion the very young kids will come and stare at us with wide eyes and amused smiles. Once or twice they've asked to be allowed a turn with the paddleball bats and we've generally obliged, watching anxiously from the bench lest they knock each other senseless with their exuberant swings. But in the main we are simply ignored, and that seems like sufficient acceptance for us to feel very much at home at the Gertrude B. After all, paying no attention whatsoever to someone, that's family.

In the winter months, when it's too cold to play outside, A. and I take our bats to the welcoming warmth of the McBurney, a YMCA gym where paddleball can be played inside on Monday and Thursday nights, and in the afternoon on Saturdays and Sundays.

The McBurney recently relocated from its previous premises on 23rd Street, down the street from the Chelsea Hotel. The old place was the first permanent home for the YMCA in New York City, opened in 1869 with support from, among others, the financier J.P. Morgan and the merchant philanthropist William E. Dodge. The gloomy exercise halls and broad stone stairways of the old building were more redolent of a church than a gymnasium, echoing a time when godliness and good health were very much part of the same programme, a far cry from the wall-to-wall mirrors and personal trainers of today's temples to muscled narcissism.

The new McBurney is located just nine blocks further south, on the ground floor and basement of an apartment building on 14th Street. Though its purpose-built premises, with their gleaming white exercise rooms and brightly tiled swimming pool, could hardly be in starker contrast with the previous building, the clientele has remained largely the same. Leaving those dedicated to fitness and physique to the city's commercial gyms, the emphasis here is more on the sociable than the cardiovascular. The crowd is generally neither young nor fit. These people would rather spend time turning radioactive pink in the steam room than labour on a StairMaster or exercise bike. They converse in high decibel on clusters of stools between the lockers, or watch baseball from sticky plastic armchairs arranged around a small TV in a corner of the room. The scene resembles an exhibit of Lucian Freud's work, with yards of drooping grey flesh in every direction.

The public display of such physical decrepitude is a source of great comfort to those who, like me, don't get to the gym as often as we should. Even the briefest exposure to this parade of sagging stomachs, hair-matted backs and varicose veins makes one feel not so out of shape after all, and perhaps not even that old. It's a psychosomatic workout involving no physical exercise.

It's rare, too, not to come across a conversation worth listening in on. This is the New York soundtrack as the British immigrant of my age always imagined it, the city of Damon Runyon and Jimmy Breslin, of tough-sounding guys with accents that could cut through steel talking about, well, what on earth are they talking about? On one occasion, perhaps five years after *Titanic* had swept the Oscars, I overheard two elderly regulars of the McBurney discussing the film as they towelled off after a steam bath.

'I hear there's a new movie out about that ship that went down in the Atlantic.'

'You mean the one that hit an iceberg?'

'That's right. What was it called, that ship?'

'I can't remember, but it's a disgrace they would make a film about it. All those poor people who drowned . . .'

It was in the corridors between the grey metal lockers of the Y's changing room that A. and I first ran into the couple we've come to know as 'the other brothers'. The kinship of this pair is not hard to spot. Though one man is much thinner than his sibling, to a degree that suggests some kind of wasting illness, a characteristic slope of the shoulder and distinctively round eyes with prominent black pupils betray a common genetic inheritance. They are older than we are, probably in their early sixties, and it is difficult to tell who is senior of the two; perhaps they are even twins. They certainly dress differently, as twins often do. The stockier one favours clothes that are far from age-appropriate. With a broad headband pressing his forehead down over protuberant eyes, he looks like a cross between an ageing John McEnroe and the late Marty Feldman. The thinner brother, more conventionally attired but always appearing drawn and tired, projects an air of ineffable sadness, as though in perpetual mourning for his sibling's lost dress sense.

The brothers are part of a group of men, maybe eight in all, who have been playing paddleball at the Y since long before we started going there. We call them 'the regulars'. The group demonstrates the sharp disjuncture between aptitude and athleticism that is possible when it comes to this particular sport. Although the standard of play among them is high, the physique of these players is far from impressive. One, a cherub-faced man, is of such enormous rotundity that when he sits naked in the locker room his stool disappears beneath him so that he appears to be hovering above the floor like a levitating swami. He is extraordinarily adept at thwacking the ball low and hard, though the accompanying loud grunts indicate that this prowess is not effortless. Another player, with a rough beard and lank hair retained by a headscarf, has a compact, wiry build, apart from a sharply bulging stomach, an incongruity emphasized by his preference for skintight Lycra tops. He has a curious serving technique where one leg slips backwards while his shoulders fall forwards, so that he appears to be making an effete bow as he hits the ball, a gesture which, given the surprising effectiveness of the stroke, appears to be earned.

The regulars' approach to their game could not be more at variance to ours. Unlike us, they follow the actual rules and compete in the regulatory group of four. Their garb is characteristically American in its obeisance to the uniform of the specialist. Just as no builder is complete without his tool belt, no cyclist without his Lycra shorts with reinforced gusset, the regulars display all the accoutrements of the dedicated paddleballer: knee pads, wristbands, headscarves and, above all, refulgent plastic goggles, the bigger the better. In contrast, A. and I sometimes don't even bother changing out of our long trousers. The regulars' game is conducted with open ferocity, quite at variance with our English politesse. Disputed points and the supposed shortcomings of partners are the source of prolonged bouts of yelling and exaggerated gesticulation. Heads are held, hands placed on hips, eyes rolled; on occasion bats are flung to the ground. I've even seen one of the brothers, the bulkier of the two and clearly the more aggressive, on his knees in front of the other, arms akimbo and face scarlet, loudly excoriating his sibling for the incompetence of a misplaced shot.

On those unavoidable and uncomfortable occasions when we're forced to share the courts with the regulars, A. and I will cast sidelong glances in each other's direction during these histrionics, perhaps raising an eyebrow of silent disapproval. We would never conduct ourselves in that fashion, we wordlessly confirm. In our contests, disagreements arise only from a mutual wish to concede points, not to win them. Our verbal exchanges are confined to quiet calls of 'fine shot' and apologies when a poorly hit ball goes out of bounds or makes a return impossible.

It's clear that, over the years, the regulars have come to regard the paddleball courts as their private domain. Whatever time we turn up at the Y, unless it's late at night, they'll be there, generally occupying both courts. No matter how long we hover outside the glass doors, or noisily bat the ball against an outside wall, they will leave only when they are good and ready to go. The idea that we might be entitled to a turn is a foreign land to them, beyond even imagination.

This lack of concern for what seems reasonable is a source of great annoyance to us, and to A. especially. As we descend the stairs from the lobby of the Y, he will bend down to look through the windows onto the court to ascertain whether there is a vacancy. Likely as not a bitter declaration will follow: 'The other brothers are here again.'

The Y encourages membership participation in the running of the facility with a noticeboard in the lobby where written comments and complaints are displayed, together with responses from appropriate members of staff. Though evidently ignored by most of the membership, I find the scrawled paper slips compulsive reading, not least because of the intemperate tone of many of the writers, a group sufficiently exercised to request one of the comment slips available at the front desk. THE SWIMMING POOL HAD A GREASY SCUM LINE AROUND THE WATER'S EDGE TODAY. PLEASE CLEAN THIS IMMEDIATELY! Or, SOMEONE HAS BEEN CUTTING HAIR IN THE MEN'S CHANGING ROOM. THE FLOOR NEAR THE WASHSTAND WAS COVERED! The responses, composed by members of staff on the bottom of the slip before it is pinned to the board, are as solicitous as the complaints are shrill. WE ARE VERY SORRY THAT THE CLOCKS WERE NOT ADJUSTED FOR SUMMER HOURS LAST WEEK AND WILL ENSURE THAT THIS DOES NOT HAPPEN AGAIN.

One night, after a particularly lengthy and frustrating wait for a vacant paddleball court, it occurred to me that we could use the suggestion box in pursuit of a fairer system. As we were leaving, I asked at the front desk for a slip and, leaning on the counter, wrote PLEASE CAN WE HAVE AN ADVANCE BOOKING SYSTEM FOR PADDLEBALL? THIS WILL GIVE EVERYONE A FAIR CHANCE AND WILL PREVENT HOGGING OF THE COURTS. I filled in A.'s name at the bottom, showed him what I'd written with what I hoped was a playful flourish and handed it in before he had a chance to object. Outside, bent over the lock on his bike, he looked at me upside down and said, 'I'm not sure that was a good idea, especially the hogging bit.' 'It'll be fine,' I said breezily and pedalled off up 14th Street.

A few days later we returned for another game. The man to whom I had given the complaint slip was on duty again. He always looks pleased to see us. We're brothers after all and building families is right up there next to healthy bodies and healthy minds on the Y mission statement. 'Good evening, gentlemen.' He looked up from the computer where he had just swiped my membership card with a broad, welcoming smile. 'And how are you guys tonight?'

I replied that we were fine. He swiped A.'s card and we headed for the stairs down to the changing room. 'By the way,' he called out before we began to descend, 'I told the other paddleball guys about your note. Things should be all right now.'

We stopped and swivelled round with simultaneity that only brothers and well-trained infantry can affect. As we did so I caught A.'s fleeting look, a study in consternation. 'Er, what did they say exactly?' he asked.

'Oh, they just wanted to know who you were, so I told them. They said it was no problem . . . You know, they're brothers too,' he added as an afterthought, evidently relishing the convocation of fraternal cooperation that he had achieved.

Before I had a chance to reply, A. called back to me from halfway down the stairs, next to the window looking onto the paddleball court. 'They're there again,' he shouted, before dashing to the men's changing room with uncharacteristic alacrity.

We began to get changed, in no rush because we knew it might be a while before we could get on the court. We were down to underpants and socks when familiar voices, still arguing loudly, announced the arrival of the other brothers. I felt myself tensing. A. put his head in his locker, muttering something about having left his watch in his trouser pocket. He looked as if he was about to climb in and close the door behind him.

One of the brothers, the burlier of the pair, walked up the aisle and started twiddling with the combination on the locker just one away from mine. Silently cursing the luck that had resulted in me picking a locker so close to his, I nodded in his direction. There was no acknowledgement on his part; he merely took out his towel and a plastic bag of toiletries and placed them on an adjacent stool before sitting down heavily on another. I moved my stuff back a couple of feet to give him more room. He looked over, a sneer across his lips. 'Sorry if I'm HOGGING the locker space,' he said, spitting out the words. 'I don't want to be a HOG,' he repeated again for emphasis. I shrank back at the vehemence of these utterances and half-turned to A. in search of support. All I could see were his legs and backside as he burrowed still deeper into his locker.

'What do you call that game you play anyway?' the burly brother enquired in a deliberately sarcastic tone as he slipped off a vest with armholes running from the shoulder almost down to the waist. I noticed with satisfaction that the mass of hair on his chest was whiter than mine.

'Well, it's our invention really,' I replied, trying to sound jocular. 'It's a sort of British version.'

'I don't get it.' I couldn't see his face now because he was bending down to loosen the Velcro straps on a pair of trainers that wouldn't have looked out of place on a pimp, all lime green with shiny yellow trimming, but I could tell it wasn't bearing a friendly expression.

'I mean, you're supposed to play with both hands and keep the ball low,' he continued, 'not send it up into the sky.'

'I know, I know. We're not very good . . . But it's the best we can do,' I mumbled, hoping that humility would encourage him to back off. It didn't.

'Well, it's not paddleball. I don't know what it is, but it's not paddleball. And –' his voice took on a triumphal tone of someone delivering an irrefutable logical deduction '– it's a *paddleball* court. That's what it says on the schedule.' He enunciated the word 'paddleball' with such emphasis that I almost fell backwards from my stool.

With that, he took his towel and, not bothering to wrap it around his waist, stood up and headed off for the showers. Only at this point did A. re-emerge from his locker, pulling on his New Balances with evident urgency. 'I told you it was mistake to hand in that slip,' he hissed. 'Now we've got a war on our hands.'

The battle of the brothers over the paddleball court was never resolved. Now that hostilities had been declared, even the previous tactic of hanging around making our presence known through the window of the court was more assertive than either A. or I felt comfortable with. It wasn't just that we wanted to avoid another confrontation. We both felt that the scorn that had been directed at our version of the game was to some degree justified. It *was* pathetic that our shots looped so high and that we couldn't play ambidextrously. Certainly we didn't want anyone who knew the proper rules to be watching what we were up to. And so we took to coming down to the Y late at night. The facility stayed open till eleven o'clock and we found that if we showed up around 9.45, the brothers and their pals would by then have cleared off and we could have the place to ourselves.

With the arrival of spring we were able to return to the outside court on 18th Street where the audience, to the extent that anyone took notice of us at all, was more uncomprehending than derisive. Arriving there one brisk April evening we found the park full of kids playing basketball and mothers watching their toddlers on the climbing apparatus. A man dressed from head to foot in what appeared to be black plastic bags, including an improvised beret, which looked uncomfortably hot even for a chilly day, was reading a newspaper on one of the benches behind the water play area.

A game of five-a-side soccer was underway on one of the ball courts, played by Latino restaurant workers evidently on a break before the evening rush in their kitchen began. They were all dressed in their cook's uniforms, white smocks and trousers, so it was hard to tell who was on which side. They looked like a campesino army from a Diego Rivera mural. At the other end of the courts was Jimmy, by himself as ever, smacking a ball with his hand against the wall in a lackadaisical fashion. We gave him a cheerful wave from the benches. 'Hey, how's it hanging?' he enquired in his customarily shy manner, without stopping his one-man contest.

We took the middle court, between him and the soccer players, and warmed up with a few energetic but wildly inaccurate swings. We played for forty minutes or so and, as usual of late, my attempts to deploy the guile and insider knowledge of the older player against the vim and stamina of the younger man were proving fruitless. I had one special move, a crafty serve that I could loop directly down the left-hand sideline so that A. was forced to play a backhand return, the weakest shot in his armoury. It was a tactic that had accumulated many hundreds of points over the years, though I sometimes felt guilty playing it because it seemed tantamount to cheating. But latterly I'd noticed that A. had adjusted his stance so that he started out far over on the side of the court and was thus able to return pretty well anything with his forehand, which was a much stronger stroke. I was three games to one down, my back ached every time I bent to pick up the ball, and I could see that if A. was at this stage vulnerable to anything, it was probably only the ennui of the confident winner. Dusk was drawing in and I was already beginning to think of where we might go for a drink afterwards, a sure sign of tiredness.

A. served the ball with a mediocre stroke that delivered it invitingly in front of me. I pounced, aiming my return at the intersection of the wall and ground, the money shot of the effective paddleball player. Whether it was the fading light, my mounting enervation or perhaps a combination of the two, I cannot tell. But the net result was that the ball hit the edge of my paddle and soared skywards, only coming to a halt when it got stuck twenty-five feet up in the fence that ran at an angle along the top of the wall separating the western side of the park from a neighbouring backyard. It took me a moment to realize what had happened but then, looking up, I could see there were a number of other balls, of various colours and sizes, lodged there, together with a variety of sticks and half-bricks that had evidently been deployed, unsuccessfully, to free them.

I asked A. if he had a spare ball. He went to look in his bag, returning a minute later empty-handed. We were standing there gazing helplessly at the unreachable ball when Jimmy wandered over. He pushed his cap back on his head.

'Let's try this,' he said, holding his own ball up for inspection and demonstrating with a practice throw how it could be used to dislodge ours.

'Be careful,' A. warned him. 'You might get that one stuck too.'

'It's cool,' Jimmy took careful aim and, with an elegant flick of his wrist, hoisted his ball skywards. It missed. He caught it expertly and tried again. After maybe half a dozen shots of consistent accuracy, his ball bounced off the fence perhaps a foot behind ours, and rolled slowly down towards it. The three of us craned upwards in breathless anticipation. Jimmy's ball had dislodged ours but before we had a chance to celebrate both balls became stuck, nestling next to each other a couple of feet further down.

'Sheeit!' Jimmy exclaimed, more animated than I'd ever seen him. He squinted up at the wall, his shoulders hunched with frustration.

'I'm sorry,' I said. 'I'm going to buy you a replacement. When will you be down here next? I'll give it to you then.'

'Hey, no sweat, man,' Jimmy mumbled. 'Maybe we can still get them back.'

He hitched up his voluminous jeans and climbed through a hole in the fence leading to the nearby projects. I'd noticed a rat skeleton there a few weeks after poison had been put down, but it was gone now. In less than a minute he was back, carrying a sizeable lump of concrete. He moved to within a couple of feet of the handball-court wall and flung it towards the stranded balls with the practised arm of a man who must have played a lot of baseball. On the first couple of occasions, he missed altogether and the concrete crashed back into the tarmac of the court. On the third time, it hit the plastic-coated wire just inches from its target. The balls shook tantalizingly but remained on their lofty perch.

'Sheeit,' Jimmy exclaimed again.

Now A. stepped forwards, squinting skywards and rubbing his hands together to warm them in the cold of the spring evening.

'Let me have a go,' he said eagerly and bent down to pick up the man-made rock. His technique was quite different from Jimmy's. He held the projectile in both hands, thrusting upwards from bent knees with a sharp grunt, as a Highlander might toss a caber at the Perth country fair. The lump of concrete disappeared into the gloom of the darkening sky. By the time it returned to visibility, it was too late for the frantic shout of warning that, in unison, Jimmy and I let out. A. stood below, immobile and directly in its path. A second later he let out a sharp yelp, like a dog being hit by a car.

My first reaction, and I'm ashamed to recount it, especially because I'm aware I've instinctively responded in similar fashion to quite awful accidents that have befallen him previously, was to laugh. Big, uncontrollable gasps of merriment shook me, even as A. fell silently to his knees on the tarmac. I couldn't help myself.

I subsequently tried to analyse why I reacted in such a heartless way. Of course, the cruelty of slapstick is always entertaining. And the surge of relief that disaster has struck nearby but avoided you can often create a wave of hysterical relief, a spasm of acute *Schadenfreude* that may take the form of transient laughter. But I'm uncomfortably aware that I may have a particular capacity for finding mishaps funny when they befall my brother. It's a momentary pleasure, soon replaced by concern if the incident proves serious. But it's there and it appears perverse. Why would I especially enjoy misfortune that afflicts someone so close to me? It seems a particular and vicious form of sadism. It harks back to something in our childhood that is difficult for me to talk about.

The scene is our family home near Liverpool in the north-west of England, a compact detached house where our father still lives today, alone now that our mother has died. The year is 1968. I'm upstairs in my bedroom, desultorily rereading *Henry IV Part I* for an English O level that I have to resit, having failed it the first time. Through the thin plasterboard walls I can hear from downstairs the sound of the TV, a new acquisition in a household that didn't get one till long after most of our neighbours. The theme song to *Gilligan's Island*, a show I like, strikes up. I abandon Harry Hotspur and amble down to the living room. A., eight years old, is stretched out on the floor, his chin cradled in his hands, staring up at the set. I can hear our mother in the kitchen preparing the evening meal.

I throw myself on the sofa and A. and I watch Ginger, the Skipper and the rest of the gang caper around their desert isle to intermittent studio laughter. The mid-programme commercial break comes up and I tumble over to where A. is lying, grabbing him by the hair and forcing him to roll over onto his back. I climb astride him, my knees under his armpits, and twist his nose between my forefinger and thumb. I can see his brow furrowing under his Beatle fringe.

'Getoff!' he squeals. 'Let me go.'

'So what number is it to be tonight?' I say in an affected sing-song sort of voice.

'Leave me alone,' he begs, attempting to force me off, quite uselessly. I'm eight years older after all; he doesn't stand a chance.

'Come on. You know the score,' I say, smiling down at him. 'You've got to pick something. One to five. If you don't choose, you get them all.'

We have a system, my brother and I, a notation of different forms of torture that I can inflict on him at will. Each technique has a number attached to it so that when I ask him to pick a number we both know what it refers to. One is 'finger bends' where I interleave my fingers with his and bend them until he believes they are about to break. Two is 'small spaces'. Here I crouch down low over his face, blocking out the light with my arms and legs, in a way that induces claustrophobia. Three is 'chest kneely' where I kneel with my full weight on his chest until he can no longer breathe. This is an especially pernicious torment for someone who, in those days, was acutely asthmatic. The affliction was sufficiently serious for him to be sent for six months to a nearby children's hospital where he and other fellow sufferers slept in a ward with a roof that could be retracted when the weather allowed, a sort of junior Magic Mountain sanatorium. The other patients included a number of quite rough boys, though none of the family fully appreciated how coarse they were until at breakfast a couple of mornings after A.'s return home he casually requested my father, much to the suppressed delight of my sister and I, to 'Pass the fucking butter'.

Number four, 'hair pull', is, as its name indicates, more straightforward. Number five, which completes the roster, is the most elaborate and terrifying of all. 'The banister hang' requires my marshalling A. to the top of the stairs, no easy task because as we ascend he will struggle like an innocent man on his way to the gallows. Once there I manhandle him over the banister, keeping hold of his ankles so that he dangles upside down over the vertiginous drop to the lower hallway.

It's hard to execute number five with my father in the house because A.'s screams will generally attract his attention and a stern order to desist, even if he's in the garage or garden. But tonight he has not yet returned from work so the full selection is available.

'What's it going to be?' I repeat, stretching A.'s ears sideways as an encouragement for a quick decision.

'OK, OK,' he whimpers. 'Number two, make it number two.'

'Small spaces', one of his favourites. I crouch down over his head, practically smothering him with my stomach. He doesn't struggle but lies there perfectly still, waiting for me to stop. He is rescued by the theme song for *Gilligan's Island* signalling the end of the commercial break. I clamber back on the sofa, leaving him where he lies on the carpet. Wordlessly he rolls over and props his head, once more, in his hands. Mum shouts from the kitchen, 'Here comes Dad,' and seconds later we hear the front door opening.

Though he had every justification for doing so, A. never complained about this cold-blooded and sadistic ritual, not then as a child, nor later as an adult. It was left to me to bring it up, in a formal expression of regret, which I delivered over dinner at a Mexican restaurant in New York a couple of years ago. I tried to downplay a gesture that could easily seem grandiloquent by self-mockingly comparing it to Bill Clinton's apology for the existence of slavery. A. just shrugged his shoulders and muttered, 'Forget about it,' as he concentrated on his chile relleno. Now, as he crouched on the floor of the paddleball court, head lowered and breathing heavily, he must have been aware of the deep draughts of mirth I could not contain. It still makes me shudder to think that I could be so unkind at such an awful moment.

By the time I had composed myself and begun to realize what should have been immediately obvious, that this was a serious accident, Jimmy was crouching next to A.

'You all right, man?' I heard him say, with a tenderness that stays with me still. He put his arm under my brother's elbow and gently helped him to his feet. Wincing, A. pulled the neck of his T-shirt down over his other shoulder. There was a large dark patch where the skin had been scraped off. He touched the wound tentatively and held up his fingers. Despite the gathering gloom we could clearly see the blood.

'Fuck, I'm sorry,' I said. 'I know it's not funny. We'd better get you to hospital.'

As we left the court I noticed that the two previously stuck balls had returned to earth and lay next to each other by the side of the back fence. I picked them up and returned Jimmy's to him.

Before its recent closure as a result of the hospital's bankruptcy, the emergency room at St Vincent's, just north of Greenwich, was a prominent neighbourhood landmark. Many of the victims of the 9/11 World Trade Center collapse were brought here, and a poignant display of ceramic tiles painted by children to commemorate those dark days still adorns the wire fence around an empty lot facing the hospital. Dylan Thomas, after protracted drinking sessions at the nearby White Horse Tavern, met his end here.

A scene of diverse human suffering greeted A. and me as we arrived. There were perhaps sixty people in the room, in various states of distress. On a bench near the entrance, a young man, with an arm poking out from his shoulder at an ominously odd angle, was being comforted by an elderly woman in a knitted hat, probably his mother. Further back, a man in clothes of Rabelaisian filth was pacing along the wall, holding a blood-soaked pad to his eye and cursing under his breath to no one in particular. Glowering in his direction, a father protectively gathered in his two toddlers. One of the children was screaming at a volume only a little less ear-shattering than the sirens of the ambulances periodically arriving outside.

I assisted A. into a plastic chair near the reception counter, below a wall-mounted statue of a devotional Virgin Mary, and went to seek help. The desk was being manned, with stoical disregard for the chaos that surrounded her, by a heavy black woman with a stern face above a gold crucifix that rested on top of her substantial décolletage like Jesus's cross on the hill at Calvary. A middle-aged mother with elaborate braids leaned against an adjoining wall with the weariness of someone who had been waiting a long time. She was holding a baby whose sallow face and perspiration-plastered hair suggested something infectious. I resolved to keep a good distance.

I manoeuvred myself directly in front the receptionist but she remained focused on her computer screen. I tried thrumming my fingers on the countertop, and then whistling, which experience has taught rarely fails to attract attention. Eventually she looked up and, as if I was the one who'd been keeping her waiting, snapped impatiently.

'Coverage?'

'I'm sorry?' I said.

'Coverage. Do you have in-sur-ance?' She emphasized each syllable of this last word separately, as though she were teaching a halfwit its name.

'Oh, sure,' I said eagerly. 'Blue Cross.' I handed over A.'s card with a flourish. At that instant I realized that my lifelong commitment to socialized health care had evaporated, replaced by a fervid and ruthlessly selfish hope that my brother's health scheme would provide a head start in the race for medical attention against the probably uninsured hoi polloi who filled the room.

'What's wrong with him?' she nodded curtly towards A., swiping the card through her computer.

'A rock hit his shoulder. I think he may have fractured it,' I said, and then, reflecting that this diagnosis was perhaps too mild to forestall a wait of several hours in this hellhole, added, 'It's really quite bad, it's bleeding. Maybe it's broken.'

She looked at me sceptically and, pointing to where A. was sitting, barked, 'Tell him to wait there.'

I returned to A. who was half hidden behind a copy of the *New York Post* he'd found in a nearby chair and was trying to read without bending his bad arm. His face was ashen but at least the bloodstain on the shoulder of his shirt was no longer spreading.

'Are you all right?' I said, suddenly feeling close to tears.

'Not too bad,' he replied. 'Are we going to have to wait long?'

'I don't think so.' I tried to sound as hopeful as the circumstances allowed. 'She's already swiped your card.' I slipped it carefully into his trouser pocket.

'Can you do me a favour?' he said, lowering the paper.

'Anything you want.' I put a hand on his good shoulder. 'Just name it.'

'See that machine over there?' He nodded in the direction of a vending machine, brightly lit in the corner. 'See if it has any crisps in it.'

'I'll be right back,' I said. As I picked my way through the sea of fractured bodies that surrounded us I heard my brother's shout.

'Salt and vinegar, if they've got any.'

It was a while before we were able to play paddleball again. It turned out that A. had not broken his shoulder, nor even fractured it, but it swelled up in a large livid bruise that took several weeks to subside. Even today, months later, he says it still feels stiff sometimes.

But we did eventually get back down to the Y, on a wet late afternoon in early February. A. practised his swing as we walked down 14th Street, testing his shoulder. It seemed to be holding up.

'Long time no see, gentlemen.' Our friend on the front desk looked genuinely pleased to see us.

'He busted up his shoulder,' I said, nodding at my brother. 'But it's good to be back.'

'Gotta stay fit.' He winked at me and smiled as he handed my card back in a way that indicated he knew that *getting* fit was first on the agenda.

A. had already headed down the stairs and was waiting for me on the half landing, still swinging his bat in practice strokes. He pointed with his thumb through the window onto the court below.

'The other brothers are there again,' he said gruffly. 'I'm going for a swim.' ∎

Postscript

I am out in the snowy woods,
trying to find a signal

to phone a friend.
Night's drawing in; the trees

are slender in the way that things
are almost, though not quite

absent, on the cusp of transformation.
There's only one path

and that leads back to the road
where I left the car.

When I get there,
I'll drive home slowly

and brew some tea;
no promises to keep,

only the moment,
passing,

and somebody quiet,
moving about the house,

locking the doors
and switching off

POEM | JOHN BURNSIDE

the porch light that I left
burning, while infinities of snow

unfold across each window
like a veil.

THE LOYALTY
PROTOCOL

Ben Marcus

The phone call said to come alone, but he couldn't just leave his parents behind. Perhaps they'd been called too and didn't remember the procedure, which would only figure. His father was not good with instructions. Worse, his father was fatally indifferent to what people said. Other people spoke and the man's face went blank, as if all voices but his own were in a foreign language. Perhaps his father had not picked up the phone. Or maybe he mistook the message for a prank and hung up.

Later, his helpless parents in tow, Edward could explain the mistake, if necessary. By then it'd be too conspicuous to leave them stranded on the road while everyone else left town.

Owing to the roadblock that would be set up on Morris Avenue, Edward parked at Grove and Williams and trekked through muddy backyards to his parents' apartment complex. He cursed himself, because he'd have to lead them back the same way, down a wet, grassy slope where his car would be waiting. In all of the configurations they'd rehearsed at the workshop, somehow he had not accounted for this annoying obstacle: moving his parents in the dark down a steep, wet slope.

His father was awake and packed already, wandering through the apartment. When Edward walked in, his father started to put on his coat.

'Where's Mom?'

'Not coming, I guess,' his father said.

'Dad.'

'You try. I tried already. You try if you want to. I'm disgusted. I'm ready to go. Do you know how many times I've had to do this?'

'Did they call you?' Edward asked.

'Did who call me?' His father was on the defensive. Had he slept at all? Had he simply been up all night, waiting?

'Did your phone ring tonight?' Edward asked, trying not to sound impatient. There were cautions against this very thing, the petty quarrels associated with travel, which only escalate when evacuation is a factor.

'I don't know, Eddie. Our phone doesn't work. I'm just ready to go. I'm always ready.'

Edward picked up the phone and heard a dial tone, but it was in an odd pitch, high and scratchy. More like an emergency signal than a dial tone.

'You don't believe me?' his father said. 'I tell you the phone doesn't work and you don't trust me?'

'I trust you. Let's just get Mom and go.'

His mother was in bed, sheets pulled over her face. It felt wrong to sit on his parents' bed, to touch his mother while she was lying down. Standing up, he could hug and kiss his mother with only a shred of awkwardness, but once she was prone it seemed inappropriate, like touching a dead person. He shook her anyway.

'C'mon, Mom, let's go. Get dressed.'

She answered from under the sheets, in a voice that was fully awake. Awake and bothered.

'I'm too tired. I'm not going.'

They'd been told that, at times like this, old people dig in their heels. More than any other population, old people refuse to go. They hide in their homes, wait in the dark of their yards while their houses are searched for stray occupants. Often they politely request to die. Some of them do not request it. They take matters into their own hands.

But there were a few little things you could do to persuade them, and Edward had learned some of them in the workshop.

'Mom, you don't know what you're saying. You really don't want to be here, I promise you.'

'See,' said his father from the doorway. 'See what I told you?'

'Tell him to shut up,' said his mother.

'You shut up,' his father barked. 'Don't ever tell me to shut up.'

'Shut up,' she said, still under the sheets, and she laughed.

'Mom, if you don't come with us, they'll be here to get you, and who knows where you'll sleep tonight. Or you won't sleep. You'll be stuck with them and I can guarantee that you won't like it. It will be horrible. Do you want me to tell you what will happen?'

He could hear his mother breathing under the sheets. She seemed to be listening. He paused a bit longer for suspense.

Something wordless, passing for surrender, sounded. A kind of huff. Edward left the room to give her time and it wasn't long before she joined him and his father in the front hallway, scowling. She'd thrown a coat over her nightgown and carried a small bag.

'OK?' said Edward.

They didn't answer, just followed him outside, where the streets were empty.

'Where's your car?' his mother grumbled.

He explained what they'd have to do and they looked at him as if he were crazy.

'Do you see any other cars here?' he whispered. 'Do you know why?'

'Don't act like you know what's going on,' his father scolded as they trekked out. 'You're just as much in the dark as we are. You have no idea what's really happening. None. Fucking hotshot. Tell me one fact. One. I dare you.'

When they reached the hill and had to navigate the decline, his mother kept falling. She'd fall and then cry out so loudly it seemed she'd been gravely wounded, except she was just falling on her rear end in the grass, falling and slipping a little, as if she were on a sled. How much could it hurt? He'd never heard her cry in pain before, and it was horrible. His father was right there holding her arm, but she was considerably bigger than he was and when she slipped he couldn't hold her up. He lost his temper and kept yelling at her, and finally, softly, she said she was doing her best. She really was.

'Well, I can't carry you!' he yelled.

'Then don't,' she said, and she stood up and tried to walk on her own, but she slipped and fell again, sliding further down the hill.

In the car she wept and Edward felt ashamed. This was the easiest part of the drill, and it had not gone well at all.

There were multiple settlements stationed throughout the gymnasium, organized by neighbourhood, and when Edward brought his parents to theirs he could not get them admitted. A young woman he knew as Hannah had the clipboard. After scanning her pages, she shook her head.

'They're not on my list,' she said.

'They live in this neighbourhood, at 429 Sheldon. Apartment 4C.' He looked at the crowd that had already registered, recognizing several of his parents' neighbours, huddled now against a wall. There were retirees from his parents' building. Neighbours who knew his parents. This was certainly the right place. He waved, but those who saw him looked away.

Hannah stared at him from behind the clipboard. He could sense the protocol overwhelming her. A street address, recited anecdotally, was no kind of evidence. Anyone could deliver that information. This was only a man talking.

'Do you want to see their driver's licences?' he asked, a bit too curtly. Not that he'd brought them.

'No. I want to see their names on this list, and since I don't, I can't let them in. I have the most straightforward job in the world. If you have a problem you should discuss it with Frederick.'

From under her shawl Edward's mother said, 'Eddie, it's OK, we'll go with you to yours.' She sounded relieved. That would solve everything and they could all be together.

Edward looked at Hannah, who simply raised her eyebrows. She and Edward had been on a practice team together at the beginning of the workshop. She had seemed nice. Very smart, too, which explained her promotion to settlement leader. Unfortunately, Hannah was far too gorgeous for his comfort. He had been so desperately compelled by her face that he had instantly resolved never to look at her or show her any kind of attention. Everything would be much easier that way. It was troubling now to discover that Hannah ran his parents' settlement. It meant he'd have to see a lot of her and regularly be reminded that she would never be his. She would never kiss him or get undressed for him or relieve his needs before work or stop trying to look pretty for him, which was the part he liked best, at least when he played out futures with women he'd never even speak to. When someone like Hannah, not that there'd ever been someone like Hannah, let herself go and showed up on the couch after dinner in sweatpants and a long, chewed-up sweater. It was unbearable.

Edward knew that he shouldn't do this, but Hannah would have to understand. He broke character and pleaded with her.

'There's nowhere else to go. Can you please take them? Please? Is someone really going to come by later and match each person to a name on your list?'

She hardened her face. She wasn't going to drop the act, and she seemed disgusted with Edward for having done so himself.

'Did they get a phone call?' she asked.

He started to answer, figuring he could lie, when from behind him his father blurted out that their phone was broken. How could you get a phone call with a broken phone?

'I assumed they did,' he confided to Hannah. 'That's the truth. Why wouldn't they get a call? Look, their neighbours are here. People from the same building.'

'They're not supposed to be here,' Hannah said to Edward. 'You shouldn't have brought them. You might consider . . .' She paused. She seemed reluctant to say what she was thinking. 'At this point you've made a serious mistake and you need to decide how to fix it with minimal impact on the community.'

She glanced pitilessly at his parents, then muttered, 'I know what I would do.'

Edward figured that he knew what she would do, too.

He leaned in so he could speak into her ear. 'Are you carrying?' he whispered. 'Because if you are, and I could borrow it, I could kill them right here, and it would be a lesson for everyone.'

She was stone-faced. She didn't think that was funny. 'There are people behind you. I have a protocol to run.'

Don't we all, Edward thought.

'OK, well, thanks for your help,' he said, sneering. 'Good teamwork. Way to go.'

She kept her cool. 'So you want *me* to make a mistake, arguably a bigger one, because you did? Let's say your mistake was an accident, which possibly it was, although I can't say. I'm guessing you're not a complete imbecile. You want me to *consciously* break the rules. You want your error, a stupid error, if you ask me, to beget other errors so we're both somehow to blame, even though I do not know you and have no responsibility for you? How does that do you a favour? How does that help you? At this point, sir, you need to fall on your sword. I don't understand what's so hard about that.'

Just then the lights switched on in the gymnasium and a hush fell. Frederick, leader of the readiness workshop, walked in with his wireless microphone. Everyone watched him. He stood at centre court, tucked the microphone under his arm, and started to clap methodically, as if he were killing something between his hands.

Soon everyone was applauding, moving in close to hear what Frederick would say. The drill, apparently, was over.

He thumped his mic, said hello, hello, and everyone fell silent. He was such a cock, Edward thought. An impossible cock.

'So,' he said, in his quick, high voice. 'Good stuff tonight, good stuff. We made OK time. Maybe we're a half-hour slow, and I don't need to tell you what that means.'

'Boom!' someone yelled from the crowd, to an eruption of laughter.

'Boom is right,' replied Frederick. 'But it's not funny.'

The laughter stopped.

'This is supposed to be the easy leg. We didn't even do the highway drill tonight. Do you all know how much time we'll lose on the highway?'

'Too much!' the crowd yelled.

'That's right. The highway is an ugly variable. You do not disrespect the highway. It murders your plan. You can't control it, whereas this . . .' Here Frederick gestured into the gymnasium. 'This you can control, down to the second. Which means I'd like to see us shave off that half-hour. Maybe forty-five minutes. We need breathing room. We need to be joining our settlements without panic, with time to kill. Next time we do this I want time to kill. Tonight we had no time to kill at all. And you know what?'

Someone from far in the back of the gym shouted, 'What?'

'I'm disappointed,' Frederick said, and he hung his head. The gymnasium seemed to groan.

'But do you know what else?' Frederick asked, brightening.

No one responded.

'I'm proud as hell of all of you. Every single one of you.'

Except me, thought Edward. He was pretty sure that Frederick wouldn't be proud of him.

They broke out in groups for the critique and Edward sat in a circle with his neighbours. His parents, because they weren't meant to be part of tonight's drill, were dismissed. Since they had no way to get home, they were probably waiting for him outside.

The group leader for Edward's neighbourhood was Sharon, and she led them through the discussion. Everything had gone fine, although Edward, she pointed out, had not registered, even though he was here in the gym. He was on time but he had never registered. Did he have trouble finding them? No. Was something wrong with Edward, was he perhaps injured or confused? No. Edward was fine. Edward didn't register with his own settlement because he'd brought unscheduled evacuees with him, and these unscheduled evacuees had turned out to be a serious liability.

'I hate to see our neighbourhood disgraced,' said Sharon.

'I hardly think –' Edward started.

'Hold up, Eddie,' warned Thom. 'You don't talk during your critique.'

'What's a good punishment for Edward?' said Marni. She was joking, but people seemed to take the question seriously.

Geoff jumped in. 'I think we should do something humiliating to his parents. That's much more disturbing, because he'd have to see them get hurt. I think that's a good punishment. I mean, I don't want his parents to be seriously harmed, but I think there's really nothing worse than watching your parents, who are essentially defenceless, get hurt in some way.'

Everyone laughed. Everyone except Sharon, who glared at Edward.

'OK, guys, I get it,' said Edward. 'If there's ever a real crisis, I'll be sure only to look out for myself. Don't worry, I've learned my lesson.'

'Unfortunately, Edward, this is not about you learning a lesson,' said Sharon. 'I'm glad your neighbours think it's funny, but this is about deterring others from suddenly deciding they can bring friends with them on an evacuation.'

'My parents aren't my friends,' he said. 'We're not friends. They're my parents. I thought they'd gotten a call, too. I didn't realize some people didn't get called. Who here with parents in town wouldn't have done the same thing?'

Some hands went up.

'Yes, Liz?' said Sharon.

'Me,' said Liz, putting her arm down. 'My parents are at home asleep right now. It would never have occurred to me to bring them along.'

A few people echoed this. They'd left their parents behind.

Good for all of you, Edward thought. You murderous fucks.

'Does anyone think it's strange,' Edward ventured, 'that the parents weren't called tonight?'

'Honestly, Edward,' said Thom. 'This is the second time you've spoken during your critique. We shouldn't have to warn you about this. You can't learn from what happened tonight unless you're completely silent now.'

'I thought that what I learn doesn't matter,' Edward snapped.

'Isn't this about all of you learning not to be like me?'

'No chance of that,' said a young woman on the opposite side of the circle, who stared at Edward so defiantly that he looked away.

On Edward's way out, Frederick broke from a mob of admirers and grabbed his arm.

'Edward, a word.'

He'd never been this close to Frederick, or even had a private conversation with him before. As much as he disliked him, he couldn't deny how compelling Frederick was. Impossibly handsome, confident, with the body, for some reason, of a small gymnast. His trademark jumpsuits could double as children's pyjamas.

'What you did tonight was incredibly brave. You demonstrated a priority for love and loyalty. You protected two fragile people who had no other saviour, even though technically they were not in danger, and would have been much safer at home. You made a choice, and on the individual level, that choice was courageous and selfless, even if at the level of the group you risked destabilizing our entire operation. If those had been my parents, and I didn't have the years of training that I happen to have, and I also didn't have the elaborate set of instincts and survival habits that I happen to have, it's possible I would have done the exact same thing. In other words, if I were you, and knew next to nothing about how to succeed at this, I might have brought my parents here tonight as well. It is completely possible. It's precisely because I can relate, however abstractly, to what you did that you won't see any lenience from me. Not a trace. On the contrary, you will meet great resistance from me, and if you do anything like that again, I promise I will crush you. But I want you to know, face to face, how much I admire you.'

When he got outside, his mother was asleep in the car, his father leaning on the door.

'I bet you're expecting an apology from me,' said his father.

Edward was tired. He said that he wasn't, that he just wanted to get home. He had a big day tomorrow.

'Because I didn't do anything wrong,' his father continued.

'I know that, Dad.'

'It doesn't really seem like you know it.'

'I do. I would like to go home now, that's all.'

'OK, go. Go straight home. Your mother and I will walk.'

'You're not going to walk.'

'Katherine! Katherine!' his father shouted into the car, banging on the window. 'Wake up! We have to walk home. Eddie refuses to drive us.'

'Dad, get in. Please. I'm driving you home. Don't worry.'

'Because we wouldn't want to put you out.'

They waited in the line of cars revving to leave the high-school parking lot. Some people took these evening drills – hellish and deeply pointless as they were – as social encounters not to go to waste. So Edward and his parents waited in traffic – his mother asleep, his father grinding his teeth – while athletically attired settlement leaders strolled up to cars and leaned against drivers' windows, chatting it out.

Edward didn't dare honk. These glad-handing semi-professional tragedy consumers would turn on him, attack the car, eat his face off. Or, worse, they'd stare at him and start to hate him slightly more, if that were possible.

His father, on the other hand, hadn't registered that they weren't moving.

'That Hannah is a Nazi cunt,' his father said.

'Dad, you can't say things like that about people.'

'She's a Nazi cunt with a tiny cock.'

'OK, Dad.'

'What, you don't agree? You don't like her, either. Tell me you don't agree.'

'I don't agree. She's in a tough position. She's just doing her job.'

That set him off.

'Just doing her job! Gandhi was just doing his job.'

Gandhi?

'Not Gandhi, that other one. That other one!'

His father was in a rage.

'Which other one? Hitler?'

'No!' yelled his father. 'The other one! The other one!'

At work the next day, a receptionist fell from her chair and died. The paramedics set up a perimeter around her desk while colleagues from the office looked on, whispering. Edward couldn't understand why the paramedics wouldn't touch her, even if it was clear she was dead. What was the protocol in cases like this? One of them squinted through a monocle at her corpse. The others pushed back her cubicle partition, then staked a low net around her body. They took pictures and air samples and questioned the co-workers who sat nearby, but they stayed away from the body.

The paramedics consulted a two-way radio, then turned to question the assembled onlookers.

Had anyone touched this woman? Her clothing? Her hair? Her skin?

No one answered, but of course they had touched her. Edward had still been in his office when she collapsed, but he understood that they'd tried to revive her. They'd loosened her clothing, breathed into her mouth, pounded on her chest. The usual hopeless tricks, taught by sad specialists at colleges and adult education centres. And, one year ago, at this very office, for a reasonable discount. Were you not supposed to touch someone who died?

A few hands went up, and these people were escorted to a private office.

'What's going on?' someone yelled. 'Where are you taking them? What are you going to do?'

'Calm down, they'll be fine,' someone else answered, and this set things off.

'How do you know? You don't know anything. You have no idea what's going on.'

The paramedics announced that the office would need to be

cleared at once. Everyone out, quickly and safely, and this quieted people down. They were to please follow their evacuation drill. Employees could wait across the street in the park. They wanted to be able to see everyone from the window.

For what? Edward wondered to himself. So they can take aim and shoot us?

It would be a little while before this was resolved, the paramedics explained, so employees were free to go get coffees if they wanted to.

Edward hung back until most of his employees had filed out. It was really not appropriate for a paramedic, or anyone, for that matter, to tell *his* employees to take a coffee break. But he would let it go.

He introduced himself as the owner and asked what was going on, what did they think?

They stared at him.

'Because we thought it was an aneurysm,' he went on. 'Except she's so young. A stroke, maybe? At any rate, it's horrible. Was it a heart attack? Probably not. What do you guys think?'

When they didn't answer he continued to theorize out loud, naming ailments. They were leaving him stranded. He couldn't handle this conversation by himself.

'Sir,' said a paramedic, 'we'll have to ask you to leave with the others.'

'OK,' Edward said. 'But do you know how long this will be? I want to know what to tell my employees. We have kind of a crazy day ahead.'

It was true. Edward had five job candidates to interview after lunch, and he had been planning to spend the morning in preparation.

The paramedics shook their heads and stared at him again, as if they were baffled that Edward expected them to know anything at all.

Edward wasn't finished. This was his office, and they were sprawled out in his chairs, and they'd moved and probably broken office equipment he'd paid for, while then completely ignoring him. Or, at the very least, failing to take him seriously.

'It's Kristina,' he said.

Again they looked at him in their queer way.

'Kristina is her name,' Edward said, gesturing at the dead woman. 'She's from Ditmars. I hired her about six months ago. She went to college . . . I forget where. She was a terrific employee. Here's her emergency contact information, if you want it. But maybe you don't want it. Maybe you guys don't care. Maybe this is simply too boring for you and that's why you can't speak. You're bored. Well, her name is Kristina. Show some fucking respect.'

One of the paramedics stood up.

'Sir,' he said, gesturing at an officer holding a cellphone. 'This is Deputy Arnold Sjogren, and Kristina was a close friend of his sister's. We know exactly who she is, we grieve her passing, and now we are doing our jobs. The longer you stand here yelling at us, the greater risk you place yourself in. I can't speak for my colleagues, but I personally do not require a lesson in respect. We are risking our lives today, and you are not. Who should be showing respect to whom?'

It was cold outside, not yet ten in the morning. Kristina must have only just started work when she died. In truth, Edward reflected, she had been a detached presence in the office. When she was trained, including a short session with Edward himself – since he tried to impress upon all new employees the larger aims of the company – she seemed indifferent to the joy that sometimes escaped from Edward when he articulated their mission.

Across the street stood his employees, some of them shivering and coatless, holding their arms. Others huddled together, hugging, crying.

His team was standing in the little patch of dirt that passed for a park. When Edward approached they fell silent. Edward knew he made them uncomfortable. He shunned public spaces at work for this very reason, protecting his employees from the destabilizing effect of his terrible presence. A broad swing set creaked on the other side of the square. As the boss, it seemed that he should speak. To sum up, or lead them in prayer, or say something, perhaps, cheerful? Maybe it was too soon for that.

'Well, poor thing,' said Edward, finally.

'Did you call her family?' someone asked, and the others nodded, leaning in.

This alarmed him. Was he supposed to do that? How could he call Kristina's family if he didn't know what was going on? At any rate he'd left the emergency contact card with the paramedics.

'They're taking care of it,' Edward said, gesturing up at the building.

But were they? He could feel them thinking that this was his job. He was supposed to take care of it, not some asshole paramedics who didn't even know her. What if one of *them* had died? he imagined them thinking. Would Edward, the so-called boss of this outfit, neglect to call their families, leaving it to some rookie EMT who might not even be able to pronounce their names? What kind of boss was he? Any one of them could have died today. They could die tomorrow, or next week.

After they stood there for a time looking at their feet, someone volunteered that they'd been discussing how Kristina might have died.

They looked to Edward again, and again he hated being in charge.

'Did you learn anything? What did they say in there?'

Edward shook his head. 'I shouldn't really comment,' he said, adopting an air of secrecy. 'They asked me not to say anything. I'm sorry. I'd better not.'

Oh, was he something. For a few moments Edward's employees could – wrongly! wrongly! – see him as a person with exclusive information, entrusted with a secret. An insider. And in exchange, what? What did he get for this lie? Well, for one, Edward would never forget what he'd said here today, how low he'd fallen. That seemed fair. A fair deal. He might as well bask in their awestruck sense of his power. Why not enjoy it for a while?

People started to drift off. Jonathan took a sandwich order, but when it grew too complicated someone suggested that they all go, and they looked at Edward expectantly. This was going to take a while. He sent them off with his blessing – explaining that he should really stay here in case they needed him – and he was left alone in the park, staring up at the window to his office, where, for some reason, the shade had been drawn.

The first job candidate showed up at 1 p.m., right on time, minutes after the hazmat truck and the mayor's motorcade pulled away. Edward and his employees had only just been cleared to return to the building. Elise Mortensen was announced when Edward got to his office, where he had discovered that his papers had been disturbed. His filing cabinets were open, in great disorder. On his shelves the books had been spread apart. A smell ran through the room, too, something floral that he hadn't noticed in the outer offices. He didn't have time to take stock of what had changed, nor to wonder what they had been doing in his office, so far from where Kristina died, when Elise Mortensen came in, adopting an exaggerated tiptoe, as if she were disturbing him, which she kind of fucking was, and asked where to sit.

Edward fumbled through the interview. He actually started with the dreaded opener, *Tell me about yourself*, so he could collect his thoughts. Elise Mortensen saw the green light and stepped on it, telling Edward about herself at good length. She acquitted herself of a monologue of qualifications that kept rising in tone, which assured Edward that it wasn't going to end any time soon. He kept his eyes fixed on hers and established a pattern of interested nods, then withdrew his attention entirely, to the place where it rightly belonged. On himself.

Edward tried to piece the morning's events together. What interest would the mayor have in Kristina's death, and why would Frederick from the workshop be part of the mayor's entourage? This was arguably the worst part of the morning, standing across the street watching the mayor exit his car, followed by business-suited staff spitting into their phones, and then, what the fuck, small-boned

Frederick from the workshop, wearing his jumpsuit, carrying a gym bag. At that point Edward figured it was OK to bring his employees back across the street so they could wait at the entrance. In truth it offered Edward another chance to discuss the situation with officials, perhaps get back in there and establish his authority. This was his office! He paid rent here, and the death had happened during working hours at his business. But of course he was rebuffed at the door by a police officer, even while his employees looked on, knowing – how could they not know? – that Edward had no influence here. No role to play. He was merely a bystander like they were.

When the mayor came back out, Frederick pointed at Edward in the small crowd.

'There he is!' yelled Frederick, and the mayor's entire entourage peered into the crowd, as if a rare animal had been sighted.

Edward froze.

'That's the man! What's up, buddy? How are you doing?'

Edward raised a hand, said, 'Hi.'

But next to Edward stood Philip, who met Frederick's greeting more forcefully, said things were good and what the hell?, a tragedy, right?, to which Frederick smiled and shrugged, pointing at the mayor with a knowing look, and it was suddenly clear that Philip and Frederick knew each other well, had lots to say. This wasn't about him. Edward lowered his hand and stepped slowly behind Philip, where it was warm and safe, waiting for the motorcade to leave.

There was a final interview, and then he could go home. Edward thought he would die. At times like this, when he didn't want to be seen by anyone in the office, and with the bathroom so conspicuous at the other end of the office, the entire staff watching him go in and come out, Edward peed in a tall jar that he kept in his drawer. He was sealing the lid when the last candidate was announced: Hannah Glazer. Oh dear God. It was Hannah, his parents' settlement leader.

On his desk was Hannah's résumé, which he couldn't focus on, but he willed himself into the conversation. As ever, it was difficult to look at her and be reminded of an enormous segment of life – the segment in which you were naked with a beautiful person and she was not repulsed by you – that was not available to him. She wore sharp black clothes, her eyes clear and mean, and her hair was arranged in one of those old-fashioned styles, pasted to her head at the top and then curled out at the bottom. Quite lovely.

'What interests you about the position?' Edward started.

'You're kidding, right?' Hannah said, glaring at him.

So he would have found no viable candidates today. A receptionist had died, and he'd have to interview for *her* replacement, and now he'd need to schedule another day of interviews for this position as well.

He had to hold up appearances, or else his appearances would turn deranged. 'I'm not kidding, no.' Maybe they could keep this short.

'Are we going to be pretending today?' Hannah asked.

'Pretending what?'

Edward looked longingly at his window, wondering if he could get up enough speed for it to shatter if he threw himself against the glass.

Hannah stood up. She spoke calmly, but she was seething. 'I seriously question your ability to be fair here, given what happened. Last night I did my job. I did my job. And today when I very much need this position, a position I am ridiculously qualified for, here you are, mister fucking policy dodger, ready to dole out a punishment because I followed instructions in a difficult situation.'

'I'm sorry,' said Edward. 'What punishment have I doled out?'

'Not hiring me,' she said. 'I saw your eyes when you knew it was me. You knew you weren't going to hire me.'

'That's not true.'

It was, for the most part, true.

Hannah sat down. She seemed miserable. 'I wonder if I could interview with someone else. Is there someone else on the hiring committee so I could be assured a fair shake?'

'Well, it's just me. There's no committee. This is my company. If I recuse myself from the interview, for my intense bias, my inability to evaluate your suitability for a position in the company that I created from nothing, a company I understand better than anyone else in the world, you'll be in this room alone. Shall I do that?'

Hannah didn't laugh. 'I'd like to continue this interview under protest,' she said.

Was that a real thing? Was there a form you could fill out?

'Listen,' said Edward. 'I would understand completely if you didn't feel comfortable going forward, if you maybe wanted to try somewhere else.' Please, please, try somewhere else.

'You sound like Frederick now. Get the person to believe her rejection is actually her own idea. Classic Frederick. Old school. I bet you've been told that before.'

'Never.'

'I guess it's no secret about me and him,' Hannah said, grinning.

Edward stared at her, waiting.

'That we're involved. I mean, everyone must know at this point.'

He wished he didn't. That was knowledge he'd very much rather not have. He picked up her résumé, waving it at her. 'Shall we?' he said. 'An actual interview, and to hell with the past?'

Hannah Glazer was right. She was ridiculously qualified for the position. Edward was crestfallen. She was sharp, articulate, preposterously experienced and when he queried her with difficult production scenarios – bottlenecks on the front or back end, human error, acts of nature – she produced a staggering arsenal of troubleshooting techniques, more sophisticated than any he'd ever heard, which she rattled off casually, as if they were too simple to be of interest any more. To deny her the job now would be impossible.

On her way out Hannah looked at his couch. 'Is that where you do it?' she asked.

'Do what?'

She leered at him.

'What?'

'All of the desperate people who come looking for work. Is that your casting couch?'

'This isn't like that. It's a couch.'

'You didn't think, when I walked in, that within twenty minutes, if everything went well, you'd have me down on it?'

Edward couldn't answer. Was that an option that he'd somehow missed? Twenty minutes into the interview she was yelling at him about his bias. Was that some deeply veiled flirtation?

'So you've fucked no one there? I'm curious.' She didn't seem curious. She seemed irritated.

He looked at the brown couch and thought back, and back, and back. The tally, indeed, on that particular activity, in that particular location – or, in fact, on any couch ever – was, indeed, zero.

His phone rang that night and this time he wasn't going to screw it up. He grabbed his bag and headed over to the high school, alone.

The roads were quiet, street lights shining so hard the neighbourhoods were bright as day. A siren issued into the night, deep and low. He'd not heard this before, and the closer he got to the high school, the more the sound became like an engine rather than a siren, rumbling beneath the ground. When he reached the turn-off, he came upon a sea of abandoned cars, doors jacked open, hazards flashing.

Edward stopped fast. The cars behind him closed in, trapping him there. He could do nothing but leave his car and walk, as the others must have done. When the drill was over, it would be one hell of a mess driving out of here, but for now he had to get inside.

He was one of the first to check in with Sharon, and it seemed she almost smiled at him. Maybe he could show her that last night was a fluke.

From across the gymnasium he watched Hannah's settlement grow, waiting for a sign of his parents. Now that he had checked in, he wasn't supposed to leave, and since this was a drill, since it didn't matter, he resolved not to care. Probably his parents hadn't been called. This was some new thing they were doing. Anyway, he'd long ago given up trying to understand the methods of the workshop. Even if his parents had been called, the phone was broken, and how would they know? It couldn't matter. But Edward couldn't stop looking over to Hannah, even as the gymnasium filled with bundled-up people, and children, and, of all things, animals, a few of them wandering sleepily across the hardwood floor, moaning. He'd never seen it so crowded here. The generator roared over the chaos – something felt different tonight.

To be fair, he'd had that feeling before. They were good at making you believe that this was the real thing, at last.

Finally, Edward spotted his father joining Hannah's settlement. He was alone. Hannah waved him in and he disappeared into the crowd.

The lights never switched on and Frederick never appeared to praise and chastise them. Instead the settlements headed outside to get in line for buses, which were departing from the back field of the school. The siren was so loud that when he tried to speak nothing came out. Some terrible noise cancellation was at work. Was this intentional? Edward looked at Thom – who was terminally available for eye contact, lying in wait for it – and Thom smiled, giving a thumbs up. Thom was excited. He'd wanted to leave for years. He was ready to roll.

Only one other night had the drill run this long. To Edward, that night seemed like years ago, when the workshop began. But probably it was only last winter. It was a viciously cold night and they'd waited in this exact spot while the buses revved up. He'd been so scared! But then Frederick's girlish voice had rung out through a megaphone and everyone had hurried back for their critiques.

So there was still time. Frederick could call this off and get them back inside.

As the settlements filed behind him, headed to their own buses, Edward waited and waited and waited, until finally Hannah approached, and, behind her, her settlement, mostly old-timers from Wellery Heights and whatever other neighbourhoods bordered nearby. He had only a moment for this, but he had to do it. There was nothing in the protocol about it, anyway. The protocol hadn't been written this far. It was a blank fucking chapter. Edward grabbed his father, who looked startled, and then the two of them opened their mouths soundlessly at each other. They couldn't hear each other, couldn't hear anything. It was his mother Edward needed to know about. His mother. He shrugged *where* and he mimed other things, things to indicate his mother, which anyone else from any country in the world would understand, but it was no use, it was stupid. Or his father was stupid, because he either did not get it, or did not want to, smiling dumbly at Edward. Finally Edward grabbed his father's left hand, isolating the ring finger, and held it up to him, tapping on the ring.

Do you get it now, you stupid old man? Where is she?

Edward's father smiled, put his palms together, closed his eyes and leaned his head against his hands. A universal sign. His mother was home sleeping. His father had left her there asleep, and don't worry, she was doing fine.

His mother was asleep, alone, at home. In an empty city. She was fine.

The buses travelled south. Frederick had been wrong about the highway. It was not an ugly variable. It didn't present a problem at all. In a caravan the buses climbed the on-ramp, entering a freeway that seemed reserved for them alone. They drove for hours. The driver was in radio communication, but otherwise the bus was quiet. Edward sat by himself in a rear seat, staring from the window. At this point, he reasoned, the drill should have been called. They'd not even rehearsed this far, so what on earth could they be testing? Wasn't it, after all, a pain in the ass now that they were so far from home, and how exactly were they going to get back? The buses, of course, could be ordered to turn around. But as the sun started to come up, and as muffins wrapped in brown paper were sent back down the line, that didn't seem so likely.

During the second day of driving, after he'd slept and woken and then slept a little bit more, he heard a commotion at the front of the bus and the bus steamed and seized and buckled as it started to slow down and pull off the highway.

Thom slid into the seat next to him.

'Holy fuck, right?'

'What happened?' asked Edward, still waking up.

'Sharon.'

Edward tried to look, but there were too many people mobbed together.

'Is she all right?' he asked.

Thom shook his head. 'I don't think so. All of a sudden she fell from her seat. I only got a quick look. But fuck, man, I think she's dead.'

It was a pretty sight. Ten – or was it more – glittering silver buses pulled over on the side of the highway. Edward's was the only bus that had discharged its passengers, and this was spoiling a lovely image: ragged, tired travellers wandering up and down the embankment while the passengers from the other buses, from behind darkened glass, looked on. Edward found a soft, dry place to sit. What a drill this was! He wondered, surveying the fleet, which of the buses carried his father. Sharon had been removed, conveyed in a sheet by some of the younger fellows from the settlement, who'd hiked her into the woods and returned already. Now they were sharing a Thermos down in the grass, and Sharon was gone. Edward wasn't sure what the hold-up was now, even while Frederick and some others, including the mayor, huddled in conference down in the shadow of the last bus.

It wasn't long before a signal was given and the buses revved up again. Edward stood and joined the orderly line his settlement had formed to board the bus, but the door didn't open.

Frederick and his crew had boarded their bus. One by one the other buses wheezed into motion, crawling from the side of the road to join the highway. His neighbours reacted differently to the situation that dawned on them, but Edward stood out on the shoulder to watch. Of course the windows of the buses were dark, so he couldn't see, but in one of them, perhaps pressed against the glass, perhaps waving at him this very moment, waving hello and, of course, goodbye, was his father. So Edward, just in case, raised his own hand too. Raised it and waved as the other buses built up speed down the highway and disappeared from sight, leaving the rest of them alone in the grass by the side of the road. ■

THE NEW VETERANS

Karen Russell

W hen Beverly enters the room, the first thing she notices is her new patient's tattoo. A cape of ink stretches from the nape of the man's neck to his hip bones. His entire back is covered with blues and greens, patches of pale brown. But – what the hell is it a tattoo *of*? So many colours waterfalling down the man's spine that, at first glance, she can't make any sense of the picture.

Compared to this tattoo, the rest of the man's skin – the backs of his legs and his arms, his neck – look almost too blank. He's so tall that his large feet dangle off the massage table, his bony heels pointing up at her. Everything else is lean and rippling, sculpted by pressures she can only guess at. Beverly scans the patient's intake form: male; a smoker; 6'2"; 195 lb; eye colour: brown; hair colour: black; twenty-five. Sergeant Derek Zeiger, 4th Infantry Division's Company B, 1st Battalion, 66th Armor Regiment.

In the billing section, he's scribbled: THIS IS FREE FOR ME, I HOPE AND PRAY . . . ? I'M ONE OF THE VETERANS.

And it is free – once she fills out and faxes in an intimidating stack of new forms. Ten sessions, 100 per cent covered by military insurance. Sergeant Zeiger is her first referral under the programme created by H.R. 1722 bill, Representative Wolly's triumph for his constituency: Direct Access for US Veterans to Massage Therapy Services. At the Dedos Magicos massage clinic, they'd all been excited by the bill; they'd watched a TV interview with the blue-eyed congressman in the office break room. Representative Wolly enumerated the many benefits of massage therapy for soldiers returning home from 'the most stressful environments imaginable'. Massage will ease their transition back to civilian life. 'Well, he's sure preaching to our choir!' joked Dmitri, one of the oldest therapists on staff. But Beverly had been surprised to discover her own cellular, flower-to-sun hunger for exactly this sort of preaching – in the course of a day, it was easy to lose faith in the idea that your two hands could change anything.

On the table, her first H.R. 1722 referral from the VA hospital has yet to budge. She wonders how long this soldier has been home for – a month? Less? Dark curls are filling in his crew cut. Only the back of his skull is visible, because he is lying face down on the table with his head fitted in a U-shaped pillow. She can't tell if he's really asleep or just pretending to be completely calm for her; often new patients *try* to relax, a ruse that never works – they just disperse their nervousness, spring-load their bones with guile.

With the man's bright tattoo for contrast, the rest of the room looks miserably generic. The walls are bare except for a clock lipped in red plastic, which feels like a glowing proxy for Ed's mouth, silently screaming at her not to go a penny over the hour. The young sergeant's clothes are wadded on the floor, and she shakes out and folds them as she imagines a mother might do.

'Sir? Ah – Sergeant Zeiger . . . ?'

'Unh,' moans the soldier, shivering inside a good or a bad dream, and the whole universe of the tattoo writhes with him.

'Hullo!' She walks around to the front of the table. 'Did you fall asleep, sir?'

'Oh, God. Sorry, ma'am,' says the soldier. He lifts his face stiffly out of the headrest and rolls onto his side, sits up. 'Guess I zoinked.'

'Zoinked?'

'Passed out. You know, I haven't been sleeping at night. A lot of pain in my lower back, ma'am.'

'Sorry to hear it.' She pats his shoulder, notes that he immediately tenses. 'Well, let's get you some help with that.'

How old was Sergeant Derek Zeiger when he enlisted? Seventeen? Twenty? As she heats the oils for his massage, Beverly becomes very interested in this question. Legally, nowadays, at what age can you do business with your life's time – barter your years on the free market for goods and services? A new truck, a Hawaii honeymoon, a foot surgery for your mother, a college degree in history? In Esau, Wisconsin, you have to be eighteen to vote, purchase cigarettes, legally accept a marriage proposal or a stranger's invitation to undress; at twenty-one, you can order a Cherry-Popper wine cooler and pull a slot lever; at twenty-five, you can rent a family sedan from Hertz. At any age, it seems, you can obtain a room by the hour at the Jamaica Me Crazy! theme motel next to the airport, which boasts the world's dirtiest indoor waterfall in the lobby.

At eighteen, Beverly had no plans for her future. All that year her mother had been dying, and then in April, two months before her high-school graduation, her haunted-eyed father had been diagnosed with stomach cancer, a double hex on the McFadden household. Six months to a year, the doctors said. Mr Blaise McFadden was a first-generation Irishman with hair like a lion and prizefighter fists, whose pugilist exterior concealed a country of calm of which Beverly secretly believed herself to be a fellow citizen, although she had never found a way to talk to her dad about their green interior worlds or compare passports. His death was not the one for which she'd been preparing. She'd spent her senior year cramming for the wrong test.

'Go to school,' said Janet, Beverly's older sister. 'Daddy doesn't need you underfoot. They can take care of themselves. Nobody wants you to stay.'

But Beverly didn't see how she could leave them alone with the Thing in the house. Beverly's parents were coy, demurring people. If they heard Death mounting the stairs at night, footsteps that the teenaged Beverly swore she could feel vibrating through the floorboards at 3 a.m., nobody mentioned this intrusion at breakfast.

Beverly enrolled in the 'Techniques of Massage' certificate programme at the Esau Annex because it required the fewest credit hours to complete. She'd surprised herself and her instructors by excelling in her night classes. Beverly felt that she was learning a second language. As a child she'd been excruciatingly shy, stiffening even in her parents' embraces, but suddenly she had a whole choreography of movements and touched people with a purpose. 'I can't believe I'm telling you this,' a body might confide to her. Spasming and relaxing. Pain unwound itself under her palms, and this put wonderful pictures in her head: a charmed snake sinking back into its basket, a noose shaking out its knots. In less than six months, Beverly had passed her tests, gotten her state certification and found a job in downtown Esau, and she was working at Dedos Magicos before her twentieth birthday. She'd felt smugly certain that she'd made the right choice.

Six months after his diagnosis of stomach cancer, right on schedule, Beverly's father died; her mother hung on for over another decade. She'd flummoxed her oncologists with her fickle acrobatics, swinging over the void and back into her body on the hospital bed while the life-recording machines telegraphed their silent, electronic applause. Beverly arranged for the sale of the farmhouse and used the proceeds to pay down her mother's staggering medical bills. For three years she lived in Beverly's apartment. In remission, then under attack again; in and out of the Esau County Hospital. Beverly tracked the rise and fall of her blood-cell counts, her pendulous vitals. She was thirty-four when her mother entered her final coma, accustomed by that time to a *Twilight Zone* split between work and the ward.

In her mother's final days, massage was the last message to reach down to her – when her sickness had pushed her to a frontier where she could no longer recognize Beverly, when she didn't know her own face in a mirror, she could still respond with a childlike pleasure to a strong massage. Beverly visited the mute woman in the hospital gown every day. She gave this suffering person a scalp-and-neck massage, and swore she could feel her real mother in the shell of the stranger smiling up at her. Marcy McFadden was gone. But Beverly could read the Braille of her mother's curved spine – it was composed in the unspeakable, skeletal language that she had learned at school.

Beverly smiles down at her new patient, rubbing the oil between her hands. She pulls at his trapezium muscles, which are dyed sky blue. Beverly is amazed that this level of detail is possible on a canvas of skin. Practically every pore on his back is covered: in the east, under his bony shoulder, there's an entire village of squat huts, their walls crackled white and black with the granular precision of cigarette ash. South of the village there is a grove of palm trees, short and fat. A telephone pole. A river dips and rises through the valley of his lower back. Tiny cattle with dolorous anatomies are grazing and bathing in it, bent under black humps and scimitar horns. The sky is gas-flame blue, and right in the centre of his back a little 'V' of birds tapers to a point, creating the illusion of a retreating horizon. Several soldiers occupy the skin below Zeiger's spine. What kind of ink did this tattoo artist use? What special needles? He dotted a desert camouflage onto the men – their uniforms are so infinitesimally petalled in duns and olives that they are, indeed, nearly invisible against Sergeant Zeiger's skin. Now that she's spotted them, though, she can't stop seeing them: their brown faces are the size of sunflower hulls. Somewhere a microscope must exist under which a tattoo like this would reveal ever-finer details – freckles, sweat beads, bootlaces. Windows that open onto sleeping infants. The cows' tails swatting mosquitoes. Something about the rice-grain scale of this world catches at Beverly's throat.

'What's the name of this river back here?' She traces the blue ink.

'That's the Diyala, ma'am.'

'And this village, does it have a name?'

'Fedaliyah.'

'That's in Iraq, I'm assuming?'

'Yup. New Baghdad. Fourteen miles from the FOB. We were sent there to emplace a Reverse Osmosis Water Purification Unit at JSS Al-Khansa. And to help the Iraqi farmers to feed their *jammous*.'

'*Jammous*?'

'Their word. Arabic for water buffalo. We're probably mispronouncing it.' He wiggles his hips to make the bulls dance. 'That was a big part of my war contribution – helping Iraqi farmers get feed for their buffalo. No hamburgers and fries in Fedaliyah, Bev, in case you're curious. Just *jammous*.'

'Well, you've got some museum-quality . . . *jammous* back here, Sergeant.' She smiles, tracing a buffalo's ear. She can see red veins along the pink interior. Sunlight licks at their dark fur.

'Yeah. Thanks. My artist is legendary. Tat shop just outside of Fort Hood.'

The brightest, largest object in the tattoo is a red star in the palm grove – a *fire*, Derek Zeiger tells her, feeling her tracing its edges. He doesn't offer any further explanation, and she doesn't ask.

She begins effleurage, drawing circles with her palms, stroking the oil onto his skin. The goal is to produce a tingling, preparatory warmth – a gentle prelude to the sometimes uncomfortably strong pressure required for deep-tissue work. Most everyone enjoys this fluttery feeling, but not Sergeant Zeiger.

'Christ, lady,' he grumbles, 'you want to hurt me that bad, just reach around and twist my nuts.'

Effleurage is a skimming technique, invented by Swedes.

'Sergeant, please. I am barely applying any pressure. Forgive me for saying this but you are behaving like my nieces.'

'Yeah?' he snarls. 'Do you twist their nuts, too?'

Healing is a magical art, said the pamphlet that first attracted the nineteen-year-old Beverly to this career. *Healing hands change lives*.

'Healing hurts sometimes,' Beverly tells the soldier briskly. 'And if you cannot hold still, we can't continue. So, please –'

People can do bad damage to themselves while trying to Houdini out of pain. Beverly has seen it happen. Recently, on a volunteer visit at the county hospital, Beverly watched an elderly woman on a gurney dislocate a bone while trying to butterfly away from the pins of her doctor's hands.

But ten minutes into their session, Beverly can feel the good change happening – Zeiger's breathing slows, and she feels her thoughts slowing, too, shrinking into the drumbeat of his pulse. Her mind grows quieter and quieter within the swelling bubble of her body, until all of her attention is siphoned into her two hands. The oil becomes warm and fragrant. A sticky, glue-yellow sheet stretches between her palms and the sergeant's tattoo.

'How does that feel now? Too much pressure?'

'It's fine.'

'Are you comfortable?'

'No,' he grunts. 'But keep going. This is free, right? So I'm getting my money's worth.'

Bulls stare up at her from the river. Under her lamp, the river actually twinkles. It's amazing that a tattoo needle this fine exists. Beverly, feeling a bit ridiculous, is genuinely afraid to touch it. She has to force herself to roll and knead the skin. For all of its crystalline precision, the soldier's tattoo has a fragile quality – like an ice cube floating in a glass. She supposes it's got something to do with the very vibrancy of the ink. Decay being foreshadowed by everything bright. Zeiger is young, but he'll age, he'll fade – and he's the canvas. Zeiger is now breathing deeply and regularly, the village rising and falling.

At a quarter to four, Beverly begins to wind down. She makes a few last long strokes along his spine's meridian. 'Time's up,' she's about to say, but then she notices something stuck beneath her pinky. When she moves her hand she slides the thing across the sky on Zeiger's shoulder, still tethered to her finger like a refrigerator magnet. Only it's flat – it's inside the tattoo. No, she thinks, impossible, as she continues floating it around his shoulders. An orange circle no larger than a grocery sale sticker. It's the sun. Beverly swallows hard and blinks, as if that might correct the problem. She draws her pinky halfway down his spine, and the sun moves with it. When she lifts her little finger, the sun stays put. She can't stop touching it, like a stubbornly curious child at a stove top – well, this is trouble, this is a real madhouse puzzle. The sun slides around, but the rest of the tattoo stays frozen. The buffalo stare at the grass, unalarmed, as it zings comet-like over their horns. The soldiers' faces remain stiffly turned to the west, war-blasé, as the sun grazes their helmets . . .

She gasps, just once, and Sergeant Zeiger says in a polite voice,

'Thank you, ma'am. That feels nice.'

'Time is *up!*' Ed raps at the door. 'Bev, you got a four o'clock!'

The door begins to open.

'Ed!' she calls desperately, pushing the door back into its jamb. 'He's changing!'

And when she turns around, Derek Zeiger *is* changing, standing behind the hamper and hopping into his pants. His arms lift and pull the world of Fedaliyah taut; Beverly gets a last glimpse of the sun, burning in its new location on the Diyala River.

Beverly swipes at her eyes. When she opens them, the tattoo is gone from view. Now Sergeant Derek Zeiger is standing in front of her, just as advertised on his intake form: 6'2", a foot taller than Beverly, and he is muddy-eyed indeed, squinting down at her through irises that are brown, almost black. He draws a hand from his pocket.

'Well, thank you, ma'am.' Inexplicably, he laughs, scratching behind one ear. 'I guess I don't feel any worse.'

'Sergeant Zeiger –'

He waves her away.

'Derek,' he says. 'Derek's good.'

She notices that he winces a little, just walking around. He pushes a hand to the small of his back like a brace.

'Oh, it's been like this for months,' he says, waving her concern away. '*You* didn't do this. You helped. It's a little better, I think.'

And then she watches him straighten for her benefit, his face still taut and bloated with pain.

She can feel her face smiling and smiling at him, her hand shaking in his.

'Then you have to call me "Beverly". None of this *ma'am* stuff.'

'Can I call you Bev?'

'Sure.'

'What about Beav?' He grins into the distance, as if he's making a joke to people she can't see. 'Beaver? Can I call you the Beav?'

'Beverly,' she says. 'Can you do me one favour, Derek? The next time you're in the shower –'

'Beverly!' He swivels to give her a big, real grin. 'I'm shocked! It's only our first date here . . .'

'Haha. Well.' Beverly can feel the blood tinting her cheeks. 'Just be sure to get all of the oil off. And should you notice – if you feel any pain? Or – anything? You can call me.'

She's never given her home number out to a patient before. As the sergeant turns his back to leave, shouldering his jacket, she mumbles something about muscle adaptation to deep-tissue massage, the acids that her hands have released from his trigger points. How 'disruptions' can occasionally occur. The body unaccustomed.

At Hoho's Family Restaurant, Beverly treats herself to peanut-butter pancakes and world news. She grabs a menu and seats herself. She's a long-time patron, and waiting for service always gives her a crawling, uncomfortable feeling. Beverly often finds herself struggling to stay visible to waitstaff, taxi drivers, cashiers. She tries hard to spite the magazines and persist in her childhood belief that ageing is honourable, to wear her face proudly, like a scratched medallion, the widening circles of purple under her eyes and the trenches on her brow. To be that kind of veteran. A woman ageing 'gracefully', like the church ladies she sees outside of Berea Tenth Presbyterian, whose yellowed faces are shadowed by wigs like cloudbursts. In truth, Beverly can never quite adjust to her age on the calendar; most days, she still feels like an old child. She spends quite a lot of time trying to communicate to strangers and friends alike that her life situation is something she chose: 'I never wanted anything like that, you know, serious, long-term. No kids, thank God. My patients keep me plenty busy.'

But it's been years, Beverly thinks. And whatever need starts knuckling at her then is so frightening that she can't complete the sentence. It's been decades, maybe, since she's been really necessary to anybody.

That night, emerging from the fog of her own shower, Beverly wonders what the soldier is seeing in his mirror. Nothing out of the ordinary, probably. Or almost nothing.

She places her hand against the green tiles and cranes around to peer at her back. She can't remember the last time she's done this. Her skin is a ghostly white, with a little penguin huddle of moles just above her hip, looking lost on that Arctic shelf. She can imagine her sister rolling her eyes at her, telling Beverly to get some colour. Dmitri, whose skin is an even shade of ginger root all year round, *tsk*-ing at her: 'Beeeverly, quit acting like the loneliest whale! Go to a tanning salon!'

Her hand glides along the curve of her spine, bumps along her tail bone. These are the 'rudimentary vertebrae': the fishy, ancient coccygeal bones. The same spine that has been inside of her since babyhood is hers today, the exact same bones from the womb, a thought that always fills her with a kind of thrilling claustrophobia. So much surface wrapped around that old stem. She watches her hands smear the water droplets on her stomach. It's strange to own anything, Beverly thinks, even your flesh, that nobody outside yourself ever touches or sees.

That night, under the coverlet, Beverly slides her hands under her T-shirt and lets them travel up and up, over her ribcage, over her small breasts and along the hard ridge of her collarbone, until she is gently wringing her own stiff neck.

Monday morning, Ed greets her with a can of diet soda. Eduardo Morales is the owner of Dedos Magicos, and he's been Beverly's boss for nearly thirty years. He is a passionate masseur whose English is so-so.

'Beverly. Here. On accident, I receive the diet soda,' Ed murmurs. 'The machine made a mistake.'

Beverly sighs and accepts the can.

'I hate it, you drink it.' He says this with a holy formality, as if this transaction were underwritten by the teachings of Christ or Karl Marx.

'OK. It's 8 a.m. Thank you, Ed.'

Ed beams at her. 'I really, really hate that one. Hey, your first appointment is here! Zeiiiiger.' He gives her a plainly lewd look. 'Rhymes with *tiiiger*.'

'Very funny.' She rolls her eyes.

But Beverly's hands are lifting to fix her hair, like a teenager. She hasn't felt this kind of nervousness in years.

Sergeant Derek Zeiger is waiting for her, lying shirtless on the table, and once again the tattoo burns like a flare against the snowy window. The first thing Beverly does is lock the door. The second thing is to check his tattoo: all normal. The sun is back at its original o'clock. When she breathes in and rubs at it the skin wrinkles but the sun does not move again.

Today, she tells Zeiger, she's trying 'cross-grain strokes' – bearing down with her forearms, going against the grain of the trapezium muscles. He says he's game. Then he shouts a curse that would shock even Ed, apologizes, curses again. She tries to lift his left hip and he nearly jumps off the table.

'It's not my fingers that are causing you the pain,' she says a little sternly. 'These muscles have been spasming, Sergeant. Working continuously. I'm just trying to release the tension. OK? It's going to hurt a little, but it shouldn't *kill* you. On a scale of one to ten, it should never hurt worse than a six.'

'Ding, ding, ding!' he yells. 'Eleven!'

'Oh, come on.' She can feel herself smiling, although her voice stays stern. 'I'm not even touching you. Tell me if you're really hurting.'

'Isn't that *your* job? To know that kind of stuff?'

She exhales through her nostrils. Knots, she tells the sergeant, are 'myofascial trigger points'. Bony silos of pain. Deep-tissue massage is a 'seek-and-destroy' mission, according to one of her more macho instructors at the Annex, a big ex-cop named Federico – a guy who used to break up race riots in Chicago but then became a massage therapist, applied his muscle power to chasing pain out of tendons and ligaments. Her fingers feel for the knots in Zeiger's large muscle groups. Her thumbs skate over the oil, entering caves between his vertebrae and flushing the old stores of tension. She pushes down into the fascia, the atlas bone that supports the skull, the top and centre of each shoulder blade, the triangular bone of his sacrum, his gluteal muscles, his hamstrings. She massages the trigger points underneath the tattooed river, which seems to pour from his lowest lumbar vertebrae, as if the Diyala has been wired into him. Beverly imagines the *whoosh* of blue ink exploding into real blood . . .

Her fingers find a knot underneath this river and begin to pull outward. Out of the blue – so to speak – Sergeant Zeiger begins talking.

'The tattoo artist's name was Applejack. But everybody called him "Cuz". You ask him why, he'd tell you: "Just Cuz." Get it?'

Well, that *was a mistake, Applejack!* Beverly silently rolls her knuckles over Zeiger's shoulders. With a birth name like 'Applejack', shouldn't your nickname be something like 'Roger' or 'Dennis'? Something that makes you sound like a taxpayer?

'Cuz is the best. He charges a literal fortune. I blew two disability cheques on this tattoo. What I couldn't pay, I borrowed from my friend's mom.'

'I see.' Her knuckles sink into a cloud over Fedaliyah. 'Which friend?'

'Arlo Mackey. He died. That's what you're looking at, on the tattoo – it's a picture of his death day. April 14, 2009.'

'His mother . . . paid for this?'

Under the oil the red star looks smeary and dark, like an infected cut.

'She lent each of us five hundred bucks. Four guys from Mackey's platoon – Vaczy, Grady, Belok, me, we all got the same tattoo. Grady draws real good, and he was there that day, so he made the source sketch for Applejack. After we got the tattoo, we paid a visit to Mrs Mackey. We lined up back to back in her yard in Lifa, Texas. To make a wall, like. Mackey's memorial. And Mrs Mackey took a photograph.'

'I see. A memorial of Arlo. A sort of skin mural.'

'Correct.' He grins, perhaps mistaking her echo for an endorsement of the project.

'That must be some picture.'

'Oh, it *is*. Mackey's mom decided she'd rather invest in our tattoos than some fancy stone for him – she knew we were his brothers.'

The sergeant's head is still at ease in the headrest. Facing the floor.

Which makes it feel, eerily, as if the tattoo itself is telling her this story, the voice floating up in a floury cloud from underneath the sands of Fedaliyah. As he continues talking, she pushes into his muscles, and the tattoo seems to dilate and blur under the oil.

'She circled our names in his letters home – Mackey wrote real letters, not emails, he was good like that – to show us what he thought of us. He loved us,' he says, in the apologetic tone of someone who feels they are bragging. 'Every one of us shows up in those letters. It was like we got to peel back his mind. She said: *You were his family and so you're my family, too.* Grady told her all the details of the attack, and then she said: *We will join together as a family to honour Arlo.* She said, *Now, I want you boys to put the past behind you* – that was her joke.'

'My God. That's a pretty dark joke.'

His shoulders draw together sharply.

'I guess it is.'

Thanks to the tattoo, every shrug causes a fleeting apocalypse. The 'V' of birds gets swallowed between two rolls of blue flesh, springs loose again.

'And – stop me if I've told you this – Mackey's ma had another kid. A girl. Jilly. She's a minor, so Mrs Mackey had to sign a piece of paper to let Applejack cut into her with his big power-drill crayons.'

'His sister got the tattoo? Her mother let her?'

'Hell, yes! It was her mother's idea! Crazy, crazy. Fifteen years old, skinny as a cricket's leg, a sophomore in high school, and this little girl gets the same tattoo as us. April 14. Arlo in the red star. Except, you know, scaled down to her.'

His head shakes slightly in the headrest, and Beverly wonders what exactly he's marvelling at, Jilly Mackey's age or the size of the tragedy or the artist's ingenuity in shrinking the scenery of her brother's death day down to make a perfect fit.

He waits a beat, but Beverly cannot think of one word to say. She knows she's failed because she feels his muscles tense, the world of Fedaliyah stiffening all at once, like a lake freezing itself.

'Plenty of guys in my unit got tattoos like this, you know. It's how the dead live, and the dead walk, see? We have to honour his sacrifice.'

Pride electrifies the sergeant's voice. Unexpectedly, he gets up on his elbows on the massage table, cranes around to meet her eye; when he says 'the dead', his long face lights up. It's like some bitter burlesque of a boy in love.

'What does your own mother say about all this, if you don't mind me asking?'

He laughs. 'I don't talk to those people.'

'Which people? Your family?'

'My family, you're looking at them.'

Beverly swallows. 'Which one is Mackey? Is this him, in the palm grove?'

'No. That's Vaczy. Mackey's burning up.' Zeiger pudges out a hip bone.

'He's – this red star?'

'It's a *fire*.' The sergeant's voice trembles with an almost childish indignation. 'Mack's inside it. Only you can't see him.'

The truck has just run over a remotely detonated bomb and exploded. Still burning inside the truck, he explains, is Private Arlo Mackey.

Why on earth would you boys choose this moment to incarnate? Beverly wonders. Why remember him – your good friend – dying, engulfed?

'You were with him on the day he died, Derek? You were all together?'

'We were.'

And then he fills in the stencil of April 14 for her.

At 6.05 a.m., on April 14, Sergeant Derek Zeiger and a convoy of four Humvees exited the wire of the FOB, travelling in the northbound lane of Route Roses, tasked with bringing a generator and medical supplies to the farm of Uday al-Jumaili. The previous week, they had driven out to Fedaliyah to do a school assessment and clean up graffiti. As a goodwill gesture, they had helped Uday al-Jumaili's son, a twelve-year-old herder, to escort a dozen sweaty buffalo and one million black flies to the river.

Pfc Vaczy and Sgt Zeiger were in the lead truck.

Pfc Mackey and Cpl Al Grady were in the second vehicle.

From the right rear window of the Humvee, Sgt Zeiger watched telephone poles and crude walls suck backwards into the dust. Sleeping cats had slotted themselves between the stones, so that the walls themselves appeared to be breathing. An orangish-grey goat watched the convoy pass from a ruined courtyard, heaving its ribs and crusty horns at the soldiers. At 6.22 a.m., a click away from the farm in Fedaliyah, the lead truck passed a palm grove within view of the Diyala River and the wise-stupid stares of the bathing *jammous*. Zeiger remembered watching one bull's tremendous head disappear beneath the dirty water. Perhaps fifteen seconds later, an IED tore through the second Humvee, in which Pfc Mackey was the gunner. Sgt Zeiger watched in the mirrors as the engine compartment erupted in flames. Smoke blindfolded him. On his knees in the truck he gagged on smoke, its oily taste. Incinerated metal blew inside the vehicle, bright chunks raining through the window. His head slammed against the windshield; immediately, his vision darkened; blood poured from his nostrils; a tooth, his own, went skidding across the truck floor.

'This front one is a fake,' he tells Beverly, tapping his enamel. 'Can't you tell? It's too perfect.'

He remembered picking up the tooth, which was a shocking, foreign white, etched in space. He remembered grabbing the aide bag and the fire extinguisher and tumbling from the truck and screaming, directing these screams nowhere in particular, down at his own laced boots, then skyward – and then, when he got his head together, he remembered to scream for the intervention of a specific person, the medic, Specialist Belok. He saw the gunner from the third truck running over to the prone figure of Corporal Al Grady and followed him.

'Well, OK: the bomb was a ten-inch copper plate, concave shape, remote-detonated, so when it blows there's about fifty pounds of explosives behind it. I heard over the radio: "There is blood everywhere," and I could hear moaning in the background. The blast shot Corporal Grady completely into the air, out of the vehicle – and Grady is 6'5", Beverly . . .'

Beverly pulls at the wispiest clouds along the cords of his neck.

'Where's the trigger man? Are we about to get ambushed on the road? Nobody knows. There's no one around us, there's no one around us, and do you think maybe Uday al-Jumaili came running to help us? Guess again. His house is dead quiet, it's just our guys and the palm grove. Behind the truck, the *jammous* are staring at us. Three or four of them, looking as pissy as women, you know, like the attack interrupted their bathing plans. Grady is responsive, thank God. The door is hanging. Mackey is screaming and screaming, I'm kneeling right under him. Some of his blood gets in my mouth. Somehow even in my state I figured that one out: I'm coughing up Mack's blood. And whatever he's screaming, I don't understand it, it's not words, so I go: Mack, what you're saying, man? What are you saying? I cut his pants to see if the femoral artery was severed. I remove his IBA looking for the chest wound. I wrap the wound to his head and his neck with a Kerlix . . .'

Zeiger's head is buried in the cushion – all this time, he hasn't looked up from the floor. Jigsaw cracks spread through the tattoo where his muscles keep tensing.

'Hours later, I'm still hearing the screaming. That night at the DFAC – the chow hall – we're all just staring at our food, and I'm telling people: "I didn't catch his last words. I lost them, I didn't catch them."

'And Lieutenant Norden, I didn't see him standing there, he goes: "Hey, Zeiger, I'll translate: goodbye. He was saying: *bye-bye.*" Norden's like a robot, no feeling. And I almost get court-martialled for breaking Norden's jaw, Bev.'

'Bev,' he says, like a strand of hair tucked behind her ear. Incredibly, in the midst of all this horror, she can still blush like a fool at the sound of her own name. She's terrified of setting him off again, knuckling down on the wrong spot, but at no point during his story does she halt the exploratory movements of her hands over the broad terrain of Zeiger's back.

'So now we all hump Mackey around like turtles. That day, April 14, it's frozen for all time back there.'

'Well, for *your* lifetimes,' Beverly hears herself blurt out.

'Right.'

Zeiger scratches at a raw spot on his neck.

'You know,' she says, adjusting the pressure, 'I think it's a beautiful thing you've done for your friend –' She traces the 'V' below the tight cords of his neck. Silent birds migrating into the deeper blues. 'You're giving him your, ah, your *portion* of eternity.'

Portion of eternity. Christ, where did she get that one?

'No, you're right.' He laughs sourly. 'I guess I'm only good for a short ride.'

A long silence follows. Fedaliyah heaves and falls.

'How long do you think, Bev?' he asks after a while. 'Fifty, sixty years?'

Beverly doesn't answer. After a while she says: 'Are you still being treated at the VA down the road?'

'Yes, yes, yes –' His voice grows peevish, seems to scuff at the floor under the headrest. 'For PTSD, the same as everybody. Do I seem traumatized to you, Beverly? What's the story back there?'

Instead of answering his question, Beverly lets her hands slide down his back. 'Breathe right here for me, Derek,' she murmurs. She eagles her palms outward, pushes in opposite directions until she gets a tense spot above his sacrum to relax completely. Beneath the sheet of oil, the tattoo's colours seem to deepen. To glow, grow permeable. As if she could reach a finger into the landscape and swirl the *jammous* into black holes, whirlpools in the tattoo . . .

Soon Zeiger is snoring.

She works her fingertips into the skin around the fire, and she can smell the flowery scent of the oil becoming more powerful; just briefly, she lets her eyes close. Suddenly the jasmine smells of her room are replaced by burning rubber, diesel. Behind her closed eyelids, she sees a flash of beige light. Spidery black palms, a roadside stand. A pair of heat-blurred men waving at her as if from the other end of a telescope. Sand ticking at a windshield.

Beverly hears herself gasp like someone emerging from a pool. When her eyes fly open, the first thing she sees are two hands, her own, rolling in circles through the oil on the sergeant's shoulders. She watches, astonished, as her hands continue the massage on autopilot, rotating slickly all the way down the man's spine. She feels a disorientation that is very close to her childhood amazement during the ghostly performances of her uncle's player piano: the black keys and the white keys depressing in sequence, producing music. Sergeant Zeiger moans happily.

What just happened? *Nothing happened, Beverly,* she hears in the no-nonsense voice of her dead mother, the one her mind deploys to police its own sanity. But her nostrils are stinging from the burning petroleum. Her eyes are leaking. Tentatively, Beverly strokes the red star again.

This time when she shuts her eyes, the flashes she gets are up close: she sees the clear image of a face. Behind the long windshield of a Humvee truck, a sunburned, helmeted soldier smiles vacantly at her. 'Hey, Mackey –' someone yells, and the man turns. He is bobbing his chin to some distant music, drumming his knuckles against the stiff Kevlar vest, uneclipsed.

Beverly has to stop the massage to towel her eyes. Where are these pictures coming from? It feels like she's remembering a place she's never been before, reminiscing about a face she's never seen in her life. Somehow a loop of foreign experience seems to have slotted itself inside her brain. Zeiger's song, spinning wildly through her. She wonders if such a thing is possible. A 'flashback' – that was the word from the VA literature.

Beverly tries to concentrate on her two hands, their shape and weight in space, their real activity. If she closes her eyes for even a second, she's afraid that Humvee will roll into her mind and erupt in flames. She forces herself to massage Zeiger's shoulders, his buttocks, the tendons of his neck. Areas far afield of the red star – the fatal fire, rendered down. The star seems to be the matchstick that strikes against her skin, combusts into the vision. And yet, in spite of herself, she watches her hands drawn down the tattoo. Now she feels she has some insight into the kind of trouble that April 14 must be giving Sergeant Derek Zeiger – there's a gravity she can't resist at work here. Her hands sweep around the red star like the long fingers of a clock, narrowing their orbit. Magnetized to that boy's last minute.

At the end of the massage, she pauses with the oily towel in her hand.

Her eyes feel as if there are little heated pins inside them.

A truck goes rolling slowly down Route Roses.

'Wake up!' she nearly screams.

'Goddamn it, Bev,' Zeiger grumbles with his eyes shut. He opens them reluctantly. Under her palms, his pulse jumps. 'I was just resting my eyes for a sec. You scared me.'

'You fell asleep again, Derek.' It's an effort to ungrit her teeth. 'And it seemed to me like you were stuck in a bad dream.'

At home, Beverly licks at her chalky lips. Her heartbeat is back to normal but her ears are still roaring. Is she lying to herself? Possibly the flashback is really nothing but her own projection, a dark and greedy way to feel connected to him, to dig into his trauma. Perhaps all she is seeing is her own hunger for drama spooling around the sergeant's service, herself in hysterics, a devotee of that new genre, 'the bleeding-heart horror story'. So named by Representative Eule Wolly in his latest rant on TV. He'd railed against the media coverage on the left and right alike: prurience, pawned off as compassion! The bloodlust of civilians. War-as-freak-show, war-as-snuff-film. 'All the smoky footage on the 7 a.m. news to titillate you viewers who are just waking up. Give you a jolt, right? Better than your Folgers.'

Was it that? Was that all?

That week, Beverly sees her ordinary retinue of patients: a retired mailman with a herniated disc; a pregnant woman who lies curled on her side, cradling her unborn daughter, while Beverly works on her shoulders; sweet Jonas Black, her oldest patient, who softens like a cookie in milk before the massage has even begun. By

Friday the intensity of her contact with Sergeant Derek Zeiger feels dreamily distant, and her memory of the tattoo itself has gone fuzzy, that picture no more and no less real to her than the war accounts she's seen on television or read. Next time she won't allow herself to get quite so worked up. Dmitri, who is working with several referrals from the VA hospital, tells her that he can't stop bawling after his sessions with them, and Beverly feels a twist of self-loathing every time she sees his puffy face. No doubt his compassion for the returning men and women is genuine, but there's something else afoot at Dedos Magicos, isn't there? Some common need has been unlidded in all of them.

What a sorrowful category, Bev thinks: the 'new veteran'. All those soldiers returning from Fallujah and Kandahar and Ramadi and Yahya Khel to a Wisconsin winter. Flash-frozen into citizens again. The phrase calls to mind a picture from her childhood Bible: THE RAISING OF LAZARUS! The spine of the book was warped, so that it always fell open to this particular page. Lazarus, looking a little hung-over, was blinking into a hard light. Sunbeams were fretted together around his forehead in jagged green and yellow blades. His sandalled pals had all gathered outside his tomb to greet him, like a surprise birthday party, but it seemed to be a tough social moment; Lazarus wasn't looking at anyone. He was staring into the cave mouth from which he had just been resurrected with an expression of sublime confusion.

When, fifteen minutes into his third massage, Sergeant Derek Zeiger begins to tell Beverly the same story about Pfc Arlo Mackey and April 14, she pauses, unsure if she ought to interject – is the sergeant testing her? Does he want to see if she's been paying attention? Yet his voice sounds completely innocent of her knowledge. She supposes this could be a symptom of the trauma, memory loss; or maybe Derek is simply an old-fashioned blowhard. As her hands travel up and down his spine, he tells the same jokes about the *jammous*. His voice tightens when he introduces Arlo. His story careens onto Route Roses . . .

'Why did you call it that? Route Roses?'

'Because it smelled like shit.'

'Oh.' The flowers in her imagination shrink back into the road.

'Because Humvees were always getting blown to bits on it. I saw it happen right in front of me, fireballs swaying on these big fucking stems of smoke.'

'Mmh.' She squirts oil into one palm, greases the world of April 14. Just his voice makes her crave buckets and buckets of water.

'I killed him,' comes the voice of Sergeant Derek Zeiger, almost shyly.

'What?' Beverly surprises both of them with her vehemence. '*No. No,* you didn't, Derek.'

'I did. I killed him –'

Beverly's mouth is dry.

'The bomb killed him. The, ah, the *insurgents . . .*'

'How would you know, Beverly, what I did and didn't do?' His voice shakes with something that sounds like the precursor to a fit of laughter, or fury; it occurs to her that she really doesn't know this person well enough to say which is coming.

'You can't blame yourself.'

'Listen: there are two colours on the road, green and brown. Two colours on the berm of Route Roses. There was a *red* wire. I didn't miss it, Bev – I saw it. I saw it, I practically heard that colour, and I thought I probably ought to stop and check it out, only I figured it was some dumb thing, a candy wrapper, a piece of trash, and I didn't want to stop again, it was a thousand degrees in the shade, I just wanted to get the fucking generators delivered and get back to base, and we kept right on driving, and I didn't say anything, and guess who's dead?'

'Derek . . . You tried to save him. The blood loss killed him. The IED killed him.'

'It was enough time,' he says miserably. 'We had fifteen, twenty seconds. I could have saved him.'

'No –'

'Later, I remembered seeing it.'

Beverly swallows. 'Maybe you just imagined seeing it.'

When Beverly's mother first started coughing, those fits were indistinguishable from a regular flu. Everybody in the family said so. Her doctors had long ago absolved them. At the wake, Janet and Beverly agreed that there was nothing to tip them off to her cancer. And their father's symptoms had been even less alarming: discomfort on one side of his body. Just an infrequent tingling. Death had waited outside their door for a long time, ringing the McFaddens' bell.

'You think it's hindsight, Derek, but it's not that. It's regret. It's false, you know, what you see when you look back – it's the *illusion* that you could have stopped it . . .'

Beverly falls silent, embarrassed. After a moment, Derek lets out a hoarse laugh. He lets enough time elapse so that she hears the laugh as a choice, as if many furious, rejected phrases are swirling around his head on the pillow.

'You trying to pick a fight with me, Bev? I saw it. Believe me. I looked out there and I saw something flash on the berm, and it was hot as hell that day, and I didn't want to stop.' He laughs again. 'Now I can't stop seeing it.'

He lets his face slump into the headrest. On the tattoo, Fedaliyah is becoming weirdly distorted by the energy of his shuddering. His shoulders clench – he's crying, she realizes. And right there in the middle of his back, a scar is swelling. Visibly lifting off the skin.

'Shhh,' says Beverly, 'shhh –'

At first, it's just a shiny ridge of skin, as skinny as a lizard's tail. Then it begins to darken and swell, as if plumping with liquid. Has it been there all along, this scar, disguised by the tattoo ink? Did the oils aggravate it? She watches with horror as the scar continues to lengthen, rise.

'I saw it, I saw it there,' he is saying. 'I can see it now, just how that wire would have looked . . . Why the *fuck* didn't I say anything, Beverly?'

Quickly, without thought, Beverly pushes down on it. An old, bad taste floods her mouth. When she lifts her hand, the dark scar is still there, needling through the palm grove on the tattoo like something stitched onto Derek by a maniacal doctor. She runs her thumbs over it, all reflex now, smoothing it with the compulsive speed with which she would tidy wrinkles on the white sheet covering the table. For a second, she succeeds in thumbing it under his skin. Has she burst it? Will a fluid seep out of it? She lifts her hands and the scar springs right back into place like a stubborn cowlick. Then she pushes harder, wincing herself as she does so, anticipating Zeiger's scream – but the sergeant doesn't react at all. She pushes down on the ridge of skin as urgently as any army medic doing chest compressions, and from a great distance a part of her is aware that this must look hilarious from the outside, like a Charlie Chaplin comedy, because the scale is all wrong here, she's using every ounce of her strength, and the red threat to Sergeant Zeiger is the width of a coffee stirrer.

And then the scar or blister, whatever it was, is gone. Really gone; she removes her hands to reveal smooth flesh. Zeiger's tattoo is a flat world again, ironed solidly onto him. This whole ordeal has taken maybe twelve seconds.

'Boy, *that* was a new move,' says the soldier. 'That felt deep, all right.' His voice is back to normal.

Beverly feels woozy. Her mouth is cracker-dry. She keeps sweeping over his back to confirm that the swelling has stopped.

'Thank you!' he says at the end of their session. 'I feel *great*. Better than I have since – since forever!'

She gives him a weak smile and pats his shoulder. Outside the window, the snow is really falling

'See you next week,' they say at the same time, although only Beverly's cheeks blaze up.

Beverly stands in the door frame and watches Zeiger scratching under his raggedy black shirt, swaying almost drunkenly down the hallway. Erasing it – she hadn't intended to do that! Medically, did she just make a terrible mistake? Should she have called a doctor? Adrenalin pumps through her and pools in her stiff fingers, which ache from the effort of the massage.

Call him back. Tell Derek what just happened.

Tell him what, though? Not what she did to the scar, which seems loony. And surely not what she secretly believes: *I saw the wire and I acted. I saved you.*

The next time Sergeant Zeiger comes to see her he is almost unrecognizable.

'You look wonderful!' she says. 'Rested.'

'Aw, thanks, Bev,' he laughs. 'You too!' His voice lowers with a childlike pride. 'I'm sleeping through the night, you know,' he whispers. 'Haven't had any pain in my lower back for over a week. Don't let it go to your head, Bev, but I'm telling all the doctors at the VA that you're some kind of miracle worker.'

He walks into the room with an actual swagger, that sort of boastful indifference to gravity that Beverly associates with cats and Italian women. One week ago, he was hobbling.

'Are you done changing?' she calls from behind the door.

She knocks, enters, light-headed with happiness. Her body feels so fiercely tugged in the boy's direction that she takes a step behind the counter, as if to correct for some magnetic imbalance. Derek rubs his hands together, makes as if to dive onto the table. 'God, I've been looking forward to seeing you all week. Counting down. How many more of these do I get?'

Seven sessions, she tells him. But Beverly has already privately decided that she will keep seeing Zeiger, for as long as he wants.

She grabs a new bottle of lotion, really high-end stuff, just in case it was only the oil she used last time that provoked his reaction. Ever so lightly, she pushes into his skin. The little fronds of Fedaliyah seem to curl away from her probing fingers. Ten minutes into the massage, without prompting, he starts to talk about the day Mackey died. As the story barrels onto Route Roses and approaches the intersection where the red wire is due to appear, Beverly's stomach muscles tighten. She drapes her hands over the spot on Zeiger's back where the scar appeared last time. She has to resist the urge to lift her hands to cover her eyes.

'Derek, you don't have to keep talking about this if you . . . if it makes you . . .'

But she has nothing to worry about, it turns out. In the new version of the story, on his first pass through the fields of Uday al-Jaimali, Zeiger *never sees a wire*. She listens as his Humvee makes its way down the road, past the courtyard and the goat and the spot where the red wire used to appear. Only much later, over fifty minutes after Mackey's body has been medevacked out on a stretcher, does Daniel Vaczy locate the filthy grain sack that contains a black mask, a video camera and detonation equipment for the ten-inch copper plate that kills Mackey, fragments of whom they later recover.

'We almost missed it. All hidden in the mud like that. No trigger man in sight. Really, it's a miracle Vaczy uncovered it at all.'

Beverly's hands keep up their regular clockwork. Her voice sounds remarkably steady to her ears:

'You didn't see any sign of the bomb from your truck?'

'No,' he says. 'If I had, maybe Mackey would be alive.'

He's free of it.

Elation sizzles through her before she's fully processed what she's hearing. She's *done* it. Exactly what she's done she isn't sure, and how it happened, she doesn't know, but it's a victory, isn't it? When the sergeant speaks, his voice is mournful, but there is not a hint of self-recrimination in it. Just a week ago last Tuesday, his sorrow had been shot through with a tremulous loathing – his guilt outlined by his grief. Beverly once read a science-magazine article about bioluminescence, the natural glow emitted by organisms like fireflies and jellyfish, but she knows the dead also give off a strange illumination, a phosphor that can permanently damage the eyes of the living. Necroluminescence – the light of the vanished. A hindsight produced by the departed's body. Your failings backlit by the death of your loved ones. But now it seems the soldier's grief has become a matt block. Solid, opaque. And purified (she hopes) of his guilt. His own wavy shadow.

Is it possible he's lying to her? Does the kid really not remember a red wire?

She plucks tentatively at a tendon in his arm.

'You can't blame yourself, Derek.'

'I don't blame myself,' he says coolly. 'Did I plant the fucking bomb? It's a war, Bev. There was nothing anybody could have done.'

Then Zeiger's neck tightens under her fingers, and she has to manually relax it. She massages the points where his jawbone meets his ears, imagines her thumbs dislodging the words she just spoke. Where did the wire go? Is it gone for good now? She leans onto her forearms, applying deeper pressure to his spinal meridian. The lotion gives the pale sky on Zeiger's back a dangerous translucence, as if an extra second of heat might send the sunset-pink inks streaming. She has a terrible, irrational fear of her hand sinking through his skin and spine. All along his sacrum, her fingers are digging in sand.

'That feels incredible, Beverly,' he murmurs. 'Whatever you are doing back there, my God, don't stop.'

And why *should* he feel guilty, anyway? Beverly wonders that night. Why should she?

Did it happen when I moved the sun? Beverly wonders sleepily. It's 11.12 p.m., claims the cool digital voice of time on her nightstand, 11.17 by the wind-up voice of her wristwatch. Did she alter some internal clock for him? Knock the truth off its orbit?

Memories are inoperable. They are fixed inside a person, they can't be smoothed or soothed with fingers. *Don't be nutty, Beverly*, she berates herself in her mother's even voice. But if it turns out that she really can adjust them from without? Reshuffle the deck of his past, leave a few cards out, sub in several from a sunnier suit, where was the harm in that? Harm had to be the opposite, didn't it? Letting the earliest truth metastasize into something that might kill you? The gangrenous spread of one day throughout the lifespan of a body – wasn't that something worth stopping?

3.02 a.m. 3.07 a.m. Beverly rolls onto her belly and pushes her head between the pillows. She pictures the story migrating great distances, like a snake curling and unwinding under its skin. Shedding endlessly the husks of earlier versions of itself.

One thing she knows for certain: Derek Zeiger is a changed man. She can feel the results of her deep-tissue work on his lower back, which Zeiger happily reports continues to be pain-free. And the changes aren't merely physical – over the next few weeks, his entire life appears to be straightening out. An army friend hooks him up with a part-time job doing IT for a law firm. He's sleeping and eating on a normal schedule; he's made plans to go on an ice-fishing trip with a few men he's met at work. He has a date with a female marine from one of his VA groups. The first pinch of jealousy she feels dissolves when she sees his excitement, gets a whiff of cologne. He rarely mentions Pfc Arlo Mackey any more, and he never talks about a wire.

All of a sudden Derek Zeiger wants to tell her about other parts of his past. Other days and nights and seasons. Battles with the school vice-principal. Domestic dramas. She listens as all the former selves that have hovered, invisibly, around the epicentre of April 14 start coming to life again, becoming his life: Zeiger in school, Zeiger before the war. Funny, ruddy stories fill in his blanks.

Beverly feels a tiny sting as Derek ambles off. He looks like any ordinary twenty-five-year-old now, with his rehabilitated grin and his five o'clock shadow. It's the first time she's ever felt anything less than purely glad to see his progress. They have four more sessions together as part of his H.R. 1722 allotment. Soon he won't need her at all.

On Friday, Sergeant Zeiger interrupts a long and mostly silent massage to recount his recent dream:

'I had such a strange one, Beverly. It felt so real. You know how you can unspool the ribbon from a cassette tape? I found this wire, I had bunches and bunches of it in my arms, I walked for miles, right through the centre of the village, it was Fedaliyah and it wasn't, you know how that goes, in dreams, the houses kept multiplying and then withdrawing, like a wave, I guess you would call it. A tidal wave, but going backwards, sort of pulling the whole village away from me like a slingshot. That's how I knew I was dreaming. Because those houses we saw outside of Fedaliyah were shanties, they had shit for houses, no electricity, but in my dream all of the windows were glowing . . .'

These walls receded from him, sparklingly white and quick as comets, and then he was alone. There was no village any more, no convoy, no radios, no brothers. There was only a featureless desert, and the wire.

'I kept tugging at it, spooling it around my hand. I wasn't wearing my gloves for some reason. I followed the wire to where it sprung off the ground and ran through the palms, and I knew I shouldn't leave the kill zone alone but I kept following it. I thought I was going to drop dead from exhaustion – when I woke up I ran to the bathroom and drank from the faucet.'

'Did you ever get to the end of it?'

'No.'

'You woke up?'

'I woke up. I remember the feeling, in the dream, of knowing that I wouldn't find him. I kept thinking: *I'm a fool. The trigger man has got to be long gone by now.*'

'What a strange dream,' she murmurs.

'What do you think it means?'

His tone is one of sincere mystification. He doesn't seem to connect this wire in his dream to the guilt he once felt about Arlo. Does this mean he's getting better – healing, recovering? Beverly's initial thrill gives way to a queasy feeling. If they continue these treatments, she worries that all of his memories of the real sands of Iraq might get pushed into the hourglass of dreams, symbols.

Derek is still lying on his stomach with his face turned away from her. She rubs a drop of clear gel into the middle of his spine.

'You were looking for the trigger man, Derek. Isn't that obvious?

But it was a nightmare. It doesn't mean anything.'

'I guess you're right. But this dream, Bev – it was terrible.' His voice cracks. 'I was alone for miles and miles, and I had to keep walking.'

She pictures a dream-small Zeiger retreating after the wire, growing more and more remote from the Derek Zeiger who's awake. And a part of her thinks, *Good.* Let him forget that there ever was an April 14. Let that day disappear even from his nightmares. If the wire ever comes up again, Beverly decides, she'll push it right back under his skin. As many times as it takes for Sergeant Derek Zeiger to heal, she will do this. With sincere apologies to Pfc Arlo Mackey – whom she suspects she must also be erasing.

Working the dead boy out of Route Roses like a thorn.

She has a feeling like whiskey moving to the top of her brain. Beverly pushes down and down and down into the tendons under his tattoo to release the knots. Muscle memory, her teacher used to say, that's what we're working against.

Off duty, at home, Beverly's own flashbacks are getting worse. She shuts her eyes on the highway home, sees the mist of blood and matter on the Humvee windshield, Mackey's head falling forward with an abominable serenity on the cut stem of his neck. At the diner, her pancake meals are interrupted by strange flashes, snatches of scenery. Fists are pounding on glass; someone's voice is screaming codes through a radio. Freckles sprinkle across a thin nose. A widow's peak goes pink with sunburn. Here comes the whole face again, rising up in her mind like a prodigal moon, miraculously restored to life inside the Humvee truck: the last, lost grin of Pfc Arlo Mackey. Outside her window, the blue street light causes the sidewalk to shine like an empty microscope slide. Her bedroom is a black hole. Wherever she looks now, she sees Arlo's absence. At night, she sits up in bed and hears Derek's voice:

'So Belok gets on the radio. Blood is coming out of Mackey like a fucking hydrant . . .'

Now Beverly is afraid to go to sleep. A moot fear, it turns out: she can't sleep any longer.

Of course there is always the possibility that she is completely off her rocker. If Zeiger were to bring her a photograph of Mackey in his desert fatigues, would she recognize him as the soldier from her visions? Would he have a receding hairline, brown hair with a cranberry tint, a dimple in his chin? Or would he turn out to be a stranger to Beverly – a boy she doesn't recognize?

Derek she likes to picture in his new apartment across town, snoring loudly. There is something terribly attractive to Beverly about the idea that she is remembering this day *for* him, keeping it locked away in the vault of her head, while the sergeant goes on sleeping.

Despite her insomnia, and her growing suspicion that she might be losing her mind, Beverly spends the next month in the best mood of her life. Really, she can't account for this. She looks terrible – Ed never even yells at her any more. Her regular patients have started making tentative enquiries about her health. She's lost twelve pounds; her eyes are still bloodshot at dusk. But so long as she can work with Derek, she feels invulnerable to the headaches and the sleep deprivation, to the bobbing head of Pfc Mackey and the wire loose in the dirt. So long as only she can see it, and Derek's amnesia holds, and Derek continues to improve, she knows she can endure infinite explosions, she can stand inside her mind and trip the red wire of April 14 forever. When Derek comes in for his eighth session, he brings her flowers. She thanks him, embarrassed by her extraordinary happiness, and then immediately presses several of the purse-lipped roses when she gets back to her apartment.

She stops wasting her time debating whether she's harming or helping him. Each time a session ends without any reappearance of the wire, she feels elated. That killing story, she excised it from him. Now it's floating in her, like a tumour in a jar. Like happiness, her souvenir of their time together, laid up for the long winter after the boy heals completely and leaves her.

Derek misses his appointment three weeks in a row. Doesn't turn up outside of Beverly's door again until the last day of February. He's wearing his unseasonably thin black T-shirt, sitting in a hard orange chair right outside her office. With his skullcap tugged down and his guilty grin he looks like a supersized version of the jug-eared kid waiting for the principal.

'Sorry I'm a little late, Bev,' he says, like it's a joke.

'You missed three appointments.'

'I'm sorry. I forgot. Honestly, it just kept slipping my mind.'

'I'll see you now,' says Beverly through gritted teeth. 'Right now. Don't move a muscle. I have to make some calls.'

Through the crack in the door she watches Zeiger changing out of his shirt. Colours go pouring down his bunched bones. At this distance his tattoo is out of focus and only glorious.

'So, American Hero. Long time no see.' She pauses, struggling to keep her voice controlled. She was so worried. 'We called you.'

'Yeah. Sorry. I was feeling too good to come in.'

'The number was disconnected.'

'I'm behind on my bills. Nah, it's not like that,' he says hurriedly, studying her face. 'Nothing serious.' His lips keep puckering and flattening alarmingly. She realizes that he's trying to smile for her.

'You don't look too good,' she says bluntly.

'Well, I'm still sleeping,' he says, scratching his neck. 'But some of the pain is back.'

He climbs onto the table, smoothing his new cap of hair. It's grown and grown. Beverly is surprised the former soldier can tolerate it at this length. The black tuft of hair at his nape is clearly scheming to become a mullet.

'Is the pressure too much?'

'Yes. But no, it's fine. I mean, do what you gotta do to fix it, Bev.' He takes a sharp breath. 'Did I tell you what's happening to Jilly?'

Beverly swallows, immediately alarmed. Jilly Mackey, she remembers. Arlo's sister. Her first thought is that the girl must be seeing the pictures of April 14 herself now. 'I don't think so . . .'

In Lifa, Texas, it turns out that Jilly has been having some trouble. Zeiger found out about this when he spoke on the phone with the Mackey women last Thursday; he'd called for Arlo's birthday. 'A respect call', he calls it, as if this is a generally understood term.

'Her mother's upset because I guess Jilly's been "acting out", whatever the fuck that means, and the teachers seem to think that somehow the tattoo is to blame – that she should have it removed. Laser removal, you know, they can do that now.'

'I see. And what does Jilly say?'

'Of course she's not going to. That's her brother on the tattoo. She's starting at some new school in the fall. But the whole thing makes me sad, really sad, Beverly. I'm not even sure exactly why. I mean, I can see to where it would be hard for her – emotionally, or whatever – to have him back there . . .'

Beverly squeezes his shoulders. A minor-key melody has been looping through her head since he began talking, and she realizes that it's a song from one of her father's records that she'd loved as a child, a mysterious and slightly frightening one with wild trumpets and horns that sounded like they'd been recorded in a forest miles away, accidentally caught in the song's net: 'The Frozen Chameleon'.

'It's probably a weird thing to explain in the girls' locker room, you know? But on the other hand I almost can't believe the teachers would suggest that. It doesn't feel right, Bev. You want a tattoo to be ah, ah . . .'

'Permanent?'

'Exactly. Like I said, it's a memorial for Arlo.'

Grief freezing the picture onto him. Grief turning the sergeant into a frozen chameleon. Once a month Beverly leaves flowers in front of her parents' stones at St Stephen's. Her sister got out twenty years ago, but she's still weeding for them, sprucing daffodils.

'You don't think the day might come when you want to erase it?'

'No! No way. Jesus, Beverly, weren't you listening? Just the thought makes me sick.'

She smoothes the sky between his shoulder blades. The picture book of Fedaliyah, stuck on that page he can't turn. After an instant, his shoulders flatten.

'I was listening. Relax.' She shifts the pressure a few vertebrae lower. 'There. That's better, isn't it?'

By March 10, she estimates she's survived hundreds of explosions. Alone in her apartment, she's watched Pfc Mackey die and reincarnate with her eyes shut, massaging her own jaw.

From dusk until 3 or 4 a.m., in lieu of sleeping, she's started watching hundreds of hours of cable news, waiting for coverage of the wars. Of course Zeiger and Mackey won't be mentioned, they are ancient history, but she still catches herself listening nightly for their names. One night, spinning through the news roulette, she happens to stop on a face that she recognizes: Representative Eule Wolly, the blue-eyed advocate of massage therapy for the new veterans.

Who, she learns, never served abroad during the Vietnam War. First Lieutenant Eule Wolly was honourably discharged from the navy while still stationed in San Francisco Bay. He lied about receiving a Purple Heart. The freckled news anchor reading these allegations sounds positively gleeful, as if he's barely suppressing a smile. Next comes footage of Representative Wolly himself, apologizing on a windy podium for misleading his constituents through his poor choice of wording and the 'perhaps confusing' presentation of certain facts. Such as, to give one for instance, his alleged presence in the nation of Vietnam from 1969 to 1971. Currently he is being prosecuted under the Stolen Valor Act.

Beverly switches off the TV uneasily. Just that name, the 'Stolen Valor Act', gets under her skin. She pushes down the thought that she's no better than the congressman, or the rest of the pack of liars and manipulators who parade across the television. In a way his crime is not so dissimilar from what she's been doing, is it? Encouraging Derek to twist his facts around as she loosens his muscles; trying to rub out his memories of the berm. Thinking she can live the boy's worst day for him.

'He's doing amazingly well,' Beverly hears herself telling her sister, Janet, during their weekly telephone call. Bragging, really, but she can't help herself – Zeiger is making huge strides. His life is settling into an extraordinarily ordinary routine, she tells Jan, who by now has heard all about him.

'He's got a full-time job, isn't that exciting? He signed the lease on a new apartment, too, much nicer than the cockroach convention where he's been living. I'm really so proud of him. Janet?'

She pauses, embarrassed – it's been whole minutes since her sister's said a word. 'Are you still there?'

'Oh, I'm still here.' Janet laughs angrily. 'You think I don't know what you're doing? You want to throw it in my face?'

'What?'

'Nice to hear you're still taking such *excellent* care of everyone.' Fury causes her sister's voice to crackle in the receiver. For a second, Beverly is too stunned to speak. 'Janet. I have no idea what you're talking about.'

'Don't pretend like I didn't do my part. I was there as often as I could be, Beverly. Once a month without fail – more, when I could get away. And not everybody thought it was a good idea to skip college, you know.'

Beverly stares across her kitchen, half expecting to see the dishes rattling. Once a month? Is Janet joking?

'Do you want me to get the calendar out?' Beverly's voice is trembling so hard it's almost unintelligible. 'From September to May one year,' she says, 'I was alone with her. Don't you dare deny it.'

'Every other weekend, practically, I was there.'

'You did *not* –'

'Dad thought you were crazy to stay, Mom practically begged you to go, so if you stayed, you did it for your own reasons. OK? And I came to help plenty of times. I'm sorry if it wasn't every fucking weekday like you. I'm sorry we can't all be saints like you, Beverly. *Healers* –'

Now she sounds like the older sister that Beverly remembers, her voice high and wild, stung, making fun.

'And I had my own family.'

'The girls only met their grandmother once –' Beverly sputters. *You got the girls*, she manages not to say, although now her outrage is actually blinding.

'You're not remembering right. We were out there a bunch of times . . .'

'Janet! You can't be serious!'

'We *were* and you know it.'

Beverly swallows. 'But that's simply not true.'

'I know I'll regret saying this, OK, I've held my tongue for twenty years, I should get a damn medal like your little buddy out there. But who else is going to tell you? You are like a dog, Beverly.' Beverly can almost feel her sister's fingers clawing into the telephone, as if they are wrapped around Beverly's neck. 'You're like a sad dog. Your masters aren't coming back. Sor-ry. Mom's been dead for over a decade, do you realize that?'

Beverly takes a breath; it's as if she's been punched.

'You have no idea what I sacrificed –'

'Oh, give me a break. Die a martyr, then. Jesus Christ.'

For many years, Beverly will remember every word of this conversation while failing to recall, no matter how hard she tries, who hung up first.

Quaking, alone in her apartment, Beverly's first impulse is to dial their old home phone number. She's always assumed that she and Janet agreed on this point, at least: the basic chronology of their mother's fight with cancer. What happened when. Who was present in which rooms. Beverly doesn't know how to make sense of who she is today without those facts in place. With a chill she realizes there are no witnesses left besides herself and Janet. She has a sense memory of steering her mother down a long corridor, her wheelchair spokes glinting. Janet missed knowing that version of their mother. If Beverly stops pushing her now, or loses her grip, she will roll out of sight.

With her hand still tangled in the telephone cord, Beverly decides that she doesn't want to be yet another of the cover-up artists. Can't.

She won't go on encouraging the sergeant to lie to himself, just so he can sleep at night. She's warped the truth, she pushed the truth under his skin, but she won't allow it to go on changing. Suddenly it is vitally important to Beverly that Zeiger remember the original story, the one she has stolen from him. Whatever she's wiped from his memory, she wants to restore. Immediately, if that's possible.

'Derek? It's Beverly. Can you come in tomorrow? I have a slot at nine . . .'

She gets a melting flash of obscenely blue sky, fire. A large bull is standing in the river, in chest-high green water, chains of mosquitoes twisting off its bony shoulders like tassels. Its eyes are vacuums. Placid and hugely empty. The animal continues lapping at its reddish shadow on the water, oblivious of the bomb behind it, while a thick smoke rolls over the desert.

When she sees Zeiger in person the following morning, with his big grin and his smooth, unlined face, she can feel her resolve fading. She knows she's got to help him to recover his original memory, to straighten out the timeline of April 14 now, before she loses her nerve completely. He lies down on the massage table, and she's glad his face is turned away from her.

'I was thinking about you a lot this weekend, Derek,' she says. 'I saw a news show where they interviewed an army general about IEDs . . . I thought of your friend Arlo, of course. That story you told me once, about April 14 . . .'

Derek doesn't react, so she babbles on.

'This general said it was almost impossible to spot tripwires. He called them these "tiny wires in the dirt". And I thought, I'll have to ask Derek if that was, ah, his experience . . .'

'Of course it's hard to spot the wires!' Derek explodes at her. There is no warning contraction of his shoulder blades. He shakes off her hands, sits up. 'You need TV to tell you that? You need to hear it from some general? Jesus Christ, it's 9 a.m., and you're interrogating me?'

'Derek, please, there's no need to get so upset –'

'No? Then why the hell did you bring up Arlo?'

'I'm sorry if I – I was only curious –'

'That's right, that's everyone. You're "only curious",' he snarls. 'None of you has any idea what it was like. Nobody gives a shit.'

Derek rolls his legs away from her and stands, struggles into his shirt and pants, knocking into the massage table. Then he goes stumbling out of the room like a revenant, half dressed, trailing one sleeve of his jacket. Walking away from her so quickly that it's impossible to tell what, if anything, changed on the tattoo.

Six thirty on Monday morning: Beverly is brushing her teeth when the phone rings. It's Ed Morales, of course, who else would it be this early on a workday but Ed, his voice spuming through the receiver? Lance Corporal Eric Ilana is dead, Ed tells her. Has been dead for two days. In the mirror, Beverly watches this information float on the surface of her grey eyes without penetrating them.

'Oh my God, Ed, I'm so sorry, how terrible . . .'

Not Derek, is her only thought as she hangs up.

It remains that, beating in her head like a bat, a tiny monster of upside-down joy: *not-Derek, not-Derek.* Then the bat flies off and she's alone in a cave. Eric. She remembers who he is – was, she corrects herself. Another of their H.R. 1722 referrals. One of Ed's patients. He'd survived three IED blasts in Rustamiyah. She'd chatted with him once in the waiting room, a lean man with glasses, complaining about how pale he'd gotten since coming home to Wisconsin. He'd passed around a photograph of his two-year-old daughter. For a new veteran, he'd seemed remarkably relaxed. Cracking himself up.

The news of Lance Corporal Ilana's death turns out to be hidden in plain sight in her apartment, spread out on her countertop, gathering leaky drips from her ceiling. After Ed calls her, she finds the Saturday newspaper where his suicide was reported:

THE SOLDIER DIED IN HIS CAR OF AN APPARENTLY SELF-INFLICTED GUNSHOT WOUND TO THE HEAD AT 11.15 P.M. AT 11.02 P.M. HE REPORTEDLY SENT A TEXT MESSAGE TO HIS WIFE INFORMING HER OF HIS PLANS TO HARM HIMSELF.

Beverly cancels every appointment in her book except for Derek Zeiger. Then Zeiger fails to show. For the first time in three years, Beverly skips work. Beds down straight through noon with the blinds half drawn, the sunbeams rattling onto her coverlet. Through the mesh of light she can still see Arlo Mackey's ruined face. *Go away,* she whispers. But the ghost is in her body, not her room, and scenes from his last day continue to invade her.

'It all came at you like you didn't have a brain,' Derek told her once, describing the routine chaos of their patrols.

Beverly has never been a drinker. But on the evening of Eric Ilana's death she returns from the liquor store with six bottles of wine. Between Monday and Friday four bottles disappear. Into her, it seems, as unlikely as she finds these new hydraulics of her apartment. It turns out the dark cherry stuff doesn't help her to sleep, but it blurs the world she stays awake in. What a bargain for ten bucks a bottle, she thinks, on her tiptoes in the liquor store. Maybe she can fix the problem by moving the sun again. How far back would she have to rewind it, to instil a permanent serenity in Derek? Hours? Aeons? She imagines blue glaciers sliding over Fedaliyah, the soldiers blanketed in ice. It seems incredible to her that she ever thought she might do this for him – wring the whole war from his tissue and bone. In Esau, night lightens into dawn. Cars begin to jump and whine across the intersection. When an engine backfires, she flinches and grinds down on her molars and watches the Humvee erupt in flames.

Enough, she tells herself – but it turns out these commands don't clear the smoke from her brain. Beverly uncorks a second bottle of wine. She cracks open her window, lights a cigarette pinched from Ed. Smoke exits her lips in a loose curl, joining the snow. She wonders if this will become a new habit, too.

Nobody blames massage therapy for the young soldier's suicide exactly, but Representative Wolly's H.R. 1722 programme gets scuttled, and plenty of the commentators add a rueful line about how the young lance corporal had been receiving state-funded deep-tissue massages at a place called Dedos Magicos.

At Dedos, it's surprising to see how much everyone is affected, even those on staff who only briefly met Ilana. There are lines of mourning on Ed's face. He spends the week following Eric's death walking softly around the halls of the parlour in black socks, hugging his arms around his ice-cream scoop of a belly. He doesn't curse or scream at anybody, not even the clock face. A gentle hum seems to be coming from deep in his throat.

And where is Derek? His phone is still disconnected. She tries another number listed on one of his intake forms, and discovers that he's been AWOL from his regular groups at the VA hospital. The counsellor there reports that she hasn't heard a peep from him in five or six days. Beverly replays her last words to him until she feels sick. She keeps waiting for him to show up, staring down at the Dedos parking lot. It occurs to her that this vigil might merely be the foretaste of an interminable limbo, if Derek never comes back.

Outside the window, geese with sunshine pooling on their wings like wet paint are flying westward. Beverly has been noticing many such flocks moving at fast speeds over Esau, and whenever she sees them they are as gracefully spaced as writing. She can't read any sense behind their dissolving bodies. Then the red parchment of the Wisconsin sunset melts, black space erases the geese, it's night.

Early Sunday morning, the phone startles Beverly awake. This time, thank God, it's not Ed Morales. It's not Janet calling with the weather report from Sulko, Nevada, or the joyful percolations of her twin nieces, wearing their matching jammies under Gemini stars in the American desert. Nobody else calls her at home. No stranger has ever rung her at this hour.

'Hello?'

'Hi, Bev. Sorry to call so early.'

'Derek.'

Beverly sinks under her coverlet. The relief that washes through her leaves her feeling boneless, jellied.

'Were you up? You sound wide awake.'

'You scared me. The last time I saw you –'

'I know. I'm really, really sorry. I didn't mean to explode on you like that. I honestly don't know why that happened. It's weird because I've been feeling so much better lately. And for that I wanted to say, you know: *thank you.* To be honest, I was never expecting much from you. My real doctor at the VA made me enrol in the programme. Massage therapy, no offence, I was thinking: hookers. Happy endings, la-la beads.'

'I see.'

'But whatever you do back there *works*. I've been sleeping like a baby ever since. I sleep through the night.'

The wall clock says 3 a.m.

'I sleep good,' he maintains, as if wanting to forestall an argument. 'Tonight is an exception to the rule, I guess.' He laughs quietly, and Beverly feels like a spider clinging to one bouncing line – their connection seems that frail.

'Well, we're both awake now.' She swallows. 'Why are you calling me here, Derek?'

'I'm not cured, though.'

'Well, Derek, of course you're not,' she says, fighting to get control of a lungeing pressure in her chest. 'Massage doesn't "cure" people, it's a process . . .'

'Beverly . . .' His voice breaks into a whimper. 'Something's wrong –'

There are a few beats of silence. In the mysterious, unreal distances of her inner ear, Pfc Arlo Mackey continues screaming and screaming inside the burning truck.

'I'm in pain, a lot of pain. I need to see you again. As soon as I can.'

'I'll see you on Monday, Derek. Ten o'clock.'

'No, Beverly. Now.' And then there is shuffling on his end of the receiver, and an awful sound like half a laugh. 'Please?'

E d Morales has never fired anybody in his thirty-year tenure as the owner of Dedos Magicos, and he always mentions this a little wistfully, as if it's a macho experience he's always dreamed of having, the way some men want to summit Everest or bag a lion on safari. She doesn't doubt that he will fire her if he finds them out.

Still, where else are they supposed to go? Beverly is a professional. She is not going to confuse everything even further at this late hour by beginning to see patients in her home.

Beverly has keys to the building. She drives beneath a full, icy moon, following the chowdery line of the Esau River. All the highways are empty. When she pulls into her staff slot, the sergeant's blue jalopy is already there.

'Thank you,' he mumbles as they climb out of their cars. His eyes are red hollows.

'Don't be scared, promise? I don't know what went wrong the other day.'

Beverly, who has some idea, says nothing.

'Are you afraid of me, Beverly?'

'Afraid! Why would I be? Are you angry at me?'

Kind *no*s are exchanged.

There is the fat moon behind him, one white ear eavesdropping brazenly in the Midwestern sky.

Beverly fumbles with the car lock, gets them both inside the building. Something is moving under his shirt, on his back, she can see it, a dark shape. In the moonlight, his snowy boots look almost silver. Nothing else stirs in the long hallway, their shoes mewl on the tiles, sucked along by slush. They speak at the same time.

'Lie down?'

'I'll go lie down –'

'Thank you for meeting me, Beverly,' he says again, sounding so much like a boy about to cry. 'Something's wrong, something's wrong, something's *wrong*.' He groans. 'Ah, Bev! Something feels twisted around . . .'

He pulls off his shirt, lies down. Beverly sucks in her breath –

his back is in terrible shape. The skin over his spine looks raw and abraded; deep blue and yellowish bruises darken the sky of Fedaliyah. And a long bright welt, much thicker and nastier than the thin scar she erased, stretches diagonally from his hip bone to his shoulder.

'Jesus, Derek! Did someone do this to you? Did you do this to yourself?'

'No.'

'Did you have some kind of accident?'

'I don't know,' he says flatly. 'I don't remember. It looked this way when I woke up two days ago. It's gotten worse.'

Beverly touches his shoulder and they both wince. Maybe the welt did erupt from inside the tattoo. Maybe Derek vandalized the tattoo himself, and he's too ashamed or too frightened to tell her. She's surprised to discover how little the explanation matters to her. In the end, every possibility she can imagine arises from the same place – a spark drifting out of his past and catching, turning into this somatic conflagration. No matter how it happened, she is terrified for him.

She dips a Q-tip into a bottle of peroxide, stirs.

This time she abandons any pretension of getting the true story out of him. She doesn't try to grab hold of April 14 and reset it like a broken bone. She doesn't mention IEDs or Mackey. Her concerns about whether or not it would be better for the sergeant to forget the wire, wipe his slate clean, are gone; she thinks those debates must belong to a room without this boy hurting in it. All she wants to do right now is reduce his pain. If she can help him with that, she thinks, it will be miracle enough.

'Don't worry,' she says. 'We're going to fix you up. Hold still for me, Derek.'

She begins at the base of his spine, rolling up, avoiding the most aggravated areas. He only whimpers once. Through his neck, she can feel the strain of his gritted teeth.

'That fucking *kills*, Beverly – what are you doing?'

'Shh – you focus on relaxing. This is helping.'

She defaults to what she knows. Eventually, like in the first sessions, she can feel something shifting under her hands. Her voice needles in and out of Zeiger's ears as she tells him where to move and bend and breathe. It's dark in the room, and she's barely looking at his back, letting his fascia and muscles guide her fingers. Gradually, and then with the speed of wind-blown sands, the story of the tattoo begins to change.

A little after 5 a.m., Beverly stops the massage to button her sweater up to her neck. It's the same baggy, cerulean skin that she always puts on, her old-lady costume. Tonight her sleeves bunch at her elbows, so that she feels like a strange moulting bird – eating has kept slipping her mind. The moon is out; their two cars, viewed through the parlour window, have acquired a sort of doomed, mastodon glamour, shaggy with snow. A green light blinks ceaselessly above them, some after-hours alarm she's never here to see. She checks to make sure the windows are closed – the room feels ice cold. Beverly moves to get Zeiger's shirt, towels. She's washed and dressed the damaged skin; the tattoo is almost completely hidden under gauze. Now she doesn't have to look at the red star. Beverly cotton-daubs more peroxide onto his neck, which has relaxed. Zeiger begins to talk. With his eyes still shut, he tours her through the landscape on his back; it's a version of April 14 that is completely different from any that's come before. She listens to this and she doesn't breathe a word. She has no desire to lift the gauze, check the tattoo against this new account.

When he's finished, Beverly asks him in a shaky voice: 'Nobody died that day, Derek?'

'Nobody.'

He sits up. Perched on the table's edge, with the blanket floating in a loose bunting around his shoulders, the sergeant flexes and relaxes his long, bare toes.

'Nobody died, Bev. That's why I got the tattoo – it was a miracle day. Amazing fucking grace, you know? Fifty pounds of explosives detonate, and we all make it back to the FOB alive.'

Beverly smoothes a wrinkle in a square of gauze, tracing the path of what was, the last time she checked, the Diyala River.

'Nobody died. I lost a chunk of my hearing, but I just listen harder now.'

His face is beaming. 'I love telling that story. You're looking at the proof of a miracle. My tattoo, it should hang in a church.'

Then he slides towards her and cups one big hand behind her head. He sinks his fingers through the grey roots of her hair and holds her face there. It's a strange gesture, more gruff than romantic, his little unconscious parody of how she feels towards him, maybe – it makes her think, of all things, of a mother bear cuffing its cub. He digs his fingers into her left cheek.

'Thank you, Beverly.' Zeiger talks in a telephone whisper, as if their connection is about to be cut off at any moment by some maniacal, monitoring operator. 'You can't even imagine what you've done for me here . . .'

For what is certainly too long an interval Beverly lets her head rest against his neck.

'Oh, you're very welcome,' she says into a muzzle of skin.

What happens next is nothing anyone could properly call a kiss; she turns into him, and his lips go slack against her mouth; when this happens, whatever tension remains in him seems to flood into her. She fights down a choking sensation and turns her head, reaches for his hand.

'Beverly –'

'Don't worry. Look at that snow coming down. Time's up.' ∎

CONTRIBUTORS

André Aciman is most recently the author of *Harvard Square*, which is published in 2013. He is the chair of the PhD Program in Comparative Literature at the CUNY Graduate Center and the director of the Writers' Institute. 'Abingdon Square' is taken from a forthcoming book, *Moral Tales*.

John Burnside teaches at the University of St Andrews. His most recent books are *Black Cat Bone*, a poetry collection, and *A Summer of Drowning*, a novel.

Janine di Giovanni has reported on more than a dozen wars for nearly twenty years. She is an award-winning reporter and author, and the former president of the Jury of the Prix Bayeux for war reporters. Her latest book is *Ghosts by Daylight: A Memoir of War and Love*. 'Seven Days in Syria' was supported by funding from The Nation Institute.

Mohsin Hamid is the author of three novels: *Moth Smoke*, a finalist for the PEN/Hemingway Award; *The Reluctant Fundamentalist*, shortlisted for the Man Booker Prize; and *How to Get Filthy Rich in Rising Asia*, which is published in 2013. He lives in Lahore.

Samantha Harvey was born in England in 1975. Her first novel, *The Wilderness*, was shortlisted for the Orange Prize for Fiction, longlisted for the Man Booker Prize, shortlisted for the *Guardian* First Book Award, and won the Betty Trask Prize. Her new novel, *All Is Song*, was published in January 2012. She was recently named by *The Culture Show* as one of the 12 Best New British Novelists.

Ben Marcus is the author, most recently, of *The Flame Alphabet*. He is the fiction editor of the *American Reader*.

Darcy Padilla is a documentary photographer and lecturer living in San Francisco, California. Her awards include a Guggenheim Fellowship, an Open Society Fellowship and the W. Eugene Smith Grant for Humanitarian Photography.

Colin Robinson is the co-founder of OR Books, and previously worked for Scribner, the New Press and Verso. He has written for a range of publications including the *New York Times*, the *Sunday Times*, the *Guardian*, the *London Review of Books* and the *Nation*. He divides his time between New York, London and Liverpool.

Karen Russell is the author of the story collection *St Lucy's Home for Girls Raised by Wolves* and the novel *Swamplandia!*, a Pulitzer Prize finalist and one of the *New York Times*'s Top 5 Fiction Books of 2011. Her new story collection, *Vampires in the Lemon Grove*, is forthcoming next month. In 2007 she was named one of *Granta*'s Best Young American Novelists.

Jennifer Vanderbes is the author of three novels: *Easter Island*, *Strangers at the Feast* and the forthcoming *The Secret of Pigeon Point*. Her non-fiction has appeared in the *New York Times* and *Wall Street Journal*, and she is the recipient of fellowships from the Guggenheim Foundation and the New York Public Library's Cullman Center.

Lauren Wilkinson recently received her MFA in fiction and literary translation from Columbia University, where she is teaching a creative writing course. She is finishing her first novel and will be applying to medical school in the autumn.

Callan Wink is working on a novel and a collection of stories, forthcoming from Random House in the US and Granta Books in the UK. He lives in Livingston, Montana.

Visit granta.com for the online edition of Betrayal, featuring podcasts with contributors including Mohsin Hamid and André Aciman, new fiction from Andrès Neuman, memoir from James Lasdun, poetry from Syrian poet Nouri al-Jarrah and the announcement of two New Voices.

LONDON

BETRAYAL: A LIARS' LEAGUE STORYTELLING SALON

28 January, 7 p.m., Betsey Trotwood, 56 Farringdon Road, London EC1R 3BL. £7, tickets include a copy of Granta 122.

Performing stories marked by the sharp edge of loss, love and betrayal from an unnamed dystopia to the American West, the Liars' League, a live storytelling salon, reads new work from *Granta* 122 contributors Ben Marcus, Jennifer Vanderbes and Callan Wink. In the second half of the evening, a contributor to *Granta*'s online edition of Betrayal will join us for a reading and conversation.

THE GRANTA ART SALON

29 January, 7 p.m., Hospital Club, 24 Endell Street, London WC2H 9HQ. Seats are limited. Email publicist Saskia Vogel to check availability and to reserve your place: svogel@granta.com. Free.

Granta returns to the Hospital Club for a salon that explores the lyrical space that emerges when art and literature are in dialogue.

THE LONDON LAUNCH

30 January, 6.30 p.m., Foyles, 113–119 Charing Cross Road, London WC2H 0EB. Free.

The latest issue of *Granta* explores the sting of betrayal by a loved one, our leaders and from within our own hearts. Join *Granta*, Samantha Harvey and other contributors for readings and conversation that mark the launch of *Granta* 122. A drinks reception will follow.

NEW YORK

TRAUMA AND RESPONSIBILITY: WOMEN WRITING ABOUT RESILIENCE

29 January, 7 p.m., 192 Books, 192 Tenth Avenue, New York, NY 10011. Free.

Survivor's guilt. Does it live on in our scars, or can we overcome it? In two powerful new stories, Karen Russell and Jennifer Vanderbes explore the lives of two women who must face trauma and the responsibility they feel towards it. *Granta* editor John Freeman joins these two writers to explore how we write about trauma and if it is possible to release the guilt of a survivor.

STORYTELLING: A CONVERSATION ON TRUTH AND BETRAYAL

30 January, 7 p.m., BookCourt, 163 Court Street, Brooklyn, NY 11201. Free.

From a masseuse who secretly manipulates the scars of war with her touch to the fire that perhaps didn't have to claim the life of a loved one to a stillborn flirtation, Jennifer Vanderbes, Karen Russell and André Aciman explore the many shapes of betrayal. *Granta* associate editor Patrick Ryan joins these authors for a reading and conversation about their new work in *Granta* and the ways in which betrayal functions in a story.

THE NEW YORK LAUNCH

31 January, 7 p.m., McNally Jackson, 52 Prince Street, New York, NY 10012. Free.

Treachery lies at the heart of our most dramatic stories. Celebrate the launch of *Granta* 122 with an evening of stories and conversation exploring betrayal's many forms with Ben Marcus, Karen Russell, Colin Robinson, Lauren Wilkinson and *Granta* editors. Drinks will be served at the event.

LITERARY PUBLISHERS PRESENT: A READING WITH KAREN RUSSELL AND PHIL KLAY

8 February, 5 p.m., NYU Creative Writing Program Reading Series, Lillian Vernon Creative Writers House, 58 West 10th Street, New York, NY 10011. Free.

Phil Klay, a veteran of the US Marine Corps, and Karen Russell have written movingly in *Granta* about soldiers returning from Iraq. In a time when more and more stories of veterans are being told, these contributors join *Granta* editor John Freeman to explore why and how we narrate these experiences and the possibilities of homecoming and healing.

EVENTS TO BE ANNOUNCED

- Bath Spa, *January*
- Columbia University, *January*
- Philadelphia, *January*
- Perth International Arts Festival, *February*
- Sydney, *February*
- Tokyo International Writers Festival, *March*

For ticketing, updates and full event details, visit granta.com/events.